M U R D O C H

M Y S T E R I E S

Night's Child

THE MURDOCH MYSTERIES

MURDOCH

MYSTERIES
Night's Child

MAUREEN JENNINGS

TITAN BOOKS

Murdoch Mysteries: Night's Child
Print edition ISBN: 9780857689917
E-book edition ISBN: 9780857689986

Published by Titan Books
A division of Titan Publishing Group Ltd
144 Southwark St, London SE1 0UP

First edition: May 2012
2 4 6 8 10 9 7 5 3

Visit our website:
www.titanbooks.com

What did you think of this book? We love to hear from our readers. Please email
us at: readerfeedback@titanemail.com, or write to us at the above address.
To receive advance information, news, competitions, and exclusive offers online,
please sign up for the Titan newsletter on our website: **www.titanbooks.com**

A CIP catalogue record for this title is available from the British Library.

Printed in India.

For Iden as always, and this one for
Peter Outerbridge, the first to bring Murdoch to life

"...he is but Night's child."
(said of Tarquin, who has ravished Lucrece)

SHAKESPEARE, *THE RAPE OF LUCRECE*

PROLOGUE

SHE HADN'T LIKED LEONARD SIMS ONE BIT. HE WAS SLY and spiteful, never missing an opportunity to make a jibe at her expense. In spite of her resolve not to, she'd often been reduced to tears and he'd laughed at her in triumph.

See. You've got the backbone of a slug. You feel like one too.

No one cared enough to protect her from his unrelenting cruelty, but perhaps they didn't even notice. That was the more likely explanation, and she was used to not being noticed. So when she understood that Leonard Sims was dead, she was glad at first. Serves him right, she thought. He'd pushed just once too often. But then she had to go with them when they carried the body in a chest down to the frozen lake. They needed a cab to get there and at first none came by because it was late and the snow was thick and blowing in everybody's face. The cabbie hadn't wanted to take them, said his horse was tired and he was on his way to the stables.

This poor girl has got to visit her old aunt who lives near the shore. You can see how perishing she is. Open your heart.

The cabbie agreed when they paid him double the usual fare.

They didn't bother to tell her what they were doing and, of course, she didn't ask. After the cabbie left, she had to stand there, in her too-thin coat, shivering with cold, to keep lookout. She was so afraid, she was actually whimpering, but the swirling snow blotted up the sounds as the two men vanished into the darkness.

They hauled the chest across the lake to where a short promontory thrust out from the shore. Here they must have shoved it under the overhang. It took them almost ten minutes to trudge there and back through the knee-high snow and they both cursed the weather.

Never mind. When the ice melts, the bloody thing will sink to the bottom and never be found. Goodbye, Sins, and they had both laughed at the joke.

CHAPTER ONE

MISS AMY SLADE WAS SEATED AT HER DESK, SURVEYING her class. For the moment, the room was quiet, the only sound was of chalk moving on slate boards. By rights the children should have been writing in notebooks, but Miss Slade had taken spare slates from the lower standards and used them for rough work. "Then you don't have to worry about perfection, which as we know doesn't exist," she told her pupils. She caught the eye of Emmanuel Hart and frowned at him.

"How many times must I remind you, Emmanuel? The mind is like a muscle and must be exercised else it grow flabby and inert."

The boy bent his head immediately to the task of long

division. He was a big boy, too old to still be in the fourth standard, but he had missed a lot of school and his reading and writing was barely at the level of the younger children. In a different classroom he would have been either the bully or the butt of ridicule. Not here. Miss Slade, without ever resorting to the cane, ran a tight, disciplined ship. She was strict about what she called the rules of order, which she'd established on the first day of the term. No talking when there was work to be done; only one voice at a time when there was a question-and-answer period; absolutely no tormenting of other children. Any infraction of these rules and the offending child, almost always one of the boys, was sent to the Desk of Thoughtfulness, which was right under her nose. Here he had to sit and reflect on his behaviour while all around him the class enjoyed the games and competitions that Miss Slade used to liven up her lessons. "Learning should be the most fun you ever have," she told her pupils. And so she made it. On her desk was a large jar full of brightly coloured boiled sweets. The winner of the competition could choose one. But it was not just the succulent bribery of raspberry drops that won the children's devotion, even though that helped a great deal. What they came to respect most was Miss Slade's justice. She dispensed praise and occasional scoldings with an absolutely even hand whether it was to a hopeless case like Emmanuel Hart or to Mary, the clever, exquisitely dressed daughter of Councillor Blong. One or two of the girls, already too prissy to be saved, disliked and mistrusted her, but the others loved her.

This was Miss Slade's third year of teaching at Sackville Street School and her fourth placement. Although her pupils didn't know it, her contract was precarious. She was far too radical a teacher for the board's taste, and if she hadn't consistently produced such excellent results, she would have been dismissed long ago.

She waited a moment longer, enjoying the *put, put* sound of the chalk on the slates. Then she clapped her hands.

"Excellent. There is nothing quite as fine as the silence of the intelligent mind at work. What is it that makes so much noise? Hands up if you know the answer."

Every arm shot up, hands waving like fronds.

"Good. I would expect you to know the answer to that as I have said it innumerable times. Who hasn't answered a question lately? Benjamin Fisher, you."

The skinny boy's face lit up. "The most noise in the brain comes from the rattle of empty thoughts, Miss Slade."

"Yes, of course. You can get a sweet later. Now, wipe off your slates, everybody, and put them in your desks."

There was a little flurry of activity, desk lids lifted, as the children did as she asked.

"Monitors, open the windows wide, if you please."

Florence Birrell and Emmanuel Hart got up promptly and went to push up the window sashes. Cold air poured into the classroom, which was hot and stuffy. The large oil heater in the centre of the room dried out the air. The girls who were sitting closest to the windows wrapped their arms in their pinafores for warmth while the boys remained stoic.

"Good! Stand beside your desks, everybody, and assume your positions for cultivation of the chest."

The children stood in the aisles, their heels pressed together, toes turned out at an angle.

"Remember now, your weight must be forward on the balls of your feet. Let me see. Rise up."

One or two of the boys deliberately lost their balance, which gave them an excuse to flail their arms and grab on to the desk beside them.

"George Strongithorn, stop that. You will sit out the exercise in the Desk of Thoughtfulness if you misbehave again. You are quite capable of standing on your toes. All right, children, you may assume your correct position once more."

Miss Slade began to walk up and down, inspecting her pupils. She had her cane pointer in her hand but not to whack at any child, merely to correct.

Benjamin's older sister, Agnes Fisher, who was directly in front of the open window, shivered violently. She was wearing only a thin cotton jersey underneath her pinafore.

"Agnes, come to the front. It's warmer out of the air."

Miss Slade faced the class. "Now, all together. Inhale…and exhale as you say the word *far*. Whispers, please. *Farrr.*"

There was a soft sighing throughout the room.

"Twice more. Joseph, for goodness sake, your mouth should be closed, not catching flies."

A giggle ran through the ranks.

Miss Slade, whose chest was well cultivated, lead the way. "Inhale through the right nostril only. And exhale through the left nostril."

Henry Woolway had a bad cold and blew out some snot as he exhaled. He wiped it away with his sleeve. Without comment Miss Slade handed him a clean handkerchief from her pocket.

The children continued to breathe, first through one nostril then the other, puny chests thrust out and upward.

"All right, we will pause for a moment. Isaiah, you are still prone to making your shoulders do all the work. That is wrong. It is the lower chest that must rise."

"Sorry, Miss Slade. My chest bone hurts if I breathe in too deep."

Isaiah had a persistent dry cough.

She tapped hard on her own chest with her two fingers. "This is what you must do every day without fail, Isaiah. Firm percussion for five minutes. Then splash cold water on your neck and chest, followed by a dry warm towel. Within three weeks, we should see some improvement."

"Yes, ma'am."

There were four younger children in Isaiah's family and the closest he got to water in the morning was a damp rag that his mother made him whisk around the face and ears of the two next down. She didn't seem to notice whether he did the same to himself. Miss Slade read his face correctly.

"On second thoughts, Isaiah, we'll do the exercise when you come to school and I will be able to supervise."

"Yes, ma'am."

"Now, everyone, let us move into rapid breathing." She consulted the gold fob watch on her bodice. "I think we are ready to try for three minutes. When I say *go*, breathe in through the right nostril as rapidly as possible, then out through the left. Are you ready? Shoulders down, mouth quite closed. Begin. Quietly please."

With finger and thumb to their noses, as they had been instructed, the children began, Miss Slade keeping time like a band conductor. "And in…and out…Inhale and exhale."

The class was breathing in unison, sounding like an animal in its death throes. The two-minute mark was just reached when suddenly Agnes Fisher, with a barely audible gasp, fell backwards, gracefully and quietly as if her body had turned to cloth. She lay still, her eyelids fluttering.

"Goodness me, Agnes." Miss Slade ran over to her, knelt down, and took one of the girl's hands in hers. She began to rub it. "Agnes! Agnes! Can you hear me?"

The girl's face had turned as white as the chalk. The other children gathered around them, their faces sombre and afraid. Benjamin looked down at his sister in terror.

"It's all right, Ben. She's just fainted. See, she's coming around. She had a bit too much oxygen, I'm afraid." Miss Slade slipped her hands underneath the girl's arms and helped her to sit up. "Children, please return to your seats." She waited for a moment to make sure her order was obeyed. "Agnes, are you hurt anywhere?"

The girl put her hand to her head. "I feel a bit dizzy, Miss Slade."

"Stay where you are then. It will pass. Ben, get a sweetie from the jar, quick as you can. A barley sugar."

The boy hurried to do what she said. Miss Slade offered it to the girl.

"Pop this in your mouth and suck on it slowly."

She noticed that there were small dark bruises on the child's wrist and a larger one, already yellowing, above her eyebrow, which her hair had hidden. It was not the first time she had seen such marks.

"Can you sit at your desk now, do you think?"

"Yes, ma'am," whispered Agnes.

With her teacher's help she got up slowly, then returned to her place.

"Did you have any breakfast, Agnes?"

"No, ma'am. We were late getting up."

Miss Slade knew better than to ask why. Mrs. Fisher had died more than a year ago and the children were left to fend for themselves most days. Mr. Fisher, as Miss Slade had discovered, was a man of intemperate habits.

She regarded the worried faces in front of her.

"Children, I think it's time for recess. Yes, I know it's a little earlier than usual, Maud, but I think we all need some time in the open air. Florence and Mary, will you accompany Agnes? Walk a few times around the playground. Don't forget, heads up, breathe through your nose."

She placed her hand over the girl's. "Are you feeling better now?"

"Yes, ma'am, thank you." The girl's habitual dull look had returned. She was one of Miss Slade's least responsive pupils.

"Off you go, then."

The children made a dash for the hooks on the wall where they'd hung their coats and hats. Florence and Mary had a little scuffle as to who would link arms with Agnes. Mary won, and with a precocious maternal expression, she lead Agnes out of the room. Benjamin trailed behind.

Miss Slade sighed. Although the Fisher children weren't the only ones who came to school with bruises, they seemed to have them more often than any of the others.

She stood up and went over to her own desk, where she had left an iced cake the day before. Whenever possible she celebrated birthdays. It gave her an excuse to bring in cake for children who never had any at home. She took a clean handkerchief from the pile she kept ready, wrapped the cake, and went back to Agnes's desk. She raised the lid, intending to tuck the cake into the back of the desk as a surprise, and stopped in mid-motion. Pushed into the far corner was a photograph. When she lifted it, she discovered more. Four in all.

The top one was a stereoscopic photograph, a staged studio portrait of a young man in formal attire, who was about to embrace a woman dressed as a maid. Both of the faces had been scratched out. The maid's back was to the camera and she was nude except for apron strings and gartered stockings.

The man was naked from the waist down and was in a state of extreme sexual arousal. The caption at the bottom read, *Mr. Newly-wed meets the new maid.*

Miss Slade was no prude, but neither was she a woman of the world and she felt herself turn hot with embarrassment. She could not imagine how such a photograph had ended up in the desk of one of her pupils.

She looked at the second card, which was a single, hand-tinted photograph of a beautifully gowned baby in its cradle. At first glance, the infant appeared to be sleeping peacefully, but the photograph was bordered in black, signifying death. Along the bottom, the caption read, CALLED TO JESUS *in the year of Our Lord, 1895.* She turned the card over.

Somebody had printed words that made her gasp. Even she, a professed atheist, was not immune to such appalling blasphemy.

The third photograph was of a young man, naked except for an absurd silk turban with an elaborate brooch in the front. He was lying languorously on a Turkish couch. There was a black border around this card as well.

The last card was also a double image for the stereoscope. This caption read, *What Mr. Newly-wed really wants.*

"No!" she whispered and, in shock, she turned the card face down so she couldn't see it.

CHAPTER TWO

AS USUAL, THERE WAS A ROARING FIRE IN INSPECTOR Brackenreid's office, and cigar smoke, both stale and new, clogged the air. Murdoch waited whilst the inspector alternately drew on his pungent cigar and gulped at a mug of tea that he had fortified with a dash of brandy, "against the cold". Neither Murdoch nor Constable Crabtree had been invited to sit down and so they stood in front of the desk.

"Have you made any progress with the Smithers case?"

"No, sir. Constable Crabtree and I have taken statements from all of the servants and we also spoke to the staff at the funeral parlour, but they all swear they didn't steal the brooch."

"Where is it, then?"

"According to Mrs. Smithers's personal maid, her mistress often misplaces things these days, more so since old Mrs. Smithers died. Apparently, they have a way of showing up in unexpected places at a later date."

"What's your opinion, Crabtree?"

"I'm inclined to believe they are all telling the truth, sir. The house servants are upset at being accused because they have been with the family for a long time."

Brackenreid nodded. "The woman is probably losing some of her slates. By her own admission, the brooch isn't valued at more than ten dollars. Hardly worth making a fuss about. She and her mother-in-law both attended my church, and in my opinion, they were both mad as hatters." He drew on his cigar, remembered his manners, and added, "May she rest in peace."

He blew out a thick smoke ring, which gradually expanded so that by the time it drifted across the desk to Murdoch, he couldn't have put his finger through it however tempted he might be.

"Anyway, I don't want either of you wasting any more time with it."

"No, sir."

Brackenreid emptied his tea mug in one long gulp.

"Crabtree, you can leave. Murdoch, stay on for a minute."

Murdoch felt a twinge of uneasiness. Brackenreid usually went out of his way to avoid private interviews with his detective. On the rare occasion the inspector could find a transgression in Murdoch's performance as an officer, he preferred to administer the scolding in front of others. He wondered what he was going to be chastised for that merited privacy.

As soon as the door closed behind the constable, Brackenreid went over to the fireplace. He took the poker and banged at a recalcitrant lump of coal until flames burst out of it. Murdoch waited, watching while Brackenreid turned to warm his plump buttocks.

"What I am going to show you, Murdoch, must be viewed in complete confidence. Do I have your word?"

Obscene and insolent questions jumped into Murdoch's head, but he replied with sufficient politeness not to give offence.

"Is the matter related to our professional relationship, sir?"

"What?"

"I mean is it pertinent to you as my inspector?"

Brackenreid flushed. "Of course it is, what are you implying?"

He had an all too familiar expression of bewilderment on his face that tended to take the fun out of baiting him. Murdoch sighed.

"I'm implying nothing, sir. Just clarifying matters."

"You're going to step over the line one of these days, Murdoch."

"And what line would that be, sir?"

But he knew he'd come a little too close this time. Brackenreid could fine him for insubordination with no chance of redress if he so desired.

"I beg your pardon, sir. I was distracting you from your purpose. You wanted to show me something. In complete confidence."

Brackenreid scowled at him, but he went over to his desk, pulled open a drawer, and took out two folded sheets of paper. He handed them to Murdoch.

"Have a gander at these. Give me your opinion. I'm damned if I'll have one of my officers maligned."

Murdoch was astonished. The inspector so often acted like a half-drunken sot that he'd long ago lost any respect for him. However, on occasion, he glimpsed the kind of man Brackenreid had been before his habit conquered him. This was such an occasion.

"The top one came first."

Murdoch removed the sheet of paper from the envelope. The message was typewritten, unsigned.

JANUARY 20 '96

Inspector Brackenreid. I feel it is my duty as a citizen of this fair city to draw your attention to the reprehensible actions of one of your officers. I refer to Sergeant Seymour whose behaviour unbeknownst to you is both wicked and illicit. I suggest you ask him how he spends his leisure time.

Murdoch glanced up at the inspector, who nodded. "Read the next one."

MONDAY, JANUARY 27 '96

Inspector. I have previously warned you concerning the illegal activity of one of your officers. No action seems to have been taken. I will give you one more week. Unless the miscreant is punished I will alert the newspapers and will lay the case before the Chief Constable himself. This will bring shame on the station and the force itself.

"What do you make of them?" Brackenreid asked.

Murdoch hesitated. "What on earth are they referring to?"

"How do I know? Could be anything from buying beer on Sundays to stopping his beak at the whorehouse. Depends on what you consider to be wicked and illicit activities."

"Have you spoken to the sergeant himself, sir?"

"No. Frankly, I dismissed the first letter as pure mischief-making, but the second one is more serious."

"I think you should ask him directly, sir. Give him a chance to defend himself."

"Against what, Murdoch? What he does when he's off-duty isn't my concern. I'm not a priest who wants to hear every sin he's ever committed. Did you have naughty thoughts today, sergeant? Did you forget to say your rosemary?"

"The term is 'rosary', sir."

Murdoch knew he should have let it go. Brackenreid smirked and waved his hand dismissively.

"Whatever it is."

"The writer does say 'illegal' in the second letter. That suggests he is accusing Seymour of more than just a sin, which as you are implying, sir, can be relatively unimportant in the wider view of things."

"I've noted that, Murdoch. That is why I am discussing the matter with you. What is your impression of Seymour? I understand that of all the officers in this station, he is most friendly with you."

Murdoch wondered who had told him that. "To my knowledge, the sergeant is an officer of the highest calibre. He is decent and hard-working."

"Anybody he don't get along with who might want to make mischief?"

"Not that I know of. He keeps to himself, but I believe he is well-respected by the men."

"Damned peculiar business." Brackenreid tapped on the desk. "Anything else you can say about the letters themselves?"

"They're surprising. The fact that they're typewritten, for one thing. And the language is superior even if the intent isn't. 'Miscreant' isn't exactly a common word. Did they come with the regular post?"

"Yes. The second one was in the post this morning. As you see, the envelope is also typewritten and is addressed to me." He frowned. "The writer is out to make mischief, knows the sergeant by name, and has used it. The problem is that even if Seymour is pure as the driven snow, if the writer does send this to the papers, a lot of mud will be flung and some of it will stick."

"Unless the accusations prove to be laughably trivial."

"Somehow I doubt that, Murdoch. There's a tone to the letters. I believe the writer means business. As you say, the words are 'illegal' and 'illicit'." Brackenreid walked over to the window and looked out. "Snow's starting up again. I'll be happy when we're done with this weather." He picked up a framed miniature from the mantelpiece. Murdoch knew the painting was of Brackenreid's wife. According to the station gossip, Mrs. Brackenreid was consumed by unrelenting ambition to achieve a high social standing among the Toronto gentry and to that end she led her husband a merry dance. Brackenreid's expression was perplexed, and Murdoch wondered if he were trying to understand what he had once found appealing about the woman he'd married. On the other hand, he could have just been trying to decide if it was a good likeness and worth the money.

"Besides, it is not likely he will admit it."

"Beg pardon, sir?"

"Seymour. He's not likely to come right out and admit he's been dipping his wick in the mud pond, is he?"

"I can't say, sir."

"Of course, he won't. He knows he'll be dismissed. He has a position of superiority here. He must be an example."

With a sigh, Brackenreid returned the picture to its place on the mantelpiece. He turned around.

"The sergeant is on duty today. I'll have to speak to him. I'd appreciate it if you would stay, Murdoch, and give me your honest opinion."

Murdoch didn't relish the task. He liked Seymour, and over the years they had formed a friendship, sharing a passion for fast wheels. Last summer they had gone on a couple of bicycling trips with the Toronto Bicycling Club, to which Seymour belonged. Was he the kind of man who had a secret life that could get him into trouble? Murdoch thought it not likely, but to be honest, he didn't know much about the man. He believed he'd been married at one time but couldn't recall when he'd heard that. Now, like Murdoch, he lived in a boarding house.

Brackenreid pulled the bell rope twice and returned to his desk.

"Have you considered the possibility that the letter has been written by somebody in this station, sir?"

Brackenreid scowled at him.

"I'm not an imbecile. Of course I thought of it. That's why I wanted to discuss the matter with you. Any of the men prone to whinging? Any of them a bit too straight-laced for their own good?"

"I'd have to think about that, sir."

The station had thirty-four constables at all four levels and Murdoch only had a nodding acquaintance with most of them. More familiarity was dependent on who worked on his cases.

"It's the threat of going to the newspapers that I detest," said Brackenreid. "Surely there's enough loyalty among the men that if the sergeant is misbehaving, they would come straight to me and report him, not go through all this cloak-and-dagger nonsense."

"If it is one of our own men writing the letter, I wonder how he knows what Seymour's private proclivities are."

Although the constables might associate with each other

when they were off duty, the sergeants would never break rank.

Murdoch decided to float a tantalizing fly on the surface of the pond to see if the old pickerel would take the bait.

Shortly before the end of the year, a new constable, third class, had joined the station. The incident had caused quite a stir because he was replacing Philips, a well-liked young fellow who had been abruptly dismissed. The charge was poor work habits, based apparently on the fact that he had not come into work for three days in a row when he was suffering from influenza. Because Philips had not produced a note from a physician, Brackenreid said he was malingering. According to the unfortunate constable, he was too ill even to consult a physician and couldn't afford to have one come to his house. The inspector was adamant and the lad was cast out. The next day he was replaced by Liam Callahan, an Irishman, who appeared to have stepped straight off the boat and into the job. Rumour immediately ran riot that he was related to the inspector, although Callahan denied it.

"You mentioned loyalty, sir, and that is a good point. All of the officers have been here for two years or more. Except for Constable Callahan, that is."

Brackenreid wrinkled his nose at Murdoch as if he committed the impropriety of publicly breaking wind.

"He's a very good lad. Let's not make wild accusations."

"I wasn't making any accusation, sir, wild or otherwise. I merely pointed out that Constable Callahan is very new here. The issue pertained to loyalty."

"Yes, well…"

There was a tap at the door.

"Enter," Brackenreid called and Seymour came into the room. In some surprise, he glanced at Murdoch, who nodded reassuringly at him. Brackenreid cleared his throat.

"Sergeant, I've got some, er, unfortunate news to impart to you. I've asked Detective Murdoch to be present because the matter relates to the welfare of the station."

"Yes, sir."

"Take a look at these two letters. They are dated."

He handed them to Seymour. Murdoch watched him, feeling like a traitor even to do that.

The sergeant went very still and it seemed to Murdoch that his hand trembled a little. Not that that was necessarily a proof of guilt.

Brackenreid scowled. "Is the accusation true, Seymour? Have you been committing some illegal act?"

"What might that be, sir?"

"I don't know, sergeant. Anything. Gambling, dancing with whores, stealing apples. You know what the word means."

The sergeant's mouth was tight with anger. "If I am being accused of misdoing, I would like to know who so accuses me and of what charge."

"So would we, sergeant, so would we. Why d'you think somebody would go to the trouble of writing such letters?"

"I don't know, sir."

Brackenreid rested his head on his hands for a moment. "You

can see, I'm in a deuced awkward spot, Seymour. If the writer is as good as his word, he will send this to the newspapers and there will be the devil of an uproar."

"I realize that, sir. But the alternative seems to be to dismiss me. Unless you are in fact asking that I resign. To avoid unpleasantness."

Murdoch jumped in. "May I make a suggestion, sir? The writer has given us a week's grace. We might be able to track him down. If we know who he is, we can determine with absolute certainty what the accusations against Sergeant Seymour are and at least he will have a chance to defend himself."

Seymour looked over at Murdoch. His expression was bleak. He was a man who expected that the sentence had already been made.

Brackenreid fiddled with his moustache, which badly needed trimming.

"Certainly that would be a good move, but there are two hundred thousand citizens in this city of ours. Any one of them could have sent this letter."

Murdoch didn't challenge the inspector on the exaggeration. "May I have your permission to investigate, sir?"

"Yes, you may. See what you can find." Brackenreid drummed his fingers on the desk. He avoided Seymour's eyes. "In the meantime, until we get to the bottom of the matter, I am going to ask you to remain at home, sergeant. If the unknown letter writer is as cognizant with the workings of the station as he appears, it may mollify him for a while."

Seymour was also avoiding the inspector's face. "Is that to be without pay, sir?"

"No, no. A week with pay. If, er, if you are, er, if the charges are true, you will have to repay those wages. How does that sound?"

"I can understand the necessity. But I do have a favour to beg of you, sir."

Brackenreid nodded.

"Can we put out that I have come down with the influenza? As you say, mud sticks and I don't want gossip going around that I have been up to no good. I may never be able to completely clear my name."

The inspector hesitated, then said, "Yes, we can do that. We'll call it an informal inquiry. Why don't you get your things now? Say you are unwell. You can send for Gardiner to replace you. He and Hales should be able to manage for a few days. Murdoch can get on with his investigation."

"Thank you, sir."

He gave Brackenreid a stiff, formal bow and left. He hadn't once looked at Murdoch after he had made his offer.

The inspector waited for a moment. "Well, Murdoch, what do you think? He seemed very shaken to me."

"Who wouldn't be when faced with that?"

"Yes, you're right of course. Doesn't necessarily mean the poor fellow has a guilty conscience, does it?"

"No, sir. Not at all."

"All right then. Get on with it. See what you can find."

Murdoch stood up. In spite of what he'd said, he was ill at

ease. Sergeant Seymour had indeed appeared shaken by the letters, but he'd not seemed surprised.

CHAPTER THREE

MURDOCH RETURNED TO WHAT HE OPTIMISTICALLY referred to as his office, a cubicle off the back hallway, next to the cells. He put the two letters on top of his desk. He didn't relish this assignment. He considered the sergeant to be a dedicated police officer who did his work properly, was punctual, didn't drink, appeared clean and groomed, and was fair to the constables under his command. Surely he wouldn't be so foolish as to risk his job for some peccadillo. Murdoch grimaced, realizing what he was thinking. Seymour was right. No matter if you were clean as the fresh, fallen snow currently beautifying the city, mud stuck.

There was a tap on the wall outside. Because the cubicle

was too small for a door, Murdoch had hung a reed curtain at the threshold. Through the strips, he could see the outline of George Crabtree. The constable filled the entire space.

"Come in."

Crabtree pushed aside the curtain sufficiently to show his head and shoulders.

"There is a lady out in the front hall who wants to talk to you."

"Who is it?"

"I don't know, sir. She didn't give her name. She said you wouldn't know who she was anyway."

"Did she also refuse to say what she wanted?"

"As a matter of fact she did, sir. A personal matter was all she'd say."

"George, I've seen that expression on your face before. What's wrong with this one? Do I need you to protect me?"

Crabtree looked sheepish. "Not that, sir. It's just that…well, she's dressed sort of peculiar. Not what you'd usually see. But well-spoken."

"I'm intrigued. I'll come out."

He put the two letters in a folder and slipped it into his desk drawer.

The public area of the station was a large room called the hall. Along one wall ran a wooden bench where the public could wait while their complaints or misdemeanours were dealt with. A big wood stove in the centre poured out heat into the room. The sergeant on duty sat on a stool behind the high counter and behind him was the telephone and telegram table, manned at the moment by young Callahan. Both men were trying without much success not to stare at the woman who was standing in front of the counter. She was on the short side, slim, with fine features and blonde, wavy hair. However, her features were not the extraordinary thing about her. Her clothes were. She was wearing a loose-fitting, brown tweed jacket, belted at the waist and buttoned at the neck. The hem was at her knees and below it were visible brown pantaloons, also loose fitting, and fastened with narrow bands at the ankle. Her boots, simple brown felt hat, and the portmanteau she was carrying were unimpeachable.

As soon as Murdoch appeared, she spoke up.

"Good afternoon, you must be Detective Murdoch. I wonder if we could talk in private. It is a matter of some urgency."

"Of course. Please come this way."

She walked past him and he followed her along the corridor. Except for the strange garb, she was an attractive woman, still on the younger side of thirty, he guessed. And as Crabtree had said, she was well-spoken. She was also very upset about something.

He lifted aside the reed curtain, indicated the spare chair, and took his place behind the desk. He wished yet again that his office wasn't so shabby. The grey metal filing cabinet behind him could have come from a railway discard yard and the upholstery of the chair she was sitting on had split at the bottom. He'd never quite been able to scrub off the chalk marks on the wall where he'd periodically drawn street maps of the area around the station. The woman, however, showed no curiosity at all about her surroundings. She sat down on the chair, her back straight, her eyes fixed on his.

"May I have the privilege of knowing to whom I am speaking?" he asked.

She thrust out her hand in a somewhat masculine fashion. Her grip was firm. "My name is Amy Slade. I am a teacher at Sackville Street School." She leaned forward slightly and he had the impression of somebody on a diving board, not completely sure if they wanted to plunge into the water. He nodded encouragingly and she relaxed a little.

"Mr. Murdoch, I realize that what I have to ask you is quite unorthodox." For the first time, she smiled. "But as you can see, I am not an especially orthodox person. I have come to you for help because you are a police officer, but I must beg for your absolute discretion."

She suddenly looked as if she were on the verge of losing her composure and he sensed this was not a state that she was particularly familiar with or enjoyed. She was also waiting for an answer.

"Ma'am, I can make no promise until I know why you have come to see me. Of course I will be discreet as the circumstances warrant, but you must allow me to be the judge of that."

He thought for a moment that she might get up and leave. She studied his face, not hiding the fact that she was assessing him. He didn't speak, allowing her to decide as she saw fit. Finally, she gave a sigh and her shoulders released.

"Very well." She reached down to the portmanteau, snapped

open the catch, and took out something wrapped in a white handkerchief. She handed it to him. "Yesterday, I discovered this in the desk of one of my pupils." This time, she didn't watch his face but stared over his head. He was unprepared for what he saw.

A girl, dressed in only a chemise, was sitting on a low chair, her legs spread. The caption underneath read, *What Mr. Newlywed really wants.*

Miss Slade's voice was shaky. "The girl in that picture is my pupil, Agnes Fisher."

Murdoch put the card to one side on the desk so it wasn't directly between him and the young teacher.

"Are you sure?"

"Yes. She, er, she is of course painted in such a way as to be almost unrecognizable, but there is no doubt."

"Does she know you discovered it?"

"Yes, I fetched her in immediately and confronted her. She was unable to answer me. By that, Mr. Murdoch, I mean, literally, was unable. She went mute. She could not utter a word." This time she met his eyes. "I should explain that what the photograph depicts is utterly out of character for this girl. She is normally a quiet, withdrawn child, and I fear is not well-treated at home. I cannot convey to you, sir, how distressed I am."

"I can quite understand that, Miss Slade. This is an extremely serious matter. Have you informed your headmaster?"

She looked away and he could see her discomfiture.

"No, I have not. I have become fond of Agnes. However, I do

not know, I cannot possibly imagine, the explanation for this photograph, but I am sure Mr. Kippen would have her charged. She will be sent to the Mercer Reformatory. He is not, shall we say, a particularly kind or lenient man."

Murdoch had the feeling that in spite of her matter-of-fact tone, Miss Slade had been affected by the headmaster's lack of kindness. Given her defiant adoption of Rational Dress, he guessed her relationship with the school board would be a strained one.

"And the child's parents?"

"She lives with her father, who is a widower and, frankly, a drunkard. I have not yet decided whether he should be informed. I would be afraid of his reaction."

"What do you want me to do, Miss Slade?"

"Find out who has taken this picture. Agnes must have been coerced. There is no other explanation. The person concerned deserves to be prosecuted."

"You asked for discretion, but if I do uncover the perpetrator, the law will have to be followed. I cannot guarantee anonymity."

She sighed. "I am aware of that. I can only trust that you will be sensitive to the needs of my pupil. If this is made public, she will have no future whatsoever."

"Did she come to school today?"

"No, she did not. I am most concerned about that. Perhaps I should have acted sooner but, frankly, I did not know the best course of action to take."

Murdoch took his notebook from his pocket.

"Her name is Agnes Fisher?"

"Yes."

"How old is she?"

"She will be thirteen this birthday. She has a younger brother, Benjamin, who is also in my classroom. Agnes was held back a year, unfortunately, which is why they are in the same standard now. There is also an older sister who is in service. I don't know where or what her name is." She fished in the portmanteau again. "These photographs were also in Agnes's desk."

He looked at the other three cards.

"You will have to reverse the mourning card," she said. "I warn you, it is quite repugnant."

It was, and he winced.

"Is this the girl's handwriting?"

"I am sure it is."

"Why would she keep the cards in her desk where they could be easily found?"

"I'm sure it is a far safer place than her home and they were tucked well into the back." Miss Slade glanced down at her lap. "Unlike some teachers, Mr. Murdoch, I do not believe in inspecting my pupil's desks. A little untidiness can be a result of a creative mind."

That's not what the nuns at Murdoch's school had drilled into him.

Miss Slade handed him a folded sheet of paper. "I have written out Agnes's address, on Sydenham Street. You can get in touch with me at the school when you need to."

"I will do everything I can, Miss Slade." He got to his feet. "Let me see you out."

She too stood up. "No, no, I am quite capable of walking down a short hall. I won't lose my way."

Murdoch waited until she had left to pick up the photographs. He reread what Agnes had written on the back of the mourning card. How could she know words like that? He hoped she was not also familiar with the sexual acts she described. He turned the card over. The photograph of the dead baby had a simple setting of rear draperies, tinted blue, as was the cradle. The infant was dressed in a white-edged lace gown with matching bonnet. His eyes were closed.

The sweetness of that image was in direct contrast to all three of the other photographs. *What Mr. Newly-wed really wants.* Murdoch knew the so-called Newly-wed series was very popular, and that, typically, five cards told the story. In the first, a young servant girl and her employer, named only Mr. Newly-wed, are in a kitchen. The man, young and dapper, exclaims, *By Jove, I didn't know you were our new maid*, or words to that effect. In the second photograph, he embraces her, but she leaves tell-tale floury handprints on his jacket, which are seen in the third image. Next picture, his wife sees this evidence of misbehaviour and orders the maid out of the house. Final picture is, *Mrs. Newly-wed's new maid.* This servant was always an ugly woman or a coloured wench, presumably unattractive to the lustful Mr. Newly-wed.

Murdoch examined the version, not commonly sold, that

was in front of him. A doorway to the left offered a partial view of a dining room with flock wall covering and a patterned rug. A row of china plates sat on a shelf and above them a half-seen painting of two sporting dogs. To the right was a large clock, the hands standing at five minutes to five. The floor covering was a striped oilcloth.

Murdoch picked up the second photograph, which was tinted. A naked youth was wearing only a gold turban with a pin in the front holding a spray of ostrich feathers. The pin itself was a silver circlet with brightly coloured red jewels around the edge. He could see that there had originally been five but two were missing. The boy's lips had been reddened and his eyelids coloured violet. His body was slim and hairless and at first glance he seemed a mere child but Murdoch thought his face was too lined for that and his genitals were mature. He put him at about seventeen years of age or even older. A black border around the edge of the card had been carefully inked in.

Lastly, Murdoch turned to the photograph of Agnes, which was also tinted. The girl's cheeks and lips were rouged and her hair was loose about her shoulders, but she was unsmiling and expressionless. She was seated on a low chair and behind her was a painted backdrop, rather ill-drawn, of a panelled room. To her right was an empty birdcage and a bedraggled-looking palm in a pot. To her left, a doorway revealed the end of a Turkish couch draped with a gauzy cloth. There was a leopardskin rug on the floor.

Murdoch took a magnifying glass from his drawer and began

to examine all the ink marks. The writing on the back of the mourning card was clotted with blots, typical of cheap school ink and worn pens. Then he held the glass to the scratches on the two faces in the Newly-wed picture. The gouges were deep, and when he moistened his handkerchief and tried to wipe away the ink, the marks remained. The black ink looked the same as that used on the back of the mourning card, so he assumed Agnes Fisher was the one who had obliterated the faces. Why? So the two people couldn't be identified or because she hated them? The black border around the photograph of the naked youth seemed to also be the same ink.

For the next half an hour, Murdoch went over every detail again of the four photographs, making notes as he did so. On previous occasions, he had been called on to bring charges against young women, always in the theatre, who were supposedly revealing too much leg or bosom. He had always been glad when the charges were dismissed or the young women received only a small fine. Even though they upset some respectable citizens, he saw no harm in what they did. They were of an age to be responsible for their own decisions and mostly, they catered to adult men who rarely got beyond the leer-and-cheer stage. He felt somewhat the same way about the second Newly-wed picture. If grown men and women wanted to take off their clothes and take up lewd poses, that was up to them. Presumably they were paid to do so. The photographs of the two young people were different. Even if the youth was of the age of consent, Agnes was not. He could understand why

Miss Slade was so distressed. The way the girl had been painted and rouged like a tart, and worse, the pose she had been placed in, disgusted him and made him furious with whoever it was had exploited her.

He opened his drawer to take out an envelope and saw the folder he'd placed there earlier and he suddenly felt intensely uncomfortable. Surely, the anonymous letters and Miss Slade's photographs were unconnected. The thought they might not be was disturbing.

CHAPTER FOUR

THE SKIN ON THE BUNION, SOFTENED BY THE LONG soaking, flaked off easily as Ruby scraped at it with the knife. Mrs. Crofton flinched.

"Beg pardon, ma'am, did that hurt?"

"No, hardly at all. It's just a little tender."

"We're almost done and then you can have the nice part."

A minute later, Ruby put down the knife, poured a few drops of the oil of bergamot onto her fingers, and began to rub it on the poor deformed feet. The skin felt thin and fragile as paper but smooth and soft from the water.

"Better now?"

Mrs. Crofton leaned back against her pillow and closed

her eyes.

"It surely is."

Mrs. Crofton's Irish lilt was always more pronounced when she was relaxed. She was seated in the armchair by the fire with Ruby on the footstool at her feet. Tending to her mistress's corns and bunions had become one of the girl's tasks and they went through this ritual once a week. The elderly woman's toes were so deformed that the great one lay, almost at right angles, across the second one. The remaining toes were crowded together and curled under, making it painful for her to walk for long, even though she wore special, handmade shoes lined with soft fur. In damp weather, the bunions ached.

It was Ruby who had suggested this remedy. She'd heard it from her mother, who one day, out of the blue, had talked about tending to her own grandmother's bad feet. She so rarely spoke about her own childhood that when she did, Ruby paid attention.

What did you do for her, Momma?

I'd make her soak her feet in hot water that had sal-soda sprinkled in it. When the bunion and corns were soft, I'd scrape off the dead skin with a sharp skinning knife. Then I'd rub the entire foot and ankle with warm goose grease. It gave her a great relief.

There had been a wistfulness in her mother's voice, and Ruby had a brief glimpse of the girl she had once been, neglected by everybody except the old lady she took care of. She had rushed to comfort her. *Shall I rub your feet, Momma?* Her mother had grimaced. *Not my feet but you can rub my back.* She had been carrying yet another child. The two pregnancies after Benjamin had both ended in a miscarry, but this one was farther along. Then this child had caused both their deaths.

Ruby poked bits of soft cotton wool between each toe, then slipped on the felt slippers.

"Ah, my dear, you are as precious as your name."

Ruby was not her baptismal name. When she'd applied for the position of general servant, she had decided to change her name. First because she fancied Ruby sounded prettier, second so that she could not be traced. She'd been bold about her references, writing the letter with great care, dictated, she said, by her employer who was now blind and moving away to England. The housekeeper, Mrs. Buchanan, had looked skeptical but when she presented the girl to Miss Georgina and Mrs. Crofton, they had both been charmed.

We'll try her for a month, but in the meantime, give her some good meals, Mrs. Buchanan, she's far too thin.

Six months later, Ruby had more flesh on her bones and more colour in her cheeks, and was happier than she had ever been in her life. Mrs. Buchanan remained rather reserved, but Ruby had become the special pet of her employers, Miss Georgina in particular.

"Shall I fetch your coffee now, ma'am?"

Mrs. Crofton didn't open her eyes.

"Yes, thank you. Is Miss Georgina up yet?" she asked in a drowsy voice.

"Yes, ma'am. She was up betimes, doing some finishing touches."

"Again! I thought she did that yesterday."

"She did, ma'am. I suppose there was still more to be done."

"How ridiculous, I…"

She stopped as her daughter came into the room.

"What is ridiculous, Mama?"

Mrs. Crofton opened her eyes. "The fuss you make over your paintings. Surely even the Master himself declared something completed."

Georgina grinned, not the least perturbed. They'd had this argument many times before.

"We don't know whether he fussed or not. Perhaps the gallery owner wrested the canvas from his grasp and he ran after him with brush in hand. 'No, wait, I have to add a little more cadmium in that corner.'"

She ran across the floor, miming the painter with brush in outstretched hand and both her mother and Ruby laughed.

When she had first met Georgina Crofton, Ruby thought she was the strangest-looking woman she had ever seen. She was wearing a plain holland, ankle-length smock daubed from top to bottom with smears of paint. Her greying hair was braided with a red-and-gold silk scarf and pinned in a halo around her head. Later Ruby learned that this was what Georgina wore when she was in her studio. She was, she declared immediately, an artist. Her speciality was portraiture, preferably that of the recently dear departed. Usually, she worked from a photograph, but whenever possible she used sketches she made at the deathbed before the corpse was sealed in the coffin. The bereaved family often wanted an embellished likeness that an actual photograph could not provide. Georgina made the beloved look "as they were in life, not the least bit dead". She was successful in this career, accomplished, sympathetic, and discreet. Ruby knew all of this because, for the last four months, she had been Georgina's assistant and companion.

Georgina went over to the birdcage by the fire and clucked her tongue at the canary sitting on the perch. The bird tilted his head and chirruped.

Georgina frowned. "What is wrong with him? For all that he cost, you would think he could sing something."

She went through this ritual every day, and the bird, Rembrandt, only ever cheeped back at her.

"Whose portrait were you touching up today, dear?" asked Mrs. Crofton.

"The baby I told you about who died last month. Not that he needed much improvement. He was as peaceful as if he were asleep. Wasn't that so, Ruby?"

"Yes, ma'am. He was a dear little thing."

"May I see it?"

"It's not dry enough. I'll show it to you later. I promised the parents I'd take it over tonight. I've been too long as it is. By the way, have you done with Ruby? I had a message from a Mr. Guest over on Sherbourne Street. His wife has passed away and he would like me to see her now. It will be a good commission, he has large private grounds."

"Yes, I know the place. He was in trade for a long time. Your father and he were acquaintances. And yes, we're finished I think, aren't we, Ruby?"

"Yes, ma'am."

There was a light knock on the door and Mrs. Buchanan came in. "Excuse me, Mrs. Crofton, but there's a young lass at the back door. She says she's inquiring after her sister, Martha Fisher by name. She seems to be under the impression she is in service here."

"That's odd." Mrs. Crofton looked over at Ruby, who had turned to wiping out her bowl.

"You don't know her, do you?"

"No, ma'am. I can't say that I do."

"How strange, why has she come here?"

"You have to watch it," burst out Ruby. "She's probably spying out the place for a gang to come in and steal."

"Goodness gracious. Did you leave her in the kitchen, Hannah?"

"Of course I didn't. She's standing outside the door."

"Send her away then."

"Yes, ma'am."

Georgina called out to her. "Wait a moment. At least give the child a few pennies or a piece of bread and butter."

"Not if she's a spy, ma'am. Why should I?"

"Well perhaps our Ruby was being an alarmist."

"No, Miss Georgina," said Hannah. "I've heard from Mrs. Smithers's maid that there have been burglaries in the neighbourhood. Even poor Mrs. Collard, you know, the one who lost her husband just last month, says she's missing her gold filigree earrings."

"Losing a husband and earrings, how careless."

"Georgina, shame on you," exclaimed her mother, but she was smiling.

Ruby concentrated on tidying up her corn-cutting implements.

"Come on, Hannah," said Georgina. "Let's be Christians after all. Suffer little children. Go and give the poor gypsy child some pittance."

"Very well, Miss Georgina."

She left and Georgina walked over to Ruby and put her arm around her shoulders.

"Don't look so worried, little sprat. It's better to err on the side of caution. Such things as you described are not unknown. The girl could quite easily have been a little thief."

"Yes, ma'am. She could have been, couldn't she?"

CHAPTER FIVE

THE SNOW HAD STOPPED, BUT THE WINTER AFTERNOON was growing rapidly darker and the chill air burned Murdoch's face. He quickened his pace, huddling into his muffler for warmth. He wasn't much looking forward to questioning Agnes Fisher, especially if she were going to be as uncooperative as Miss Slade had said she was. He turned on to Sydenham Street. Lamps were lit in a few houses, but they were all meagre. On this street few people could afford the luxury of unnecessary candles or lamp oil. The street gas lights were already turned on and they flickered, sickly yellow, making little dint in the gloom. They were widely spaced, perhaps simply because the street was old, perhaps because nobody of any importance lived there.

Number seventy-six was situated in deep shadow between two street lamps. As Murdoch came up the path, he noticed that the upstairs window was clumsily draped with a blanket and a light showed through. He could hear the sound of a baby crying.

Nobody had answered his first knock and he banged the door again, louder. He was about to knock a third time when a voice called from the other side of the door.

"Who is it?"

"My name is Murdoch. I would like to speak to Agnes Fisher."

The door opened and the face of a young woman appeared in the crack. She was not what Murdoch expected, hardly more than eighteen or nineteen and from what he could see, she was pretty, with light brown hair, loosely pinned up. He tipped his hat.

"Good afternoon, ma'am. Sorry to disturb you, but I am looking for Agnes Fisher."

She scrutinized him. "Just a minute, I'll fetch a light."

The door closed with a snap and he wondered if he was going to have to use his police authority to get in. However, in a moment the woman reappeared carrying a lamp.

"Come in out of the cold," she said and stepped back so he had room in the narrow hallway. "Did the school send you?"

He nodded, glad he wouldn't have to go into an explanation. "I assume I am not speaking to a member of the family. You are not Mrs. Fisher, surely?"

The young woman smiled. "No, of course not. I'm Kate...I mean, I'm Mrs. Ralph Tibbett."

Behind her, the baby's wail grew louder and she glanced over her shoulder anxiously. Mrs. Tibbett had the full, lush figure of a woman recently confined.

"I'm sorry if I wakened the baby," said Murdoch. He listened. "Or am I mistaken? Are there two?"

She sighed. "I have twin boys. I had better tend to them." She nodded in the direction of the stairs. "Aggie lives upstairs. She's a good girl," she added, her voice sharp. "Her father is often ill and she stays home to take care of him. If that's what you've come about."

"Did you see her today?"

"No, I didn't, but then the twins have been so mardy all day, I wouldn't have heard Her Majesty herself if she came calling."

The wailing of the two infants was unabated and Mrs. Tibbett hurried toward the parlour door. Murdoch thought he was going to have to find his way upstairs in the dark but suddenly she realized that and swivelled around.

"Do you have matches?"

"Yes, I do."

"There is a sconce directly at the bottom of the stairs. You can light the candle."

She went into the front room, leaving him alone. He fished out his box of matches, struck one, and lit the candle. There was barely enough light to see by but it would do. The stairs were uncarpeted and the wall covering was a dingy brown flock. As it turned out, he didn't need the candle to guide him. From above, a man's voice erupted with all the obscene vigour of the very drunk.

Murdoch felt the muscles at the back of his neck tighten. As a child he had been only too familiar with the violence of a drunken man. Even though he had run away when he was twelve years old, the memory was like a perpetual sore that never quite healed. What he had to hold in check now wasn't fear but his anger.

The Tibbett babies had stopped crying and the man was suddenly quiet, and in the unexpected silence the only sound was the creak of the stairs. Murdoch halted at the landing. A light shone from under the door to the front room. He gave a short knock on this door and, not waiting for an answer, turned the knob and stepped inside. The air was chilly but pungent with the odour of unwashed linens and spilled ale. A weak fire gave off acrid smoke.

A man was lying on a bed pushed against one wall. He seemed to be asleep, the drunken ranting over. A boy about eleven or twelve years old was seated on a stool drawn as close to the hearth as he could get. He had the gaunt, pasty look of the malnourished, and his hair had been cut so short, he was almost bald. As Murdoch entered, the boy turned around and jumped to his feet. If there had been anywhere to run, he would have made a bolt for it.

Murdoch smiled at him. "Hello, you must be Benjamin. Your teacher, Miss Slade, sent me. I would like to have a word with your sister, Agnes."

The boy might have been deaf for all the response he gave. Murdoch walked a little closer but made sure he was still blocking the door.

"Do you mind if I warm my hands? It's nippy outside and I forgot to wear my gloves."

Ben shrank away from his spot in front of the fire. There was a grunt from the direction of the bed. Murdoch pointed. "That's your poppa, is it?"

Again, no answer, just the merest of nods. Both father and son were wearing dirty overcoats. Mr. Fisher's neck was wrapped in a red-and-black-striped muffler and his only blanket was a moth-eaten woman's fur coat. His bed took up most of the space, leaving room for only the small table and a wooden chair in the corner. Along the opposite wall was a narrow cot, neatly made up with a quilt that looked new and clean.

"Is Agnes at home?"

Benjamin shook his head. Murdoch was at a loss. The boy was like a feral dog, so frightened he would fly away at the slightest provocation. Or bite.

"I understand from your teacher you are a very bright boy."

Miss Slade had of course said no such thing, but Murdoch considered all children had that potential. Ben blinked in surprise.

"Did the teacher tell you that?" his voice was almost inaudible.

Murdoch approximated a nod. "Miss Slade seems like a very kind person."

Ben lost some of his wariness. "She gives us sweeties if we get things right. I had two yesterday."

"Butterscotch? That's my favourite."

"No. Barley sugar."

Murdoch sat down on the stool. Ben had backed off to the table.

"I didn't mean to alarm you, son. But I do need to speak to your sister about something important. Do you know where she is?"

"She fainted at school."

"Miss Slade told me that."

"Is she in trouble because she did that?"

"No, not at all. We can't help fainting."

Suddenly, there was a growl from behind him for all the world like a bear woken from hibernation.

"Who the frig are you when you're at home?"

"Good afternoon, sir. My name is Murdoch. Miss Slade, your children's teacher, asked me to come. I was hoping to have a word with Agnes."

Fisher was still so in the grip of drunkenness that Murdoch could see the man try to catch the words as they went by. He repeated what he had said.

"Are you a truant officer?" Fisher asked finally. "I'm always telling that girl…got to get education but she won't listen. Does exactly what she wants. Has she been missing school again? I'll give her what for."

Given what Miss Slade had told him, Murdoch had already

decided to wait before he showed the photograph to Mr. Fisher. The man's reaction supported this decision.

"No, I'm not here about her school attendance. It's another matter. She fainted in class yesterday and her teacher is concerned about her."

That was too much for Fisher to comprehend and he lay back on his pillow.

"Wouldn't like to do a man a favour, would you? I'm fair parched. There's some hair of the dog in the cupboard…next room."

Murdoch glanced over at the boy. "Can you fetch it for him?"

Ben scurried away at once, leaving a swirl of smoky air in his wake. Fisher started to cough and he was forced to sit upright. He aimed a gob of phlegm at the hearth but missed. However, the activity had brought him more into consciousness. Murdoch saw there was a teapot on the table with a couple of mugs. He went over to it and lifted the lid. There seemed to be some tea left in the pot. He poured some into the mug and brought it over to Fisher.

"Have a sip of this. It'll wet your whistle."

Fisher accepted the mug, took a gulp, and pulled a face as if it were bad-tasting medicine.

"It's gone cold."

He handed it back to Murdoch, as if to a servant. His hand was shaking. This close to him, Murdoch could smell his rank breath. He couldn't have been much older than Murdoch himself and might at one time have been considered a handsome man. His hair and moustache were brown and his eyes dark. However, his bloated face and puffy eyes and cheeks told their own tale.

Ben came back into the room with a bottle in his hand.

"There's only this, Poppa," he said and gave it to Fisher. Murdoch noticed the boy positioned himself to one side, out of reach of a sudden blow.

Fisher put the bottle to his lips and swallowed down whatever it was. He wiped his mouth with the back of his sleeve and belched. Murdoch actually wondered if this gross display was put on for his benefit.

"Tha's better," said Fisher. "I'm a Christian again."

And indeed some intelligence had returned to his eyes. He looked at Murdoch shrewdly.

"If her teacher's so worried about Aggie, why have you come and not her?"

"Let's say, Miss Slade thought it better if I investigated." He glanced around the shabby room. "Do you know where Agnes might be, Mr. Fisher?"

"I don't. I haven't clapped eyes on her since this morning. Ben, where's your sister?"

The boy took an involuntary step back. "I don't know, Poppa. Maybe she went to see if she could find Martha."

Fisher took another long pull from the bottle. "That's my eldest. She's in service somewhere, but the little minx hasn't told us where." He actually grinned. "Makes you wonder if she's ashamed of us, don't it? If Aggie has gone to find her sister, she won't be back for hours. No point in you waiting, Mr...?"

Murdoch didn't answer him. He was only too happy to leave. To remain any longer in this stinking, cold, smoke-filled room was out of the question even though he suspected that Ben would have welcomed it.

"You look like you could do with a bite to eat, Mr. Fisher. Why don't I stand you and Ben to some hot pies for your supper? There's an eating house not too far from here on Queen Street. Allow me to buy you some grub."

"Much appreciated, good sir." Fisher winked. "Couldn't see yourself to stretching to a spot of gravy, could you, mate? Makes the pies nice and moist, and you can hear how dry my throat is."

"I can indeed." Murdoch beckoned to the boy. "Why don't you come out now with me and fetch them. Get your hat."

Ben hurried to do as he said and took an old man's felt hat from a hook on the door. He didn't seem to possess any gloves.

"Shall I tell Aggie you was asking for her?" Fisher asked.

Murdoch shrugged. He knew it didn't matter what he said. Fisher would frighten his daughter or not as he wanted.

"She doesn't know my name," he said. "Just tell her Miss Slade was concerned about her."

"I'll do that."

An unspoken question had hovered round the edges of the conversation Murdoch had had with Miss Slade: Did Fisher know of the photograph or, worse, had he something to do with it? His lack of alarm seemed to indicate no, but Murdoch wasn't going to completely dismiss the possibility, appalling as it was. Men like Fisher had long ago lost all acquaintance with conscience and, without it, could act the innocent convincingly.

Ben was standing at the door watching him anxiously.

"Come on, lad," said Murdoch. "Let's get those pies."

He put his hand lightly on the boy's thin shoulder and led him out of the room. He was gratified the boy tolerated his touch.

CHAPTER SIX

FOR THE PAST TWO MONTHS, MURDOCH HAD BEEN shamelessly trying to buy the affections of Mrs. Enid Jones's son, Alwyn. Every couple of weeks, he brought him a small gift, another lead soldier for his collection, a bag of his favourite toffees, a new board game. Tonight he was going to give him a sled. He thought this would serve two purposes: gain him more good feelings and, secondly, give him a chance to get the boy outside so they could spend some time together. His motives weren't all self-seeking; he was becoming genuinely much fonder of the boy. He felt more tolerant of Alwyn's resentment and jealousy and he was careful to include him in conversations between himself and Enid. The boy was definitely thawing, Murdoch thought. It was he who opened the door.

"Please to come in. Mamma's upstairs." He eyed the sled, but Enid had instilled him with good manners and he didn't ask about it.

Murdoch didn't tantalize him. "This is for you. One of the constables gave it to me. It used to belong to his son, but he's outgrown it now. I know you wanted one."

Alwyn crouched down to examine the sled. Murdoch had polished the steel runners and rubbed out some of the scratches on the maple struts. He thought it was almost as good as new, but he knew better than to demand a response from the boy until he was ready.

"How old is the other fellow?" Alwyn asked finally.

"Oh, I don't know, eight or nine perhaps."

"I'll be eight next birthday."

Murdoch stared down at the boy, trying to determine what he was getting at. Many of Alwyn's proclamations to him came in some sort of code and he'd learned to be on the alert in order to get the real message.

"Well, I did wonder about that, whether it would be too small, but I thought we could give it a try and see." In fact, the sled was the perfect size. Alwyn was small for his age and self-conscious about it. "Why don't we go sledding this Sunday? We can try the riverbanks. They'll give us a good run, I bet."

Alwyn shook his head. "Not on Sunday. We're not allowed to play on the Sabbath."

Murdoch cursed to himself. Of course he knew that, and Enid's strict observation of the Sabbath day often irked him. Papists were much more lenient. As long as the faithful went to mass that morning, they could do whatever they liked in the afternoons, especially such wholesome sports as skating and sledding. The priests themselves joined in all the time, tucking their soutanes up into their belts like peasant women.

Enid was coming down the stairs.

"What are you two doing with the door open like that? Do you want to heat the outdoors then?"

Murdoch had been standing on the threshold. "I'll leave it on the porch," he said to the boy. "We can decide when to go sledding later on." He smiled at Enid. "Good evening, Mrs. Jones."

"And a good evening to you, Mr. Murdoch."

"He brought me a sled," said Alwyn.

"And who might 'he' be you're referring to?"

"Beg pardon. I mean, Mr. Murdoch brought me a present."

"Did you say thank you?"

"Yes."

In fact, the words hadn't fallen from his lips, but Murdoch wasn't about to ruin his chances with the boy by mentioning that now.

Enid caught her son's hand. "My goodness, Alwyn, you're as cold as ice. You'll catch your death. Get on upstairs and warm yourself this minute."

"Yes, Mamma." The boy raced up the stairs two at a time. Enid came over to Murdoch.

"Let me take your things."

He touched his fingers to her neck and she flinched. "You're freezing too."

"I'll be warmer for a kiss."

She gave him a quick peck on the cheek. He would have liked much more, but he knew she wouldn't while they were in the hallway where Alwyn might see them. Nevertheless, he put his arms around her and pulled her close to him.

"Is Mrs. Barrett at home, tonight?" he whispered into her hair.

"I'm afraid she is."

On cue, the door leading to the rear opened and the landlady poked her head through the portieres. Enid moved away immediately and hung Murdoch's coat on the hall tree. He straightened his necktie unnecessarily.

"Good evening, Mrs. Barrett. How are you keeping tonight?"

"Not well, Mr. Murdoch, not well. This cold weather is terrible hard on us old people."

He didn't think she was as old as Mrs. Kitchen, his landlady, but she acted as if she were an octogenarian. According to Enid, Mrs. Barrett had been widowed for more than six years but like Queen Victoria she elected to retain her widow's weeds. Murdoch had never seen her without the black bonnet and long veil that trailed down her back. Her gown was of dull bombazine.

"Sorry to hear that, ma'am."

She didn't acknowledge him further. "I want to retire early tonight, Mrs. Jones. No later than nine o'clock. Will you let me know when Mr. Murdoch leaves so I can be sure the door is bolted behind him?"

"Of course, Mrs. Barrett."

She sniffed, cast a baleful glance at Murdoch, and backed into her den.

Murdoch followed Enid upstairs to her sitting room. There were several sombre oil paintings hung on the walls, all depicting biblical scenes in which the Jews looked remarkably like modern English gentlemen. They had all been painted by the late Mr. Barrett, a keen amateur artist.

Enid ushered him into a room warm and bright with firelight and lamps. Alwyn was crouched on the rug in front of the fire playing one of his favourite board games, The Prince's Quest. The object of the game was to rescue the sleeping princess in her bower and Alwyn liked nothing better than to play against Murdoch.

"I just made a fresh pot of tea, Will. Would you care for a cup?"

"There's only one thing I'd like better."

He was treading close to the edge by such a remark, but he couldn't help it. Alwyn piped up.

"What is that, Mr. Murdoch? What would you like better than a cup of tea?"

"Two cups of course."

The boy laughed and so did Enid, but then she frowned at him in warning. She was right, and Murdoch felt guilty. He didn't really want the boy to feel on the outside of a secret adult world.

While Enid poured the tea, he went over to the fire. "I was able to get quite a good sled for Alwyn. Maybe we can all go out soon and give it a try?"

"That sounds quite splendid. Do you know I have never been sledding in my life?"

"Ah. I'd be honoured to be the first to show you how."

He wished everything he said didn't sound as if it had some sexual connotation.

"It's easy," said Alwyn. "I've seen the boys at school. You just sit on the sled and go down the hill."

Murdoch accepted the cup of tea.

Enid beckoned to her son. "Alwyn, come. It's time to get ready for bed."

"Mamma, it's too early."

Enid answered him in Welsh and Murdoch saw him swallow his protests. "Will you come and say goodnight to me, Mr. Murdoch?"

"I certainly will."

The boy followed his mother out of the room. Murdoch finished the tea and put down his cup. There was a notebook on the table, open at a page covered with pencil marks. Beside it a book, *Isaac Pitman's Shorthand*. Enid made her living as a typewriter and was presently learning to be a stenographer. She seemed to have been practising, for on the first line she had written her name, *Enid Jones*, and some pencil strokes that Murdoch assumed was shorthand. She'd repeated that a few times, then *Enid Llewellyn*. That must be her maiden name;

he'd never thought to ask her what it was. At the bottom of the page, she'd written *Enid Murdoch*. He straightened up in shock, certain he wasn't supposed to see that and not at all sure what his own response was.

He sat back just in time as Enid came into the room.

"He's actually very tired," she said. "Will you give a good-night now?"

"Yes, of course."

He went to the tiny box room at the end of the landing where Alwyn slept. He bent over, kissed the boy on the forehead, and said, "*Nos da.*" That was pretty much the extent of his Welsh, but Alwyn murmured something back to him.

Suddenly, the boy reached up and put his arms around Murdoch's neck and kissed him heartily on the lips.

"Thank you for the present. I'd like to go sledding soon."

"And so we shall."

Murdoch pulled the quilt up, feeling suddenly fiercely protective. Alwyn was a highly strung boy who was shy and withdrawn much of the time. He went to the same school as Ben and Agnes Fisher and, for a moment, Murdoch considered asking if he knew them. But then Alwyn smiled and propped himself up on his elbow.

"Mr. Murdoch, Mamma says I can go to watch the typewriting competition tomorrow. Can I sit beside you?"

"The seat is yours," Murdoch said. "*Nos da.*" He blew out the candle.

When he returned to the sitting room, he noticed that the

notebook had vanished. Enid was at her typewriter, the keys clacking.

"Do you want me to time you?" Murdoch asked.

"Later, perhaps."

"There's only one more day to go. How do you feel? Are you nervous?"

"Yes, indeed. I heard today that there's a man come up from New York to compete. He won the state contest last year."

"I can't imagine anybody typing faster than you do."

"It's not just speed. I mustn't make any errors."

He came over to her and put his arms around her. "Enid, you're worse than me when I'm preparing for a bicycle race. All you can do is your best."

She frowned at him. "I don't care about that. I want to win that fifty dollars and the cup. I don't mind at all if I do my worst and win."

He laughed. "Mrs. Jones, the next thing I know you'll be putting sand in your rivals' machines."

He kissed the top of her head. Her hair smelled of the violet-scented pomade she had rubbed in it. She touched his cheek.

"I'm sorry Mrs. Barrett is at home tonight, Will."

"So am I. Give me a kiss to comfort me."

She turned around and he held her tightly. What would it be like to be with her all the time? To not have to leave at the dictate of a bad-tempered landlady, he wondered. The notion was oddly disturbing. Liza had been dead for more than two years now and he'd thought he was ready to court another woman. Now he wasn't so sure.

Enid leaned back and looked into his face. "What is the matter, Will?" She touched his forehead between his eyebrows. "You've got your dark look on."

"Beg pardon, madam."

"Is it a case?"

"That's right," he prevaricated.

Murdoch often told her something about the case he was currently working on, but tonight he couldn't bear to relate the story of the photograph and Agnes Fisher. It was bad enough that it existed. Enid couldn't do anything about it and he knew she would only fret. As far as he was concerned, part of his job was to carry the burden of human wickedness. He wasn't about to share the other personal thoughts either.

She looked as if she were going to protest, but he stopped her with a kiss. Her response was rather cool and she was the first to break away. He didn't insist. But there was something he could tell her.

"Unfortunately, I do have work on my mind." He rummaged in his coat pocket and took out the two sheets of paper that Brackenreid had handed to him. "Enid, I wonder if you would type a sentence for me on your machine. I want to compare something."

It was her turn to seem disappointed, but she made no comment except, "Certainly."

She went over to the typewriting machine.

"Will you type, 'I feel it is my duty as a citizen.'"

She did so, almost as fast as he spoke the words.

"Let me see."

She pulled out the paper and handed it to him. He compared it with the two pieces from Brackenreid. They looked exactly the same. He showed her the letter. "I'm trying to find out who might have written it. The type looks exactly the same as your machine, so that's not much help. It's not like handwriting."

"That's not quite so. All typewriter operators have a different touch, which is fairly consistent." She held the letter up to the light. "The typing is very even, no strikeovers at all, and the print is clean and sharp. I would say the operator is professional and is working from a fairly new machine or at least one that is kept in good condition. I'd wager it's a Remington machine, which is what I have now. My old Caligraph had a different look to it."

Murdoch grinned at her in astonishment. "Well done, Mrs. Jones. Let me see."

He looked over her shoulder, leaning his chin lightly.

"Who uses Remingtons?"

"Most offices do these days."

"All right, madam detective, what else can you tell me about this letter?"

"The paper is copy paper. Look."

She riffled through the tray of blank papers on her desk and picked out two sheets.

"Invariably, good paper has a letterhead. This one is from Mr. Deacon, my last client, a lawyer. I would send that one out and keep a copy for him for his records. See, it's slightly thinner paper that has no inscription on the top. Your letter writer, I would say, therefore, is more likely to be a clerk than a private citizen who would not have much use for copy paper."

Murdoch put his arms around her waist. "How very clever."

She sighed. "I despise anonymous complainers. What do you think poor Sergeant Seymour has done?"

"I don't know."

"Oh dear, let's hope it's not serious. He's your friend, isn't he?"

"Yes, he is."

He released her and walked over to the fireplace, standing with his back to it, his feet astride, hands behind him.

"Let's forget police work...Mrs. Jones, will you be so good as to type a letter?"

She smiled and took up her position at the machine, fingers poised over the keyboard.

"Yes, sir."

"Dear Mrs. Barrett...it has come to our attention that you are retiring early tonight...it is with deep regret that we have heard this news..."

He dropped to his knees in histrionic fashion. "Dear Mrs. Jones – no, don't write it down. Dear Mrs. Jones, is there anything we can do for the next hour that is quiet enough not to disturb your landlady?"

"We can talk to each other."

To his dismay, he saw she was serious. There was also no ignoring the feeling he was being punished.

CHAPTER SEVEN

GEORGINA FLUNG OFF THE BLACK FOCUSING CLOTH, tipped the camera slightly downward, then disappeared again underneath the cloth. She fiddled with one of the right-hand knobs.

"Ruby, bring that lamp closer to her face. Good, that's my girl."

She emerged again, took up the long shutter cable, and pressed the button. After a few seconds, she pulled out the photographic plate, dropped it into her box, removed a fresh plate, and slipped it into the camera.

"I'll take another one from the other side."

Ruby waited patiently. Mrs. Guest, the recently dear departed, was dressed for the coffin in a night bonnet of white cambric and her best nightgown. The yoke and collar of the gown were of cream-coloured Valenciennes lace threaded with pale yellow silk ribbons. If, in life, Mrs. Guest had looked becoming in this gown, she no longer did. Her illness had wasted her face to a skeletal thinness and her neck emerged stalk-like from the lace collar; her skin had turned a greenish grey, which the pure white of the cambric only accentuated. She smelled dreadful.

"Try the ringlets, there's a pet," called Georgina from under the camera cloth. "Let's see how she must have looked."

Ruby put down the lamp and went over to the valise they had brought with them. She rummaged through the tools of Georgina's trade: a pot of rouge, a card pinned with several hair pieces of different colours, two or three bunches of silk flowers. She unpinned the coil of brown ringlets and went over to the bed where the corpse lay. This was the part of her job she enjoyed the least. Rigor mortis had gone, so she was able to lift the head, take off the bonnet, and slip on the band that held the ringlets. The ravaged face suddenly surrounded by shining, luscious curls on top of the wispy, grey hair was grotesque.

"Oh dear. Put the bonnet back on and pull the ringlets around her face. That's better. Can you turn her this way a little."

Georgina had rolled the tripod to the other side of the bed. "Step back. Splendid."

She emerged once again and clicked the shutter.

"That should do it." She pulled out the plate, held it up to the light for a moment, then placed it with the other one in the box. She pinched her nostrils. "Phew. She's getting a bit gamey, isn't she? Do something about it, will you?"

"Yes, ma'am."

Ruby took a vial of chloride of lime from the valise, unstoppered it, and splashed a generous amount onto two cotton pads, which she placed on the dead woman's forehead. The sharp smell temporarily overrode the odour of decay. Georgina had pulled forward a chair and taken out her sketchbook.

"Have they left her rings on, Ruby?"

Ruby reached underneath the sheet that reached to the middle of the dead woman's upper arm and gently pulled up the left hand. There was a narrow gold wedding band on the ring finger. Ruby tried not to touch the clammy skin at the wrist but she had no choice.

"Just the wedding ring, ma'am."

"Hmm. My impression of Mr. Guest is that he would relish loading his wife with visible signs of his own prosperity, wouldn't you agree, Ruby?"

Ruby really didn't know what Georgina meant, but she nodded as if she understood completely.

"Have a look on her dresser. See if she has any rings."

The mirror had been draped with black crepe, and for a moment Ruby was startled at her own reflection, a ghostlike shadow in the room. All of the bedroom furnishings were of dark mahogany, and Mrs. Guest had favoured a crimson-and-green flock wall covering with matching curtains and fabric on the chairs. Against the opulence of the room, the bed seemed stark with its white sheets and colourless body. Ruby shivered, partly at the image of herself, partly because the room was very cold. The window was open wide to the frigid winter air and there was no fire in the grate, the better to preserve the corpse. Fortunately, Miss Georgina always worked quickly.

The top of the dresser was neat and orderly, the hair ornaments, arranged on a tray lined with pink satin, were of sterling silver, as was the hairbrush and hand mirror. Both were monogrammed.

"I don't see a ring, ma'am, but there is a lovely gold watch."

She held it up. It hung from a heavy gold chain and the front was set with pearls, emeralds, and three diamonds.

"Very good, Ruby. Bring it to me."

She continued to sketch the room as she spoke. When they went to view the bodies, Miss Georgina left behind her strange, mannish clothes, and her navy blue taffeta gown, trimmed with jet, was the essence of propriety. She also insisted Ruby wear dark clothing. *Like a little postulant preparing herself for her marriage to Christ* were her words, which meant nothing to Ruby. She thought the dull grey woollen waist made her look sallow. She took the watch to her mistress.

Georgina nodded. "Slip it over your neck for a moment. Let me see it against the grey."

Ruby did so. She was surprised at how heavy the watch was, pulling her neck forward. The lamp had been turned up high and the light winked on the jewels. Ruby knew what they were now although before she came to the Croftons' she had never seen so much as a picture of a pearl or an emerald. She longed to look at her own reflection but she didn't dare do so, afraid her mistress would think it vain.

Georgina smiled at her. "I'd wager my life's savings it was a present from Mr. Guest. Let me see." She leaned forward, flicked open the front lid, and peered at it. "Yes. I was right. 'To my dearest Margaret on the occasion of our golden anniversary.'" She snapped the case closed and let it rest against Ruby's chest. "It is a vulgar piece, isn't it?"

Ruby thought she had never seen such a beautiful thing in her entire life but she nodded.

"Yes, ma'am, it certainly is."

Georgina flipped over a page and made a quick drawing of the watch, with arrows pointing to each jewel with a letter to indicate what they were in case she forgot. Ruby believed she herself would remember the design until the day she died.

Her mistress turned back to her original drawing. "What do you think? Is it a likeness?"

Ruby examined the sketch carefully. She had learned that this was the one area where her true opinion was wanted. Georgina Crofton was quite short-sighted. Her portraits, even with the help of a photographic image, were often a little off.

"She has been ill, ma'am. Perhaps in life her cheeks would be rounder and her nose less sharp."

"Quite right, as usual, Ruby."

Georgina made the adjustments. "Goodness, I almost forgot. What colour were her eyes? Have a look, there's a pet."

Ruby walked over to the body and carefully lifted one eyelid. "It's rather difficult to tell at this stage, ma'am. But I would say they were brown."

"I'd better ask Mister. People get upset if you have the wrong eye colour. You know how that young couple were with the baby. As if it mattered. I thought all babies had blue eyes."

She blew on her fingers. "It's perishing cold in here. But I'm done. I'm going to give the painting a drawing-room setting so we had better go down there next."

"Perhaps they would like to have these photographs behind her." Ruby indicated two photographs in carved silver frames that were on the mantelpiece.

"As long as they weren't taken by Mr. Notman. Why should I advertise for him?"

William Notman was developing a reputation in Toronto for his photographs, and although he didn't do the same kind of work Georgina did, she had a bee in her bonnet about him. "Uncouth, my pet. People want pretty pictures, not that nonsense."

"They are from Mr. Krieghoff's studio, ma'am." In one of the photographs, a much younger Mrs. Guest sat in a chair holding a baby in a long christening gown. Behind her was Mr. Guest, moustached, portly, obviously proprietal. The second portrait was more recent. Again Mrs. Guest was seated in the centre, but now there were six others behind her who looked as if they were further offspring. Three small children sat at their feet.

"In that case I will include it. A very good suggestion, Ruby." Georgina started to gather up her things. "We'll leave the tripod. The butler can bring it down. But let's take the box with us. I don't trust anybody not to drop it."

She stuffed her sketchbook into the valise while Ruby went to get the box.

At the door, Georgina turned. She laughed. "I think you had better return the watch to the dresser. You don't want them sending a constable after us, do you?"

Ruby turned bright red. She hadn't forgotten about the watch around her neck. How could she? She had wanted to enjoy wearing it for a few more moments. Quickly she took it off and replaced it in its satin bed. Lugging the heavy box, she followed Georgina from the room.

She'd noticed her mistress slip one of the silver-edged hair combs into her pocket, but she told herself it must be necessary for the portrait.

CHAPTER EIGHT

AS SOON AS HE GOT TO THE STATION THE NEXT MORNING, Murdoch consulted the street directory. There were forty-two photographers listed in the city, most of them on King Street in the fashionable shopping district or on the heavily commercial Yonge Street from King as far north as Bloor Street. He could do with some help if he was going to do a thorough investigation, and in spite of what he had said to Miss Slade, he was half inclined to go to Inspector Brackenreid now. He was always balancing on a knife's edge with the man, who would reprimand him one minute for acting too independently and the next tell him off for not taking care of things. By "things", Brackenreid meant anything that might reflect badly on the station or, more precisely, the inspector himself. Murdoch had the uneasy feeling that telling Brackenreid about the photographs would be like putting his hand into a lobster trap. And he knew from experience how sharp those claws were. He could understand the teacher's concern for her pupil, but it was highly unlikely the situation would be resolved quietly. And why should it? He, himself, wanted the perpetrators to be caught and punished. However, he had agreed to begin discreetly, and that's what he'd do.

He took out his chalk and, using the wall as a blackboard, sketched a rough map of the city streets as far as Bay to the west and River to the east, Bloor to the north and Front to the south. Then with the blue chalk he marked the addresses of all the studios that were listed in the directory. How had Agnes met the photographer? Was it through somebody she knew? A chance encounter? Someone who had seen her and thought she was a good possibility? If the latter, then the studio might be in the vicinity of Syndenham where Agnes lived or the Sackville Street School. He doubted she had the means to go far afield. There were two studios that qualified, one by the name of Broom and Company, on Queen Street just west of Parliament, the other, Lofts Photographic Studio on King Street, near Sackville. Both were within a few blocks of Agnes's home. It was somewhere to start anyway.

He pulled open the drawer where he kept the photograph of Liza that he had taken not long before she died. He was in the habit of taking out the picture every day, but yesterday he'd forgotten to do so. He looked at the blurred image, not a good likeness, nowhere capturing the liveliness and intelligence to which he'd been so attracted.

"You would have liked Miss Slade, Liza," he murmured. "She's a woman after your own heart." He touched the glass. Nobody compared to her. He replaced the frame in the drawer and, thrusting his notebook in his pocket, headed for the hall. On the way out, he would see if he could find out something about the anonymous letters.

As agreed, Seymour had stayed off duty and Sergeant Gardiner was at the front desk.

"Good morning, Will," said the sergeant. "Anything we can help you with?"

Here was another situation requiring discretion, thought Murdoch. He was going to become as adept at deviousness as a town councillor.

"Has the morning post been collected yet? I was wondering if there are any letters for me?"

Gardiner pointed with his pen in the direction of the constable. "Ask him."

Callahan was sorting through the new deliveries, putting them into different piles.

"I haven't seen anything so far, Mr. Murdoch."

Callahan's voice was polite and his boyish face showed his eagerness to please. His brogue was pleasant. Murdoch felt a spasm of unreasonable irritation. He wished he could like the fellow more than he did. It wasn't his fault he was Philips's replacement.

"Is this a typical day? There doesn't seem to be a great deal of mail."

"No, there isn't really. Gets heavier at the end of the month when the tradesmen send in their bills." He finished sorting through the last few letters. "Nothing, sir."

Murdoch leaned over his shoulder, feigning curiosity. "The inspector's correspondence is the majority, I see."

"Yes, it always is. He's forever getting invitations to inspect this or that."

"Do you read the letters first, then?"

"Beg pardon, sir?"

"I just wondered. You seem well-acquainted with the contents."

As far as he could tell, Callahan didn't seem discomfited. "The inspector passes them along to me to answer for him." He indicated the typewriting machine on the desk beside him.

"That thing must save you a lot of time."

Callahan shrugged. "I'm only just getting the hang of it. Eventually it will be faster than handwriting, I'm sure."

"One of my fellow boarders used a typewriter. It didn't look like that one though. What kind do you have?"

"It's a Remington. All the stations have them now."

Gardiner was leaning his elbows on the counter in exaggerated bewilderment.

"I've never before known you so interested in what goes

on behind the desk, Murdoch. Not considering a change of position, are you? I'm sure young Callahan would be only too glad to swap. He'd like to be a detective, I bet, get to go out all the time, question pretty young women."

Murdoch decided it was time to leave. "You have a totally false notion of my tasks, sergeant."

He got his hat and coat from the hook by the door, nodded goodbye, and left.

He hadn't gone far when a deluge of rain began. The winter weather had been sliding from damp and mild, with November temperatures, to the bitter cold you'd expect in January. Today was like a chill morning in autumn, and the snowfall of the previous day was already reduced to grey mounds in the gutters. Passersby were huddled under their black umbrellas, coat collars turned up. Murdoch didn't have an umbrella. The unspoken attitude of the police force was that umbrellas were unmanly. No constable was issued one and detectives were expected to show their mettle by braving the elements.

He'd hoped to arrive at the school while the children were out for their playtime, but when he got there, the schoolyard was deserted. The windows glowed with light, warm and welcome in the leaden morning. The building itself was plainer than a bank might be, with no fancy cornices or elaborate carvings. Nevertheless it managed to convey the same air of solidity and sobriety. There was a set of double doors in the centre of the front but on a whim Murdoch went in through the boys' entrance on the right. He walked through the cloakroom, which was redolent with the fug of damp, woollen coats. A man in workman's brown corduroys, a lamp in his hand, came through the door that led to the corridor.

"Can I help you, sir? Would you be in search of somebody?"

"I would indeed. Can you tell me which is Miss Slade's classroom?"

The man had a round, ruddy face with full blond side whiskers. He pursed his lips at Murdoch's question.

"She'd be on this floor. Go through this door. It's at the far end." He grinned, showing tobacco-stained teeth. "You can't miss her."

If he hadn't already met Miss Slade, Murdoch would have been puzzled by the man's leer. However, he knew why it was there and felt irritated. He nodded and went through to the corridor.

He was in a wide hall with classrooms to the left. The doors were closed but he could hear the sound of the pupils chanting their multiplication tables as he went by. A boy was standing outside the third room, leaning against the wall in boredom. He straightened up quickly as he saw Murdoch, who smiled reassuringly at him. Whatever trouble the boy had got himself into, he couldn't rescue him from it.

Near the far end of the corridor, he realized the reason for the caretaker's mocking tone. There was an extraordinary noise coming from the room. It was as if it was filled with birds, all twittering and chirping at full volume. However, as he got closer, the sounds abruptly changed into full-throated foghorns, pulsing on the sea air. He looked through the small window in the door. Miss Slade was leading her pupils in some sort of exercise. They all had their hands to their mouths, fingers cupped, and they seemed to be blowing out of the side of their mouths.

She made a chopping gesture and the foghorns died away, then he heard her call out, "Horse." As one, the children shifted to a chorus of neighs and whinnies that were startlingly real. He might have been listening to a stable of agitated equines. At that moment, Miss Slade caught sight of him. Even from his vantage point, he could see her blush. She gestured for the children to stop what they were doing and came directly to the door.

"Free practice, boys and girls," she said over her shoulder, and Murdoch was treated to a veritable barnyard of sounds as she came out to the corridor.

"Mr. Murdoch, do you have news?"

"I went to Agnes Fisher's house but she wasn't there. I'm going to check on all photographic studios but I thought I'd come here first."

Miss Slade frowned. "She hasn't come to school again today. Her brother says she is staying with their sister."

Murdoch took out his notebook and pencil. "Do you know where that is?"

"No, I don't."

"May I talk to the boy, then?"

Miss Slade hesitated. "I suppose you will have to. I'll bring him out."

She went back into the classroom to a momentary pause in

the livestock noises. However, they resumed immediately with great vigour if diminishing authenticity. Murdoch stepped to one side and Benjamin Fisher emerged, Miss Slade behind him.

"I'd like to be present if you don't mind," she said.

Murdoch knew that what she meant was she didn't know him well enough to trust him not to be indiscreet, which irked him somewhat. However, he respected her care for her pupils. As for the boy, when he saw who wanted him, he looked as if he would do a bolt right there and then. Any good feeling that Murdoch had purchased with hot pies and gravy the night before had vanished. Murdoch crouched down so as to be more on a level.

"Hello, Ben. I don't want to take you from you lessons for too long. That sounds amazingly real to me, by the way, especially the foghorns." He glanced up at Miss Slade. "I'm from Nova Scotia and believe me, I've listened to lots of foghorns warning off the ships."

She nodded, but Ben hardly seemed to have heard. He was waiting for the inevitable. The reason Murdoch wanted to speak to him.

"As I told you, I am concerned to have a word with your sister, Aggie. I understand she's missed school again today. Why is that, Ben? Is she not well?"

The boy wouldn't look at him. "She's staying with Sis."

"Does she do that very often?"

"Sometimes when…"

He didn't finish his sentence and he didn't need to. Murdoch guessed that the girl fled the home when things became unbearable with their father.

"Why didn't you go with her?"

Ben, if possible, shrank even more. "Martha only has room for Aggie."

"And where is Martha? I understand she's in service."

"I don't know where she is. She didn't want us to know."

Again his voice tailed off.

"But she told Aggie where she was? Only Aggie, not you?"

Ben's eyes flickered. "That's right."

Murdoch knew he was lying, but he wasn't about to press him. For all the boy's timidity, he had the feeling he had become inured to brutality. If he'd decided not to reveal his sister's whereabouts, there wasn't much Murdoch could do about it. He had no intention of outdoing Mr. Fisher in terms of violence. Miss Slade stepped in.

"Ben, neither Mr. Murdoch nor I mean any harm to Aggie. In fact, it is the opposite. She, er, she might be in some kind of trouble and we both want to help her."

The boy pointed at Murdoch. "Is he a frog?"

"If you mean, is he a police officer, yes he is. I have…I have consulted him because I am worried about Agnes. Benjamin, please answer truthfully, do you know what I am referring to?"

He scrutinized her for a moment, then nodded. "You think she might have one under her apron."

Miss Slade quickly hid her shock at the vulgarity of the boy's response.

"In fact, that was not what concerned me. Aggie fainted because she breathed too much air and she didn't have any breakfast. That is all."

It was Murdoch's turn to speak up. This time, his voice was firmer. Still kind but there was no mistaking that he was reaching his limit.

"Benjamin, what you just said to your teacher was rude. Gentlemen don't speak like that. Please apologize."

The boy was looking so white, Murdoch almost thought he might faint the way his sister had.

"I beg your pardon, Miss Slade. I didn't mean nothing."

"Anything," she corrected him automatically. "You didn't mean anything."

"No, Miss."

"I am in no way asking you to be disloyal to your sister, Ben, but I would like to speak to her, as would Mr. Murdoch. You say you don't know where Martha lives now. But at a guess, where might she be? Was it a grand house like the ones on Sherbourne Street or Berkeley?"

He thought for a moment. "I can't say, Miss. Martha never told us much 'cos of Pa. She's come back home a couple of times in the beginning and she said it was a swell house and they treated her good. That's all I know."

"How did she get the position, Ben?" Murdoch asked.

"She found a newspaper under a bench."

Miss Slade and Murdoch exchanged glances. "You mean she answered an advertisement?"

"Yes, sir, that's what she did."

Murdoch took the photograph of the baby boy from his envelope and held it in front of Ben.

"Have you ever seen this picture before?"

The boy's eyes flickered, but he shook his head. "No, sir. Passed on, has he, the baby?"

"Yes."

Before he left the station, Murdoch had taped a piece of paper over the genitalia of the youth in the other photograph so that he was only visible from the waist up. He showed this card to Ben.

"Do you know this lad?"

"No, sir. Why is he covered up? Is he a prince?"

"I doubt he's a prince and he's covered up because he doesn't have any clothes on."

Ben giggled nervously. "Why not?"

Murdoch decided to ignore the question. "Are you sure you've never seen him? He didn't come to your house ever?"

Ben was on safe ground here. "Oh no, sir. Nobody comes to the house."

Murdoch took the boy's chin in his hand and looked into his eyes. "Are you telling me the truth, son?"

Ben stared back at him but his brown eyes had gone blank, deliberately guileless.

"Oh yes, sir. I ain't never seen either picture before."

Miss Slade managed to bite her tongue and not correct his grammar. Murdoch let him go, unconvinced. "Thank you, Ben.

Now, listen to me. I want you to let Miss Slade know the moment Aggie returns home. Will you do that?"

"Yes, sir. But Aggie'll come to school, won't she?"

"She might be afraid to. You will be doing her a great kindness if you tell her that we want to help her. Then let Miss Slade know. Just in case Aggie decides to run off to Martha's again."

"Yes, sir."

"You can go back into the classroom, now, Ben," said Miss Slade.

The raucous attempts at imitation had died down and now there was the ordinary murmur of unsupervised children. Benjamin did as the teacher told him, but she remained in the corridor. Murdoch could see her distress.

"We'll get to the bottom of this, ma'am, I promise. Even if I have to knock on the door of every photographer in the city."

That comment won him a rather reluctant smile.

"I do appreciate your help, Mr. Murdoch."

"I will report back to you as soon as I can."

She stared at him for a moment, considering some choice he couldn't fathom.

"Just a moment," she said and went back into the classroom, returning immediately with a silver card case in her hand. She opened it. "Here is my card. I would be more than happy if you call on me at my lodgings. I don't mind what the hour. I wish to know any outcome of your inquiries."

Murdoch put the calling card into his pocket and tipped his hat.

"Good day, Miss Slade."

As he walked back toward the cloakroom, he could hear new sounds emitting from the classroom. Somebody was whistling an old folk song, sweet and tuneful as any musical instrument. Given what he had already seen of Miss Slade, he assumed it was she who was creating the sound.

CHAPTER NINE

THE FIRST STUDIO WAS ON THE SECOND FLOOR ABOVE a dry goods store, currently closed down. On each side were boarded-up vacant houses. In an attempt to combat the surrounding air of decay, the entrance to the right of the dry goods store was newly painted and a sign, GREGORY'S EMPORIUM: WELCOME AND COME IN, hung from the doorknob. There was an ink drawing of a camera on a tripod in the corner of the notice. Following instructions, Murdoch went inside. Almost directly in front of the door was a steep flight of stairs, carpeted in rush matting and, in case the customers happened to get lost between entrance and stairs, a second sign was tacked on the wall. A hand pointed upward, underneath it the words EMPORIUM, THIS WAY. Before Murdoch had even reached the first stair, however, a door on the landing above opened and a young man and woman came out. They were laughing and, not seeing Murdoch, turned toward each other. The man grabbed both of the woman's buttocks in his hands, lifting her up to press against him. Murdoch heard a cry of protest that was smothered by the man's hard kiss. Embarrassed at being an involuntary witness to this private embrace, Murdoch called out.

"Good morning, I'm looking for the photograph studio."

He might as well have shot off a gun. They leapt apart and stood staring down at him. He proceeded up the stairs.

"Good morning," he repeated and tipped his hat to the young woman. Her wide-brimmed hat had been knocked backwards by the force of the man's embrace and she straightened it quickly. She was dressed in a fawn-coloured walking suit with a corsage of fresh flowers at the breast. He had on a brown tweed overcoat and a snappy bowler hat. Everything about them said they were newly married.

"The studio is this way, I presume?" he said, indicating the door behind them.

"It is," the man replied. Recovered from his surprise and made a touch belligerent because of it, he pulled his bride toward him and they went down the stairs, his arm around her waist. Their progress was awkward because of the narrowness of the stairwell, but he wouldn't let go of her. She now belonged to him.

On the door was hung yet another sign, GREGORY'S

EMPORIUM: KNOCK FIRST. THEN ENTER. In smaller print, *Leave umbrellas in the hall*. A little drawing of a furled umbrella and an arrow aiming in the direction of a stand beside the door. Currently it was devoid of coats or umbrellas. Murdoch glanced around. So far he couldn't say he was impressed with the Emporium. The stairs and hall were dull, no paintings, no wall covering, just a dingy pale green coat of paint. Either it needed redoing or the gas light was leeching out the colour, which everybody complained it did.

He rapped sharply and went inside. Another young woman, about the same age as the shy bride he had just encountered, was sitting behind a desk facing the door. This one, however, gave him a smile brimming with confidence.

"Good morning, sir. Welcome to the Emporium."

She was dressed in a demure gown of tartan taffeta and her hair was tightly pinned in a knot on top of her head. Murdoch removed his hat and returned her smile.

"Newly wed?"

She looked at him, startled.

"I beg your pardon, sir?"

He jerked his thumb in the direction of the door. "The couple that just left. I'll wager they've just got hitched."

"Oh, yes, you are quite correct. Early this morning, I believe. They wanted to get photographed before they went to their wedding breakfast."

"Lucky man," said Murdoch.

She lowered her eyes to the piece of paper in front of her.

"Quite so. Now as for you Mr...?"

"Murdoch. William Murdoch."

"Are you interested in a wedding portrait?"

Murdoch felt a twinge of warning in his gut. It wasn't that the young woman wasn't professional in her appearance and manner, she was in a rather self-conscious way, but her reaction to his question had been too wary. There had been a momentary flash of cold suspicion in her eyes.

He gave a phony chuckle. "Oh no, ma'am, not me. I haven't had that kind of luck yet to find me a bride. I'd just like to inquire about a photo picture to give to my dear old mother."

She smiled at him. "How very thoughtful of you. A cabinet then." She consulted a notepad in front of her. "We actually have time now. It isn't usually the case, normally we are full up, but there was an unexpected cancellation." She smiled at his good fortune and handed him a card. "Here is a list of our prices. I do recommend you order the package of five. It is more economical."

Murdoch had not really expected this and he wasn't sure how he was going to pay. Or if he could pay. So far this investigation was unauthorized.

"Can you send me the bill?"

"Of course, that is our usual procedure." She allowed the smallest note of reproach to creep into her voice, as if he were impugning the integrity of the Emporium by implying that they were money grabbing.

She stood up. "I'll fetch Mr. Gregory, our photographer.

And will you be so kind as to fill out this form with your name and address."

"Thank you, Miss…?"

"I beg your pardon, I should have introduced myself. I'm Miss Hill."

She smiled again, a smile quite as false as Murdoch's overdone grinning. Then she handed him a piece of paper and disappeared through another door. Ignoring the form for the moment, Murdoch took a look around him. The room wasn't large, but a tall window allowed good light and created a pleasant airy feeling to the place. Several chairs, nicely covered in burgundy plush velvet, were around the edge of the room, a mahogany coat stand stood by the door, the carpet was a richly patterned Axminster. Perhaps the savings accrued from the sparse furnishing of the entry had been used here where it counted. The walls were lined with row on row of photographs, and Murdoch went to examine them. Gregory's seemed to specialize in wedding photographs, given the number of portraits of happy couples, sombre for the moment, all dressed in their best. Interspersed here and there were what he assumed were the cabinets, head-and-shoulders photographs of serious-looking men and a few women. He was more interested in the backdrops but at a quick inspection, he didn't see the artificial wood panelling or the leopard-skin rug and the birdcage that were in the stereoscopic picture of Agnes.

He had just returned to his seat and picked up the form when Miss Hill returned, followed by a stocky fellow whose hand was outstretched even as he came in the door.

"Good morning, Mr. Murdoch. My name is Gregory. Bartholomew Gregory. At your service, sir."

He had a strong cockney accent.

Murdoch shook hands. Gregory's grip was vigorous. Despite the formality of his black worsted suit, there was no hiding the fact he had performed manual labour at some point in his youth. His shoulders were wide and sloping and his upper arms filled the sleeves of his jacket. Murdoch could feel the hard calluses on his palm.

"I was actually looking for a Mr. Loft. I understood he had a studio here. He did some good work for a cousin of mine a while back."

Gregory grinned, revealing the glint of a gold filling in his front tooth.

"Dead and gone. Or I should say, Mr. Loft is enjoying a well-earned retirement. I purchased the business a few months ago. Decided to change the name to avoid confusion."

"From over the pond are you, Mr. Gregory?" Murdoch asked, gaping a little.

"*Horn and head*, born and bred to you," said Gregory. "Now I understand from Miss Hill that you would like our cabinet package of five."

"That's right. For my mother." He waved vaguely at the photographs on the wall. "But I'd like a nice serious backdrop. Gives a better impression, don't you think?"

"It most certainly does, sir. And you're a man of commerce, I'd wager."

"How'd you ever guess that? Let's just say I'm interested in the typewriting business."

"Good going, sir. Efficient typewriters are in great demand. I don't know what I'd do without Miss Hill."

The young woman had returned to the desk but she nodded an acknowledgement.

Gregory gestured. "Why don't we step right out and get started?"

They were interrupted by the door to the hall banging open. A young man came in with such a flurry, he might have been propelled by the wind. He was carrying an umbrella that he immediately started to shake, scattering raindrops like a wet dog.

"Frigging weather…"

He stopped in mid-sentence when he saw the room was occupied. "Oh, I beg your pardon."

Gregory barely acknowledged his presence and made no attempt to introduce him.

"You can put your bat and moat on the stand, Mr. Murdoch," he said. "Come this way."

The newcomer stood where he was. Not a customer obviously. A handsome young man by any standards, with his dark hair and trim moustache. Murdoch thought he might be Miss Hill's suitor, but she didn't acknowledge him either. He glanced curiously at Murdoch, then plopped down in one of the chairs.

CHAPTER TEN

THE STUDIO WAS NOT MUCH LARGER THAN THE RECEPTION room and had the same impoverished decor of the entrance hallway and stairs. The plank floor was uncarpeted, there was no furniture at all, and the walls were whitewashed. In spite of the three deep windows, the dull light of the rain-soaked day was not sufficient for photographic purposes and two gas chandeliers overhead had been lit. A camera on a wheeled tripod was aimed between two platforms, each curtained off by a curved rod, rather like miniature stages.

"Well, which do you fancy, Mr. Murdoch? You can have your penny dip. This setting here is what we call the Park. An exact depiction of the Allan Horticultural Gardens, which I'm sure you are familiar with."

He drew back the heavy curtains of the nearest stage, revealing a painted backdrop of depressing ineptitude. The pavilion leaned slightly and looked as if a good gust of wind would blow it away; the few shrubs in the foreground were an odd muddy green and the sky and the dirty clouds looked as if the painter hadn't bothered to clean his brush. In the centre of the platform was a flimsy wooden plinth, painted to look like a marble sundial.

"Stand here, Mr. Murdoch, if you please. Turn to the right just a titch. Good. Excellent. Don't move for a tick and a tock." Gregory went over to the camera and wheeled it to the front of the Park. He disappeared underneath the focusing cloth, moved a little closer, then reappeared. "Now that is a fine portrait as ever hit my peepers. You are most definitely an outdoor man. I must say I would never take you for a man of commerce."

Murdoch grinned, showing lots of teeth. "But that is what I am, Mr. Gregory, and I think I'd be better off with the indoor setting. What's that other one like?"

Gregory sighed, just enough to let customers know how foolish they were to question his choice. He pulled back the second curtain to reveal a stage that was bare except for a plain wooden chair in the centre and a small rolltop desk at the back. However, Murdoch could see that the painted backdrop depicted a panelled wall. Something must have shown in his expression because Gregory became hearty again.

"I know it don't look like much as is, but in a photograph, it is very realistic. You'd think you were in the Prince of Wales's study."

Murdoch pointed to the adjacent set of double doors.

"Got anything else back there I can look at?"

"I'm afraid not. That leads to my private birch and broom and the dark room. A dark room is where the plates are developed," he added.

Murdoch chortled. "Well, I didn't think it was a place you sat with the lights out." He walked around the little stage. "It'd be better with carpet on the floor. Have you got any more props or is that it?"

"Course, I do. I'm just setting you up first. Why don't you sit on the lion's lair and take the weight off your beaters."

Murdoch mounted the platform and sat in the chair while Gregory brought the camera over and focused it.

"Yes, yes, that's better. You were the Isle of Wight. I'd ask you for a loan if I thought I'd get it." His voice was muffled by the black cloth. "Shall I take the photograph now then?"

"I thought you were going to put down a piece of carpet."

Gregory's head emerged. "I was about to get it."

He headed for a large wardrobe that was in the corner of the room.

"I wouldn't mind a plant of some kind, pictures, a clock. I'm sure his Majesty doesn't sit in a bare room," Murdoch said.

He could feel the man's exasperation, but decided it was for show, intended to intimidate him. While Gregory was rooting in the wardrobe, he studied the backdrop. He couldn't be sure it was the same one that had been used in the picture of Agnes Fisher. There wasn't much to define either one.

"How's this mug?"

Gregory was throwing down a fringed rug. It was surprisingly fresh and colourful with a pattern of overblown roses intertwined with lilies.

"Is that the only one you've got?"

"Yes, it is. And it's mint as you can see." He went over to the desk. "I'll put these have a looks here like so."

They weren't real books, just the outer shells.

"What about some greenery? A fern or one of those leafy plants, asperdasters they're called."

"You mean, aspidistras. And no, I don't have anything like that."

Murdoch stood up. "Maybe I can look for myself. See what you've got."

Gregory didn't flinch. "By all means. I want satisfied customers even if it takes all May."

Murdoch pointed at the windows, which were blurry with rain. "Not likely you'll get many now."

While the photographer watched, he walked over to the wardrobe. There was in fact a piece of greenery in there, not the one he was looking for, but a basket of bent and warped ivy. He pulled it out triumphantly.

"See, you did have something. This'll look real good on the desk."

"You're right. Don't know how I overlooked it."

. He'd told the truth about the rugs. There weren't any others and Murdoch couldn't see anything else from the stereoscopic photographs. He picked up a clock with the hands perpetually set at ten to three and a framed print of a watercolour that must have been done by the same artist who had painted the sets. He seemed to specialize in dull colours and vague, lopsided shapes. It was only on second glance that Murdoch recognized Niagara Falls.

"These will do just fine," he said and brought them back to the stage.

Without a word but making no attempt to hide his impatience, Gregory took them from him. The watercolour he hung on a nail above the desk and the clock at a point just to the right of the chair. Obviously, they had been placed there before and Murdoch wondered why the man wasn't showing more care. Perhaps it was because he thought Murdoch was unemployed.

"All right then, sir. Sit in the chair and cross your arms. Good. Most impressive."

He stepped out from the focusing cloth and stood to the side of the camera, the lens cable in his right hand.

"Now I want you to keep as still as you can. Don't move a muscle. Look straight into the camera." He pressed the button. "Hold it. Don't move."

Murdoch heard a click as the lens closed.

"Good. We got it." Gregory went to remove the plate from the camera. "Now I could take another for good measure, but that is a cost that has to be borne by the customer."

Murdoch got out of the chair. "I'll leave it at that. When can I have the pictures?"

Gregory was all hearty again. "They'll be ready the day after tomorrow at the latest. Now I'd better get on with my work so I'll leave you to settle your till with Miss Hill." He held out his hand. "It's been a pleasure to take you, Mr. Murdoch. I'm sure you'll be quite satisfied."

He was smiling his broad, gold-illuminated smile, but when Murdoch looked into his eyes he saw nothing there but a cold indifference. Gregory averted his gaze immediately, stepped over to the door, and ushered Murdoch into the other room.

"See to this gentleman, will you, my dear," he called to the woman behind the desk and he went back into the studio, closing the door behind him.

"Come and have a seat, sir." It wasn't Miss Hill any more. This woman was older, thin faced with a sharp nose and chin.

"What happened to Miss Hill?" he asked. "She was the one I was dealing with before."

"She's gone to have her dinner," said the woman, apparently struggling to be pleasant.

"Pity. And who might you be, ma'am, if I may be so bold as to ask?"

"I'm Mrs. Gregory. Mr. Gregory, my husband, is the one you have just been with." She had no trace of a cockney accent.

"Very good fellow indeed even if he does talk peculiar. Knows what he's doing all right."

She nodded but without expression.

Murdoch decided to stir up a little jealousy. You never knew what would fall out when emotions ran high. He continued.

"That Miss Hill's a mighty handsome young woman, I must say. Talented too, I'd wager. Does she ever get on the other side of the desk? You know, pose for pictures herself?"

"No, she does not."

"Pity that, with her good looks she'd be very popular."

"I'll let her know your sentiments, sir. I'm sure she will be flattered."

She took a form out of the drawer. "Perhaps I can take your order now and not keep you any longer."

So much for calling on the green-eyed god. Mrs. Gregory had been impervious.

She handed Murdoch the piece of paper. "You didn't indicate which package you wanted, sir. I understand it's ten copies."

"Oh no. That's too many for me. Two will do. One for me and one for my mother."

Mrs. Gregory sighed, looked as if she would try to talk him out of it, changed her mind, and dipped her pen in the inkwell. "Two portraits then. That will be three dollars, please."

"Whoa back, ma'am. The other young lady said you would send a bill seeing as I don't have a position at the moment."

Mrs. Gregory frowned. "Miss Hill is new here and obviously not familiar with our policy. We require one half payment now and the remainder on delivery of the photographs."

There wasn't any point arguing with that chin and besides,

he wanted to come back again. He fished in his pocket and took out all the coins he had.

"I've got seventy-five cents here. You'll have to be satisfied with that."

She didn't blink and he regretted he had succumbed so easily. "Given your circumstances, I will make a concession."

She swooped up the money and put it into a cash box.

"Speaking of mothers," said Murdoch. "My dear old mother gave me a stereoscope for a Christmas present and I'd like to buy me some more cards. I wonder if you sell them, seeing as you do photographs."

He was observing her carefully but detected no reaction. Either she was completely ignorant of the possible secondary line of work of the Emporium or she was a consummate actress.

"I'm afraid we don't, Mr. Murdoch. But I understand Mr. Eaton's store has a good selection. You know where he is, don't you?"

"Yes indeed, ma'am. He's right at the corner of Queen and Yonge Streets."

"That's right. Now if you will excuse me, I must get on with my work."

She swivelled around in her chair. There was a typewriting machine on the desk that had been covered before. She inserted a sheet of paper.

Murdoch stood up, retrieved his hat and coat from the stand, and went to the door. The clacking of the typewriter's keys followed him. Mrs. Gregory sounded like an expert typewriter, he thought. Pity he hadn't been able to see what kind of machine she was using. He could have verified Enid's statement that offices were using Remingtons these days.

CHAPTER ELEVEN

"BABY BABY BUNTING, YOUR FATHER'S GONE A HUNTING,'" Kate Tibbett sang softly to the twins, whom she was carrying in the crook of each arm. Both babies were teething and her nerves were worn ragged. She had hardly soothed James and got him to sleep when Jacob would wake up, screaming, and within minutes she had both of them crying again. Her arms ached from the weight of carrying them, walking around the tiny bedroom, into the front sitting room and back, round and round. She wished she could have even one hour free, when she could fall into the sweetness of sleep. But there wasn't anybody to take over. Her family were far off and wouldn't be sympathetic anyway. *You made your bed, now you have to lie in it* would be her mother's sour words. But Ralph had pursued her so ardently, he had swept away the misgivings she'd had about surrendering to his passion before they were married. *You should have known*, he'd said angrily when she told him she believed herself to be with child. But she hadn't known anything, and had brought such shame to her mother and father, she doubted they would ever forgive her.

When they had first moved here, Ralph had been attentive and loving, but as soon as she became clumsy and heavy with the pregnancy he had spent more and more time away from their lodgings. He'd taken work in an office, he told her, general odds-body, he said, but his allowance wasn't generous and she felt the want more keenly than she could admit even to herself. There were many nights when she cried herself asleep after waiting until the early hours of the morning for him to come home. Since the birth of the twins, his absences were even more prolonged. He said he'd had to take a second job to supplement his wages and was working as a night porter at the Dominion Brewery on Queen Street.

Don't worry, little Kate. I can get catnaps throughout the night and nobody will know.

The extra work didn't seem to tire him out, and on one of the few evenings he was at home, she thought he looked as prosperous as he'd ever been. His worsted suit was of excellent quality, but when she timorously remarked on it, he told her it was a charitable cast-off from his employer. His voice was full of reproach. *You don't know how it eats at a man's pride to be forced to accept charity*, he'd said and she burst into tears, stung once again by the feeling that she was to blame.

She halted. Both babies had fallen asleep. Now the trick was to ease them into the cradle without disturbing either one. She bent over and slipped Jacob crosswise onto his end of the mattress. He made little smacking noises with his lips but didn't wake. Carefully, she placed James at the opposite end. They hadn't expected two infants and couldn't afford a second cradle so Ralph had sawed off a piece of wood and made a divider. She kept meaning to cover it with soft cloth but she hadn't yet found the time to do so. Besides, the twins were growing fast and would soon be too big for this arrangement. Looking down at them, she felt a rush of tenderness, something she sometimes feared she would never experience again. She covered them with the quilt that her oldest sister had grudgingly passed on to her. It was irretrievably stained from previous use, but it was soft and warm and she was glad of it.

She stepped back from the cradle. Rain was pelting against the window and it was so dull and cheerless in the room, she'd had to light a candle. She watched it for a moment, dancing and juttering in the draft from the door, then walked to the window and looked into the grey street. Snow would be better than this, at least after it had stopped falling, the sun would shine and the fresh white snow would glisten beneath a blue sky. She leaned her head against the windowpane and yawned as if she would crack her jaw. She was thankful that at least the room was warm. The brewery workers were allowed to take home buckets of slack from the coal furnaces, and even though the stuff was so dusty it seemed to give off more smoke than heat, it was better than nothing. Also, every time Ralph came home with a bucket, she was relieved she could believe him about his job.

She went back to the bed. Both babies were fast asleep. She lay down, covered herself with a blanket, and closed her eyes. Just a little nap while she could.

She must have dozed off because suddenly she was awake, the babies still sleeping quietly beside her. What had awakened her was the sound of a loud, angry voice overhead. Kate groaned. Fisher had come home and, as was usually the case, he was full of liquor. Sometimes, she knew he ranted at nothing, the bed, the weather, the bedbugs. Mostly though, he yelled at the children. She'd heard Ben go off to school this morning so his father must be shouting at Agnes. She thought about the man who'd come the day before, the one she assumed was a truant officer. In their brief meeting, she'd had the impression he was kind. If the babies hadn't been crying she would like to have lingered, talked to him. From the upstairs, she heard a crash and a bellow from Fisher, then a girl's voice, loud with fear, a shriek. He must have hit her. Light footsteps followed by the man's heavy tread. Another shriek, then weeping. Fisher's voice continued for a little longer, then there was silence.

She heard the sound of quick footsteps on the stairs and there was a timid tap, tap on her door. She didn't move. There was another tap, then the steps moved away and she heard the front door open.

She pulled the blanket up so that it covered her ears. There was nothing she could do. She had her own troubles to deal with.

CHAPTER TWELVE

BROOM AND CO., THE STUDIO ON QUEEN STREET, WAS so imbued with stultifying respectability that Murdoch wondered how they deigned to photograph anyone who wasn't related to the British peerage. He showed the young man at the reception desk the photograph of the dead infant, making up some story about his uncle being near death's door and could he commission a portrait? The man sniffed and said disdainfully that they did not take such pictures. There were those that did, but he did not know who they were and, he implied, he did not wish to know. Murdoch then asked if they took stereoscopic photographs with stories that were so swell these days and the man almost pulled himself by his nostrils into heaven. *No they did not, indeed.* Murdoch asked to see the studio where the photographs were taken and with great reluctance, the young man did so. The backdrop here was another painted canvas, this one well done, of a park with a manor house in the distance. Murdoch knew it was too early to eliminate anybody from his list, but his instinct was that Broom and Co. were what they appeared to be – snobbish and expensive, catering only to the affluent. He didn't bother to get another set of pictures taken.

He tried one more studio, one nearer to Yonge Street. This place was much less pretentious, owned by a placid older man, Elias Thompson, who seemed to be waiting patiently for customers, his feet on his desk, a cigar in his hand. When Murdoch held out the mourning card, he sighed for the *poor lost lambie*, but said it wasn't his. Yes, there were a few photographers who took these kind of pictures but he had no names to give him. He said he'd seen the series of Mr. Newly-wed and the maid and he thought they were hilarious; very popular as well but too expensive for him to make. Murdoch considered showing him the photograph of the naked Mr. Newly-wed but decided against it. He liked him and shifted him to the bottom of the list as a likely photographer of pornographic images.

He didn't feel he had accomplished much. Of the three photographers he'd met, the one he most disliked was Gregory but disliking a man wasn't a good reason for charging him with issuing obscene material and, so far, he had absolutely no proof that Gregory had photographed the girl. For that matter, all four pictures could have been taken by different people, although he thought that was unlikely. The three stereoscopic cards seemed linked, at least by their obscenity. Discouraged, he decided to visit Seymour's lodgings and see if he could get any further with that investigation.

"River Street! River Street!"

The conductor was calling out his stop and Murdoch sat up. He'd actually been dozing, lulled by the warmth of the streetcar. He went to the rear door and the streetcar halted just long enough for him to get down, then clanged off on its way as if it were a horse anxious for the barn.

The rain had turned to sleet, which was homing into the gap between his neck and his collar. He wrapped his muffler more tightly. River Street was at the eastern edge of the city limits, and the houses along it were interspersed with vacant lots, all weed covered and dispiriting. Ahead of him, a woman tried to handle her umbrella and two parcels, and at the same time keep her skirt raised above the wet pavement. He was reminded of Miss Slade and her odd but practical trousers. She would have no difficulty manoeuvring through inclement weather. He knew his Liza would have liked her and he felt a mixture of guilt and pleasure. Would Mrs. Jones also like the teacher? He wasn't sure but didn't think there would be an immediate compatibility. For some reason, that made him sigh.

He quickened his pace, about to offer his help with the parcels, but the woman turned into the front yard of one of the houses. The door opened even before she rang the bell, a young girl in maid's uniform came out to help her, and they disappeared inside.

As he approached the planing mill, Murdoch could hear the thump of the steam engines that drove the machinery. Scott's was obviously in full production, and dozens of logs were piled in the yard waiting to be hauled inside for planing. Murdoch halted in front of the fence, gripped by a surge of nostalgia. Ten years ago he'd had a crib at a logging camp near Huntsville. In spite of the hard work and rough company, he had been happy there. He'd filled out to manhood, physically and emotionally. Only a half-acknowledged driving ambition had pushed him away from that life, until he finally settled in Toronto and joined the police force. Early on, fretting about the lack of opportunity, he'd questioned that choice. Then, three years ago, he had been invited to join the newly established detective department, and he liked that much better. Because he was a Roman Catholic, he knew his chances for promotion were slim, but that was compensated for by interesting work and more freedom than he'd had while on the beat. He even didn't mind being expected to be on call all the time. If he were married, that might cause problems, but he'd have to tackle that question if and when it came up. And why were his thoughts constantly scurrying back to the subject of matrimony? He was like a dog returning to his buried bone, wondering whether it was time to dig it up and, if he did, whether it would be tasty.

Murdoch glanced around him. The street and yard were

deserted. With one leap he was over the low fence. He landed on one of the logs that were lying across the yard, in some places two or three deep. The rain had made the surface slippery just as it always was when the logs were dammed in the river. He skidded and almost lost his balance but he bent his knees, flung out his arms, and kept going. Damn, he needed his iron crampons, his boots didn't give him a good traction. Nevertheless, he quickened his pace, almost running now. He'd won the competition two years in a row for fastest crossing. The trick was to be balanced low over your feet and to land squarely in the centre of the log so it didn't roll. A fall was dangerous as the huge logs could shift in the water and deliver crushing blows. Two men had been injured the year he was there, one had succumbed to his injuries and died.

"Hey, what the hell do you think you're doing?" A man had appeared at the loading door of the mill and was glaring at him.

"Just doing an inspection of your goods," called Murdoch. "Making sure these logs are packed in tight, do you want one of your workers to break his leg?" He turned and ran back, hoping he wouldn't slip again and look like a fool.

"What! What inspection?"

Before the man could protest further, Murdoch had reached the fence.

"Everything seems in order," he called and hopped over the fence the way he had come.

"Hey, get back here," yelled the man, but Murdoch got out of sight fast. He was panting but he'd enjoyed the exercise.

A few houses up from the mill was number 108, and the pounding of the steam engine could still be heard, or felt, more like it – a minor perpetual earthquake rumbling beneath the street.

Murdoch stopped for a moment to get his breath and glanced over his shoulder to make sure the irate watchman hadn't come out looking for him. All clear. He opened the gate quickly and walked up to the door. He'd come here last summer to meet Seymour for a long bicycle ride but then the house had been rather drab, with brown trim and sparse bushes in the small front yard. The door was now a cheery buttercup colour and there were a couple of ornamental stands in the front that no doubt held flowers in summertime. The shiny brass door knocker was in the shape of a lion's head and he lifted the ring that the beast was holding in its mouth and rapped on the door. Nobody responded, and after the third attempt he was about to give up when the door opened a crack and a man peered out.

"What do you want?" asked a hoarse, whispery voice. Murdoch couldn't help the momentary shock at the man's appearance. The entire right side of his face was covered with livid scar tissue from a severe burn, the lips drawn down and revealing the pink inner flesh of the mouth. The fingers of his hand were fused into a claw.

"I'm calling on Mr. Seymour," said Murdoch. When he'd been here previously, a pleasant middle-aged widow was the landlady.

"Who are you?"

"My name's Murdoch. William Murdoch."

"Friend of his or what?"

"Yes."

He didn't elaborate, not wanting to start gossip by revealing he was a detective.

"He ain't in."

Murdoch forced himself to be polite. With a disfigurement like that, the man had a right to be surly.

"Any idea when he's expected back?"

Their eyes met and Murdoch realized the man was probably his own age. The hideous burn marks and the scanty hair across his seared scalp made him seem much older. He grunted, conceding a little.

"He won't be long, he just went to run an errand." He moved back. "You might as well come in."

Murdoch stepped into the hall. A lit sconce threw off a low light, showing plain, whitewashed walls. There was oilcloth on the floor, no druggets to soften the coldness. The simple, wooden coat tree was hung with a black overcoat and fedora. He had an odd sense of being in a monastic establishment, something else he didn't remember from last summer.

"Does Mrs. Pangbourn still live here?"

"No, she moved out to Calgary a few months ago." The reluctant doorman started to shuffle away. Whatever had burned him must have also broken his leg or hip, for he limped badly.

"Are you the landlord?" Murdoch called after him, wanting to engage him in conversation.

But the man didn't answer and disappeared into the room at the back. There were two other doors off the hall, but neither had draped portieres, which contributed to the austere appearance of the hall. There wasn't anywhere to sit and he hovered awkwardly by the door wondering if he should haul the sullen man out of his lair. Then the front door was flung open and in a bluster of chill air, a woman, her long mackintosh slick with rain, burst into the hall. She stopped short.

"Goodness me, it's you, Mr. Murdoch."

Murdoch tipped his hat. "I, er, I regret you have the advantage of me, ma'am."

The woman tugged off the black, mannish felt hat that was jammed low over her brows.

He smiled. "Ah, I do beg your pardon. Good afternoon, Miss Slade."

CHAPTER THIRTEEN

AMY SLADE REGARDED HIM APPREHENSIVELY. "I CERTAINLY didn't expect you so soon. What have you discovered?"

"Regrettably, not a great deal. I have not located the photographer." He saw the disappointment in her eyes and he continued hurriedly. "But I do intend to continue the search. I'll find him."

She nodded. "If Agnes does not return soon, I will have to report her absence to the truant officer." She turned away to hang up her wet waterproof. "Ugh. This rubber lining keeps out the rain all right, but you get so clammy, it's hardly any better."

"I am actually here to call on Mr. Charles Seymour," said Murdoch. "I didn't realize you were fellow boarders."

"I gave you my card."

"I must confess, I hadn't taken note of your address."

The man who had answered the door poked his head out of his room. "Oh, it's you, Amy. Is everything all right?"

"Yes, of course, John. Mr. Murdoch and I are acquainted. He is here to see Charlie."

"So he said. Charlie'll be back in a jig."

"It's so dreary out, I think a pot of tea would do wonders. Mr. Murdoch, why don't you come down to the kitchen. Will you join us, John?"

"No, thank you."

"Come and at least let me introduce you."

John emerged as reluctantly as a maltreated dog comes out of its kennel.

"Mr. Murdoch, this is John Reordan. John, this is Mr. William Murdoch. He works with Charlie."

Reordan brushed the palm of his left clawlike hand with his right and tentatively reached out.

Murdoch also offered his hand, "Yes, I'm acting detective at his station."

Reordan suddenly jumped back. "Are you, indeed? Well, Mr. Acting Detective, I only shake hands with those who earn their bread by the sweat of their brow. You don't qualify." With that he turned and hobbled away.

"John! Don't be so silly," Amy called after him, but he ignored her and slammed his door shut behind him.

She sighed. "I beg your pardon, Mr. Murdoch. I can never

predict how he will be."

"It's not your fault. He'd obviously had an unfortunate experience and can't distinguish that from me." Murdoch spoke pleasantly, but in fact he was annoyed by Reordan's behaviour. If Miss Slade hadn't been there, he would have told the man off. "Besides, he's quite wrong, if you were to see me in the height of summer, you'd think I earned my bread by the sweat of my brow."

He was gratified by her laugh, which did agreeable things to her face.

"I would still like that tea you mentioned," he added.

"Of course, come this way."

Murdoch followed her, trying not to stare at her legs. The damp woollen pantaloons were clinging to her calves.

"Please have a seat," she said, ushering him into the kitchen. "I'll stir up the fire."

The kitchen seemed to be the gathering place for the lodgers, not unusual for a boarding house. Murdoch was struck once again by the austerity of the furnishings. There was a small, scrubbed pine table in the middle of the floor, with four bare chairs around it. Two cushioned chairs were underneath the window. A large cupboard took up most of the space next to the door, across the room from a cooking range. There was the same scrupulous cleanliness he'd noted in the hallway. No plates or cups sat unwashed at the sink. The range was nicely blacked, and the large pot on one of the burners looked quite new. Something that smelled delicious was cooking in it. Amy lifted the lid and took a sniff.

"Potato soup, John's speciality."

"His Irish heritage, I suppose."

She nodded. "I believe that also accounts for his antipathy toward police officers."

"Surely he's not as disagreeable to Seymour."

"Oh no. They are the best of friends." She smoothed back some stray strands of wavy hair, unnecessarily, he thought. Not much had escaped the tightness of her severely drawn bun. She was an attractive woman in spite of a tendency to be too solemn, and he'd noticed something in Reordan's eyes when he'd looked at her. Murdoch thought the rudeness he displayed toward him, the visitor, might be more personal than historical.

"Is Mr. Reordan your landlord?"

She gave him an odd look. "No, he's not."

"Somebody takes good care of the house."

"We all live here so we all try to be considerate of each other."

For the life of him, Murdoch couldn't understand why the conversation, banal as it was, was making her so uncomfortable, but that was the case. Perhaps it was because she was an unmarried woman sharing lodgings with single men and no landlady to chaperone her.

"Are there other lodgers?"

"Yes. We are four all together. Mr. Timothy Wilkinson also lives here."

Amy was busying herself with tea making. She took down a teapot from a shelf in the cupboard and scooped three spoonfuls of tea leaves out of a caddy. Murdoch knew Mrs. Kitchen, his landlady, would not have approved of such poor tea making as Amy hadn't warmed the pot first, but he of course made no comment. She brought two cups and saucers to the table. The china was patterned with delicate flowers, gold rimmed and light as eggshells. They looked out of place on the scrubbed surface of the table.

"I think we have some cake if I'm not mistaken," she said, prying off the lid of a cake tin on the table. She frowned. "I'm afraid not. Somebody has already eaten it."

So much for mutual consideration, thought Murdoch.

She poured out two cups and he helped himself to milk and sugar lumps. The milk jug and matching sugar bowl were silver.

"I assume it was Seymour who referred you to me," he said. "I was wondering why you asked for me."

"Yes, Charlie has a lot of respect for you. I, er, I need somebody with integrity. I was most grateful he could recommend you."

"So you showed him the photograph?"

Amy sipped daintily at her tea, saucer in one hand, cup in the other, in the manner of the well-brought up.

"No, I did not. It is my opinion that every time somebody looks at that hideous photograph, no matter if their intention is benign, the child is violated again. It was necessary for you to see it, but other than you I would prefer no one else views it."

Murdoch knew that if the case came to court, which it must if he found the perpetrators, the photograph would be handled and ogled over by many men. He said nothing.

"I simply told him I had a difficult and legal matter to deal with concerning one of my pupils," continued Amy. "He suggested I speak to you."

There was an awkward silence. Murdoch was trying to determine how to proceed without betraying Seymour's predicament. She rescued him.

"He has told me about the anonymous letters and, as you know, he is currently under a cloud of suspicion. Not of his own making and dreadfully unfair." She placed her cup and saucer on the table. "I think it's shameful that some scurrilous person would stoop to such a thing."

Murdoch liked the word *scurrilous*, which he hadn't heard before. He'd add it to his vocabulary.

"I agree. If a man in his position is in fact involved in illegal activities, then his accuser should come right out and say what they are."

To his surprise, he saw Miss Slade turn rather pink. "What constitutes an illegal act is sometimes debatable, don't you think?"

Murdoch was about to reply that, no, he didn't think there was any doubt about what was on the statutes and what wasn't, but before he could wade into that murky water, he heard the sound of the front door opening and people entering.

"That's probably Charlie now," said Miss Slade, and she stood up and went to the door. Murdoch watched her, curious to see what kind of welcome she was going to give the sergeant. He was a good few years older than she, but he was unmarried after all. And quite eligible as long as he didn't lose his job.

She poked her head out. "Charlie, we're in here. Mr. Murdoch's come to see you."

Was she giving Seymour warning, thought Murdoch. Was he being overly suspicious?

The sergeant came into the kitchen. He wasn't a man given to overt expression of feeling, but Murdoch's quick assessment was that Seymour was glad to see Miss Slade, platonically not romantically, and that his reaction to Murdoch was ambivalent, a mix of pleasure and apprehension.

"Will, good afternoon to you. Chilly weather, isn't it?" He stretched out his hand. He was wearing a tweed jacket and trousers with a brown muffler around his neck. The homely clothing made him seem younger, less dour than the police uniform.

Right at his heels was a young man, tall and shambling and extraordinarily hirsute. His untrimmed brown beard covered his face from his cheekbones to the top button of his coat. His hair was thick and wiry and shot out sideward from his head, making him look as if he was standing in a perpetual wind.

"This is Tim Wilkinson. Tim, I'd like you to meet Will Murdoch, one of my colleagues."

Murdoch hesitated, wondering if this lodger was going to be as rude as Reordan had been. Wilkinson made the same hand-wiping gesture that Reordan had made and immediately offered his hand. In the thicket of his beard, his teeth gleamed in a wide smile.

"Glad to make your acquaintance, Mr. Murdoch. Our friend here has spoken highly of you."

Murdoch smiled modestly.

"Would you two like some tea? It's freshly made." Amy removed the cozy from the teapot. It was cups of tea all round, and Seymour and Wilkinson sat themselves at the table, forcing everybody into a sudden intimacy. Once again, Amy took the initiative.

"Just as you came in, Charlie, Mr. Murdoch and I were talking about the letters."

"Disgusting," muttered Wilkinson somewhat ambiguously.

Seymour drank some of his tea. "Indeed. Has anything new come up, Will?"

As this seemed to be a household with no secrets, Murdoch didn't see any point in being unforthcoming.

"Not so far. That's why I came to see you. I thought we could go over every possibility. Anybody you know who might be carrying a grudge." He took a sip of tea. "Anything you might be doing that could possibly be construed as illegal."

His companions reacted as if a shadow had gone across a summer sun, fleeting enough, but sufficient to cause them to stiffen and, ever so slightly, move closer to each other for warmth.

"I think it would behove you to define the term 'illegal,'" said Wilkinson, his tone belligerent.

Seymour smiled. "You have to forgive my friend here, Will. He is in his second year at Osgoode law school. He can't help himself."

Murdoch was struck by how much Wilkinson's words had echoed Miss Slade's. He was about to launch into a definition, but Seymour got to his feet. He went over to the sink and rinsed out his teacup. When he spoke his back was toward Murdoch.

"Tell you what, Will. I appreciate you have a job to do but I don't want to take up your time. Obviously somebody has got it in for me and is trying to make mischief, but I don't know who that would be." He returned to the table. "And despite what Tim says, I'm quite aware of what constitutes illegal activity." He picked up the other empty cups. "I promise you, my conscience is clear."

Murdoch could see a barely discernible nod from both Miss Slade and the young lawyer-to-be. They hadn't uttered the word *Amen*, but they may as well have.

CHAPTER FOURTEEN

For the past few days, Murdoch had had the impression that Mrs. Kitchen wanted to tell him something. With hovering guilt about his unsanctified relationship with Enid Jones, he rather expected his landlady was going to give him a little homily about the teachings of the Catholic Church and the dangers of involvement with those who weren't of the true faith. He was braced, therefore, when he joined her and Arthur for one of their regular after-dinner visits. Because Murdoch had to get to the typewriting competition, Beatrice had made an early dinner, going to more care than usual with his meal, an excellent roast, for once cooked to perfection. She'd even prepared his favourite sweet, a rich layered trifle. He was sated, round of belly when they sat down with hot tea in front of the parlour fire. Arthur seemed tired and somewhat withdrawn, but that wasn't unusual as his health fluctuated. Murdoch found himself searching for a topic they could discuss. He often mentioned the cases he was working on as Arthur said it kept him in touch with a world he was no longer part of. This wasn't pure altruism on Murdoch's part. He valued their observations; Arthur with a shrewd analytic mind and Beatrice always practical. However, out of consideration for his landlady, he didn't mention the photographs and Agnes Fisher. The poison pen letters were much safer territory, and both Mr. and Mrs. listened intently while he'd described Reardon and Wilkinson and what had transpired at the boarding house. He didn't tell them that the fourth lodger was a New Woman. He knew Beatrice was having enough trouble accepting that a schoolteacher was boarding with men, and he felt rather protective of Miss Slade.

"There's a difference between having a clear conscience and being a criminal," said Arthur. "According to the law, I'm a thief if I steal my neighbour's horse. But what if I know that horse is being mistreated and the only way to rescue it is to take it away from its owner? In that case I would say my conscience is clear."

"Your point is well taken, Arthur. All three of them were evasive when I asked directly if Seymour had been doing something illegal. But what that might be, I have no idea."

"Is it possible he is a bigamist?" asked Mrs. Kitchen. "You assumed he is a widower, but what if he's not? What if in his own mind he had excellent reasons for leaving his wife – she was immoral or licentious, for instance? Then he meets this schoolteacher and falls in love with her. Makes an offer of marriage, although he knows he is not legally free."

Both her husband and Murdoch gaped at her.

"Why, Mrs. K., that is an ingenious notion. And who then would be sending the letters?"

"Perhaps his real wife."

"She's got something there, Will. What do you think?" Arthur grinned.

"I must say I didn't detect any hint of romantic feeling between Miss Slade and Mr. Seymour."

"Ah, but they wouldn't want you to know, would they?"

"So you think she would be aware of the other wife and marry him anyway?"

"Why not?" said Arthur. "Women can be very foolish if they become besotted with a man."

"And so can men," added his wife.

"It's not the same," said Arthur.

Mrs. Kitchen looked as if she could argue the point but she didn't. "Well, obviously something isn't right and I have every faith that Mr. Murdoch will discover what that is."

Her tone made it clear she didn't want to go on with the discussion. She glanced over at the clock on the mantelpiece, which was just starting to chime six o'clock.

"My, time is getting on. We don't want you to be late. Have you finished with your tea, Mr. Murdoch?"

"Yes, thank you."

Here it comes, he thought and braced himself, although he wasn't sure for what.

Beatrice glanced over at her husband. "Shall I tell him, Arthur?"

"Better you."

"Tell me what?"

Beatrice clasped her hands in her lap. No, it wasn't going to be a lecture about Enid. She appeared too upset for that.

"Mr. Murdoch, you have become a dear friend to Arthur and me over the past three years, a dear friend indeed…Oh Arthur, you have to tell him."

Murdoch waited while Arthur tugged at the nightcap he habitually wore. Finally, he blurted out, "We're going to have to leave, Will."

"Leave? The house, you mean?"

"Yes," Beatrice jumped in. "You know how some doctors believe pure fresh air and rest can bring about a cure of the consumption. By sheer chance, I saw an advertisement in the newspaper that there was a hotel in Muskoka in need of a housekeeper. Apparently, it is rather like a hospital and the guests are all people with the illness. It's right on one of the big lakes and the air is as fresh as if it's just blown in from Heaven. They boast that most of the guests leave there completely cured."

She paused, the unspoken question in the minds of all three of them hovered. Would this apply to Arthur?

"I wrote to them and I heard back a few days ago. They have offered me the position. In lieu of regular wages, they are willing to give us room and board, and Arthur can take the treatment, such as it is." She looked at Murdoch, her eyes bright with unshed tears. "How could I not accept if it means Arthur gets better? But I'm worried about leaving you in the house."

Murdoch jumped up and planted a big kiss on her cheek. "Why this is wonderful news. And don't you dare give a second thought to me. There are other boarding houses, none a jot as good as this one of course."

Beatrice, still discomfited from his display of affection, but smiling now, nodded at her husband.

"Tell him the rest of it, Arthur."

"What we're wondering about is if you'd consider staying on here and sort of managing it for us. With Mother working at the hotel, we won't have any large expenses to speak of and we'd like to hold on to this house until such time as we see how I do. We'd both rest easy if we knew you were in charge of the place." He grinned. "You don't have to cook for anybody of course. They can find their own meals or Mrs. O'Brien next door could do for them. If we let out the two rooms, this one and the one next to you that Mrs. Jones had, the income could cover any extra costs quite nicely."

"And we would give you a reduction in the rent for your services."

They were both watching Murdoch's face. He beamed at them. "That sounds like the best offer since I can remember. Of course I'll do it. And forget that nonsense about reduced rent, I'll pay my proper share."

Beatrice frowned at him. "There is no agreement unless you accept the conditions as specified."

He threw up his hands in histrionic resignation. "Very well. I agree. And when, may I ask, are you planning to leave?"

"They will send us a telegram as soon as a room is available, but according to the letter it could be any day now."

Arthur had been trying to hold back a cough, but it got the better of him and for a few moments, Beatrice and Murdoch were forced to watch him fight for breath. She passed him a handkerchief and he spat out bloody phlegm, then dropped the linen immediately into the bucket of carbolic by the side of his chair. He lay back for a moment. The coughing spells exhausted him.

"Oh Will," he said softly. "I have almost forgotten what it is like to live a normal life. I hear you bounding up and down stairs and I try to imagine the time when I could do the same. I pray, make bargains with God, for just one more moment of that freedom." He tried to smile. "The best the Lord can do is send me a dream. I had one last night, as a matter of fact. I'm on my old wheel again, the Ideal I told you about. And I'm pedalling along Front Street, the wind from the lake is in my face, my legs are strong as a horse's. I'm breathing as deep and easily as I ever used to, not coughing up my own flesh. Oh it was such a sweet dream, I didn't like waking up, I can tell you."

He appeared on the verge of tears and Murdoch felt an ache in his own throat. Ever since he'd moved in with the Kitchens, Arthur had been ill, progressively worse in spite of all his wife's ministrations. Murdoch knew he'd once been an active man because they'd talked about it, but he never complained even when his physical discomfort seemed unendurable. This was the first time Murdoch had ever heard him express such feelings of sorrow and loss for the life he no longer had.

He reached over and patted Arthur's arm. "You'll be back on that bicycle and challenging yours truly here to a race before we know it."

Arthur smiled but the sadness didn't lift from his eyes. "I hope so, Will. I'd even let you win one or two if we could do that."

CHAPTER FIFTEEN

BY THE TIME MURDOCH SLIPPED INTO HIS SEAT, THE Mechanics Institute was jammed with people alive with excitement, and the air was thick with the smells of cigar-tainted clothes, pomade, and perfume. The audience had come as well dressed as if they were attending a concert instead of a typewriting competition. Alwyn and Mrs. Barrett had saved a seat for him beside theirs. The boy was in new finery, a navy worsted suit with a red spotted waistcoat. His hair was slicked down and he smelled like soap. He glanced over at Murdoch and frowned.

"They are going to start at any minute."

"Good thing I came when I did then." Murdoch leaned

forward and touched his hat to Mrs. Barrett, who responded without much enthusiasm. He knew he would never be in her good graces. Rightfully so, she suspected his intentions with her lodger.

Alwyn glanced at Murdoch. "Your moustache is wet," he said critically.

Suddenly, the electric lights in the hall all blinked off. The chatter stopped abruptly at the unexpected darkness but resumed immediately in relief when the overhead chandeliers lit up again. A man in a formal black frock coat and dark trousers walked onto the stage and held up his hand for silence. He could have been a man from any profession, dignified and rather arrogant in his bearing. When he spoke, however, his manner and booming voice were that of a circus barker.

"Ladies and gentlemen, allow me to introduce myself. Aloysius Carver at your service, and I am here to welcome all of you to the first World Typewriting Competition ever to be held in our noble city of Toronto. We are most pleased to be the host of this exciting event, which has attracted competitors from all over the world, especially our neighbour to the south, where the current world champion, Miss Mae Orr, resides. She is with us tonight, prepared to defend her title."

A burst of applause from the right side of the audience, where some people were holding small American flags. The maestro bowed at them, then continued, "We have in addition two highly qualified entrants from over the pond: one lady from England and a gentleman from Germany. But best of all, our own fair country is represented by no fewer than five competitors, two of whom are local residents."

More applause, this time from the left side. "Yes, five, and all of them capable of wresting away the cup from Miss Orr, even if I say so myself."

He turned and signalled to a man standing at the rear of the stage who immediately pulled away a black cloth draped over a table. Three large, gleaming silver trophies were revealed.

"These are for the competitors who finish in the top three places. In addition each will receive fifty, thirty, and twenty-five dollars respectively. Five runners-up will receive a cheque for ten dollars, courtesy of the Remington typewriting company..."

"Mamma truly needs that money," Alwyn whispered in a worried voice.

"Let me explain the rules to you who are uninitiated. The competition is divided into two parts. The first is a fifteen-minute dictation from a text that has been kept secret from the competitors. We can't give anybody a chance to practise. After that the papers will be collected and our honourable judges, who are at the moment also backstage, and who are all members of our Board of Commerce, will carefully mark and grade the papers. Marks will be deducted for strikeovers, uneven typing, too many words on the line. While they are doing that, the competitors will be given a text to copy, the same for all and also unknown. After fifteen minutes, our timer will ring his bell...Mr. Briggs, if you please."

His assistant dinged the button on the large brass bell in

front of him.

"When they hear that, the competitors must stop at once. Anybody observed making even *one* more stroke after the bell has sounded will be disqualified. I'm sure all you people with keen eyes and wits will make sure there is no cheating."

There was a chorus of *right on, yes, we will*, not all good-natured, Murdoch thought. This competition was taken seriously. Patriotic fervour was hovering in the air.

"Those papers will also be marked and while that's going on, you'll have a chance to stretch your legs. Gentlemen, may I remind you of the presence of our esteemed ladies, please go outside to smoke a pipe. When the judges have finished we will announce our winners."

Alwyn crossed his fingers, both hands.

The maestro signalled to his assistant, who in turn beckoned to somebody in the wings. A gangly youth shuffled in, looking self-conscious at being in front of an audience. He was carrying a large clock that he hung on a post standing on the uppermost dais, where the audience could see it. Another nod from the master of ceremonies and out came a florid-faced portly man whose hair was too long for polite society and whose garish necktie proclaimed him a man of the theatre. He had a book in his hand and Murdoch assumed he was to be the reader of dictation. He climbed to the upper dais as well, perched on a high stool, and bowed his head in intense concentration as if he were about to deliver one of the Bard's tragic monologues.

The stage had been fitted with three risers and on each level were five desks, spaced so that each competitor was visible to the spectators. Beside each desk was a stack of paper.

"Now, ladies and gentlemen, allow me to present, Miss Mae Orr from the great city of New York, the United States of America, the reigning world champion typewriter."

There was a loud cheer from the American contingent, polite applause from the rest of the audience, and the world champion walked on stage. She was young and bespectacled, and emanated complete confidence and efficiency. Her navy gown was sensibly loose fitting in the sleeves to give her ease of movement. She sat down at the front desk, acknowledged the spectators with a cool nod, placed her hands in her lap, and waited. She was followed by an assistant, who carried her typewriting machine and placed it with great reverence on the desk.

"Our next competitor, also a former world champion from New York, ladies and gentlemen, please welcome Mr. Frank McGurrin."

To more rousing applause, Mr. McGurrin strode onto the stage. Where Miss Orr was quiet containment, he was noisy exuberance. He grinned at the spectators, called out, "Hi there" to one of his friends, and took his seat at the desk next to his rival. He had no assistant and placed his own machine on the desk, then leaned over and offered his hand to Miss Orr. She shook it with a primness that made it clear she did not approve of such showy behaviour.

"Mamma says she'll win," whispered Alwyn. "She can type

up to ninety words a minute."

Murdoch nodded, although the number meant nothing to him. Miss Orr and Mr. McGurrin were the star performers, and as the rest of the competitors were called and made their entrance, they both began their own setups, not waiting until everybody was settled. Miss Orr removed her typewriter from its case, adjusted her chair, and raised her hands above the typewriter keys to make sure she was in the exactly correct position. She looked like a pianist about to launch into a concerto. She checked the stack of paper beside her and moved it an inch closer. McGurrin was doing the same kind of fidgeting. More competitors were introduced and took their places.

"Mamma said she is seated in the second row, third seat in. Oh, here she is."

"Mrs. Enid Jones from Wales, currently residing in Toronto," the master of ceremonies announced. Enid was wearing the grey silk dress that Murdoch liked best. She appeared shy, but there was no denying her attractiveness. Some rude masher at the back of the hall let out a whistle. Alwyn was clapping with all his might and Murdoch joined in. Even Mrs. Barrett softened and applauded vigorously. Enid took her place in the second row. Alwyn looked up at Murdoch and, in the tone of somebody who cannot contain the news, said, "My grandda is quite poorly."

Murdoch was rather puzzled by what seemed to be a glint of pleasure in Alwyn's eyes, but before he could respond, the maestro shouted the name of the next competitor.

"And now a young man who is intent on keeping us all law-abiding, Mr. Liam Callahan, a constable from Number Four Station."

"Good Lord," exclaimed Murdoch.

Alwyn glanced up at him. "I don't think it's fair to have a constable in the competition."

Murdoch didn't know what he meant, but wasn't about to get into a wrangle about it. Why had Callahan, who had described himself as a beginner at typewriting, entered a competition where the level of skill was bound to be very high?

The rest of the competitors, mostly men, were announced and came out quickly. Enid had positioned her chair and typewriter to her liking and was now waiting nervously for the contest to begin. Murdoch saw her quickly scan the audience, but he didn't know if she saw him or not.

Finally all the nervous scraping and shifting was done with. The impresario looked them over.

"All ready?"

Nods and murmurs. He held up his hand to the actor sitting on the stool. "Mr. Coleman, are you ready?"

"Ready indeed, sir."

He opened his book, the timekeeper checked his watch, and *ping*, the bell sounded.

"*Toronto 'Called Back'*, by Mr. Conyngham Crawford Taylor."

The typewriter keys started to clack. Coleman read beautifully in a rich, deep voice that resonated about the hall. Murdoch assumed the book was chosen because it gave the spectators something to listen to that was mildly entertaining.

BUCKINGHAM PALACE, LONDON, NOV. 24TH, 1891

Sir – In reply to your letter to the Duke of Connaught requesting a photograph of His Royal Highness, for another edition of your work, Toronto "Called Back," I am desired by His Royal Highness to forward you the enclosed photograph.

ALFRED EGERTON

Colonel, Comptroller of the Household of H.R.H.

the Duke of Connaught

The punctuation in this passage was challenging and one or two of the competitors winced, not sure of themselves. No one watched the keys, all looking straight ahead, their fingers moving rapidly and smoothly. Then virtually as one they reached the end of the page. With her right hand, Miss Orr took hold of the roller knob at the same time as her index finger unhooked the paper holder. She pushed the carriage from left to right while simultaneously rotating the roller. The typed sheet popped out and landed on the desk behind the typewriting machine. Before it even settled, she had reached down and picked up a clean sheet of paper and inserted it in the carriage. She continued to type with hardly a break in her rhythm. There was a spontaneous gasp from the spectators. This is what they had come to see, the champion in action. Only Mr. McGurrin could make the same manoeuvre. Everybody else, including Enid, turned the carriage, rolled out the paper, put it down, and then inserted the new sheet. Coleman kept reading but already it was obvious most of the typewriters were behind.

"Mamma isn't going to win," groaned Alwyn. "I think that's cheating, don't you?"

Murdoch could understand his intense loyalty, but he couldn't see anything wrong with what Miss Orr had done. In fact, it was truly remarkable. On surged the race as Coleman read on. Constable Callahan, obviously not a neophyte, seemed to have hit a rhythm. Enid's typing was fast and smooth but her page change was too slow and he was afraid she had fallen back. Frank McGurrin was sweating but wouldn't waste time by mopping his own forehead.

The clock's minute hand jerked on to the quarter-hour, the bell rang, and Coleman stopped in mid-sentence. As one, the typewriters lifted their hands from the keys. No one was going to risk disqualification.

"Assistants, collect the papers. Make sure each one is numbered." Maestro Carver addressed the audience. "To guarantee there is not the slightest whiff of favouritism, each competitor has a number. The judges do not know whose paper they are marking."

Mr. Coleman got down from his perch, bowed to enthusiastic applause, and disappeared backstage. The assistants collected the papers and the typewriters were stretching their tight necks and flexing their fingers. Miss Orr stayed cool and contained, Mr. McGurrin could now wipe his face. The assistants returned and handed folders to each person.

"At the bell, and not a second before, you may turn over your copy and begin."

Because the clock was behind them, the contestants couldn't see the hand approaching the hour but the audience could. Every one seemed to be holding their breath. Then the bell rang, there was a flurry of turning paper, and the typewriting began. This half of the contest was the real test. Miss Orr seemed to be able to open her folder before anybody else and off she went. Murdoch thought Enid had started quickly and he nudged Alwyn.

The boy shook his head. "She won't win. She doesn't have her own machine."

"Maybe she'll be a runner-up."

"I pray for it."

The only sound now was the clack of the typewriter keys and the whirr of carriages sliding. Miss Orr executed another brilliant page change and her supporters clapped. McGurrin was a split second behind her. Nobody else seemed close. Enid appeared tense but she was holding her own and didn't seem to be doing any overstriking, which would lose her marks. Murdoch watched Callahan, who was focused on the task and appeared to be doing well. As far as he could tell the other competitors were much on a level, although the poor man from Germany inadvertently knocked over his pile of fresh paper, which was disastrous, and he stopped trying completely.

The hand of the clock moved to the next minute. Two to go. Sensing the end, Miss Orr seemed to increase her speed. She could have been a mechanical piece, she was so precise. The spectators could see the clock and as the second hand moved, they began to chant.

"…five, four, three, two…"

"Stop," shouted the maestro. The bell pinged. Mr. Carver glanced around to make sure no one had slipped in an extra stroke. All clear.

"Collect the papers. Ladies and gentlemen, we will now take a break for at least one half an hour, after which time we announce the winner."

The competitors stood up, some leaving the stage at once, some waving at friends who ran up to talk to them. Miss Orr was immediately surrounded. Enid went to the wings.

"Mamma says that my grandda might die," said Alwyn abruptly.

"Is that so? I'm sorry to hear it." But Murdoch had a premonition of what was coming next.

The boy nodded. "We have to go back to Wales. We'll be going as soon as Mamma gets a passage."

CHAPTER SIXTEEN

ALWYN'S NEWS CAME AS A SHOCK, AND MURDOCH HAD A hard time concentrating on the rest of the proceedings. Miss Orr was the winner as expected, with Mr. McGurrin next and the English lady, Miss Wildin, third. To the delight of the partisan crowd, Enid was indeed a runner-up, tying for fourth place with Liam Callahan of all people. After the beautiful cups had been handed out, all the participants mingled with their supporters in the foyer of the hall. Murdoch was waiting until the group of well-wishers dispersed, but he also had his eye on Liam Callahan and as soon as he could he went over to him.

"Congratulations, Callahan. What a surprise."

The constable wasn't just surprised, he was jolted and he flushed.

"Mr. Murdoch, what are you doing here?"

"My friend, Mrs. Enid Jones, was in the competition. You both did so remarkably well. I must have misunderstood you at the station yesterday. I was under the impression you were just beginning to typewrite."

A young woman standing close beside Callahan chuckled. "Dear me, no, Liam is quite seasoned, this is his third competition."

"Ma'am," said Murdoch.

"Er, allow me to present my fiancée, Florence Gripe," said Callahan. "Flo, dearest, this is Detective Murdoch."

She clasped her hands together. "How simply splendid. Liam has spoken of you so often. It is a great pleasure to meet you."

Miss Gripe was a small woman, with a ripe, full figure shown off to advantage in a tightly fitting dark green velvet dress. Her hair was an attractive reddish brown with fashionable front curls and she had fine blue eyes, which she used effectively. She and Murdoch shook hands and she smiled up into his face as if this were indeed a memorable moment for her. Callahan, however, was clearly of the opposite opinion.

"We'd better get going Flo," he said. He took her by the elbow, and although she looked as if she were about to protest, she allowed herself to be taken away.

"Congratulations, again, Callahan," Murdoch called out as they hurried away.

He felt a touch on his arm and Enid was beside him with Alwyn.

"I wondered if you would know him," she said. "He did very well."

"I do indeed. He's our desk clerk. And the young lady is his fiancée."

"She's quite a coquette for someone who's betrothed," said Enid. She obviously had witnessed the warm greeting that Miss Gripe had bestowed on Murdoch.

He was saved from answering by another well-wisher who took Enid's hand to congratulate her. He mouthed, "I'll get your cloak," and went to collect their outdoor clothes.

Mrs. Barrett had insisted on hiring a cab for them, and on the way home, they all went over every detail of the competition, talking about how the others had fared and how Enid had felt each step of the way. Alwyn was holding the small silver cup against his chest. Back at the lodgings, Mrs. Barrett, in an unusual display of hospitality, offered them a glass of sherry, which they took. That consumed another hour until finally they could take their leave and go upstairs. Here, Alwyn declared he was too excited to sleep so Enid took him on her lap and cuddled him. Murdoch watched them, as they whispered in Welsh, cheek against cheek, laughing together. He'd have to talk in front of the boy or go home without knowing what was going to happen.

"Alwyn says your father is ill and that you will be returning to Wales."

He thought he'd succeeded in keeping his voice neutral, but

she jumped and looked at him in dismay, the glow of happiness wiped from her face.

"I was going to tell you, of course, Will. I received the letter only this morning and there was no opportunity. My brother says Da is in some danger and it would be best if I were to go at once."

They both knew what the next question was and Alwyn answered it for them.

"We might not be coming back."

"Is that true, Enid?" Murdoch asked.

She shifted her glance down. "There is nobody else to take care of him."

"Except you who have made your life in another country."

"I am the only daughter. My brothers have their own families. I am the only one who is free of such responsibilities."

Murdoch stared at her, trying to read her expression. She was continuing to focus on the top of her son's head. Alwyn kept shifting his gaze between them.

"And is that what you want to do?"

Enid finally met his eyes. "If I don't go, I dread to think what would become of him. He has been in poor health for some time now but he has managed on his own. Now, according to my brother, he has become virtually bedridden. He has to have somebody watch for him because he has to be turned every few hours as his lungs are so congested. Aled's wife has been doing the best she can, but they have five little ones and it is too much for her."

"So will you stay there?"

She sighed. "I cannot answer that question, Will. I have so few ties here in Canada and so many in Wales."

"You have me."

"Do I?"

"The fact you even ask the question tells me you doubt it."

Enid again averted her eyes. "I saw your expression, Will, when you read what I had written in my notebook. No matter what you tell yourself, you were not happy at my little fantasy."

Alwyn jerked away and looked up at his mother. "What paper, Mamma?"

Murdoch could feel his temper rising, but he struggled for some civility. "Alwyn, I'd like to talk to your mother in private. Will you go to your room for a little while?"

The boy spoke to his mother in Welsh. She answered. He wasn't happy, but after another quick exchange he got off her lap.

"I'm not going to sleep until you come in," he said and left with a sharp closing of the door.

"Thank you," Murdoch said to Enid. "I was finding it impossible to speak freely."

But there was silence between them. Murdoch refused to dissemble by pretending he didn't know what she was talking about. *Enid Murdoch*. She was right. He hadn't been happy. He supposed he could have jumped in and said that he'd reacted only out of surprise, but he didn't know if that was really the case.

"I'm sorry, Enid, I am extremely fond of you, but…"

"You don't know if that fondness, as you call it, is enough for marriage. For connection yes, but not for marriage."

He was stung by the bitterness in her voice. "I was under the impression we were equally desirous of an intimate connection. I'm sorry you seem to think I was merely gratifying myself."

She got up and walked over to her desk, where she'd placed her typewriting machine, bedecked with the silver ribbon of fourth place. "It doesn't matter what I think, Will. I have to return to Wales. I have no choice."

He stared at her back. She had made sure her thick, dark hair was firmly pinned on top of her head for the competition. He'd actually indulged in the pleasurable fantasy of taking out the combs and hairpins and letting her hair cascade around her shoulders. Not much chance of that at the moment.

"When will you go?"

"I've requested a passage as soon as possible. At this time of year it shouldn't be too difficult. Perhaps as soon as Saturday."

"You'll go from New York?"

"Yes."

He stood up. "There doesn't seem to be anything else to say. I assume you care enough to write to me."

She didn't move. "Of course."

He didn't want to leave things like this. He should rush over to her, take her in his arms and tell her that he would wait, that he did want her for his wife. But he couldn't.

"Can I come back tomorrow night?"

"Certainly, if you want to. I should have an answer by then

about the passage."

She sat down at the desk and stared at the typewriting machine.

"Good night then. And congratulations on the competition. You did very well."

"Thank you. Good night. *Nos da.*"

He was about to offer her a kiss but her ramrod straight spine was too forbidding and, besides, he felt anything but tenderness.

He left and let himself out into the winter dark.

CHAPTER SEVENTEEN

HONORIA DAVIS WAS TALL AND DARK-SKINNED, WITH long slender hands and feet and a neck as graceful as a swan's. Her mother said their forebears came from the west coast of Africa, but that was a story she'd been told by the man who owned her and there were no more details available. Neither Honoria's mother, Grace, nor her father, Ferdinand, had grown up with their parents but what little family lore they had was treasured and passed down like pieces of rich cloth. All Honoria had known was the city of Toronto where she had been born, and she was so accustomed to the behaviour that she met with all the time, she didn't really question it. Coloured people were not considered to be the same as white people, in intelligence or emotions, and it was a rare person who could bridge that gulf of ignorance. Take Mr. Gregory, for instance. He'd assumed she was illiterate and was surprised when, one day, she told him she had gone as far as the fourth standard.

"One of these days, you can sit at the desk if Clara can't do it," he said with a burst of generosity. He actually clapped her on the shoulder as if she were a man. It had never happened though. He was all too aware of how this would look to his clientele. A coloured woman receiving people, unheard of. So she'd been hired to clean the studio, every evening except Sunday, thirty cents a time. Then, shortly before last Christmas, he'd asked her if she would like to be part of one of the stereoscopic sequences he produced at intervals. He'd pay her twenty-five cents for fifteen minutes of her time. That was most generous, he thought, considering she'd never been before a camera before. All she had to do was tie a scarf around her head, put on an apron, and stand in front of the table pretending to wash a dirty pot. He didn't explain what the story was supposed to be, not out of consideration for her feelings because he didn't expect her to have any, but simply because it didn't occur to him. Honoria soon realized that she was to depict the new maid, replacing the pert and pretty French maid, played by Clara. The point was that she, Honoria, was considered so ugly, she presented no temptation to Mr. Newly-wed. Renaldo, who also worked at the studio, played this part, and Honoria was struck by how much the behaviour of her three cohorts paralleled how they were in their real lives. Gregory's wife, Prudence, who acted the part of the wife, was jealous to the point of irrationality of her husband; Clara would flirt with any male out of baby skirts; and Renaldo behaved as if every woman was put in his path for the express purpose of his gratification. Even Honoria. And therein lay her anguish. He was the only white man she'd ever met who treated her first as female, second as coloured. Initially she was offended by the casualness of his manners, the constant innuendos, the little touches he managed to get in if they were ever in proximity. Then she realized he treated the other women in the same way. The awareness that he spoke in the same tone of voice to Clara as he did to her filled Honoria with a deep, unspoken pleasure.

After the Newly-wed series of views was complete, Renaldo had winked at her. "If this were the real thing, Ria, *my* wife wouldn't be so complacent. You're as good a sauce of a girl as I've ever met."

Gregory hadn't shown her the photographs until she asked to see them. He was pleased with them, but he'd made her look hideous. Her front tooth was blacked out and she was wearing a head scarf and apron over a shapeless dress. When she had complained about it, he'd stared at her in disbelief. Renaldo, on the other hand, touched her cheek gently and whispered, "I'm trying to get the old geezer to do the story of Uncle Tom. You'd make a lovely Eliza."

Gregory wasn't interested in that, probably because the suggestion came from Renaldo, but he did do a sequence called "The slave woman's agony". Honoria depicted a woman who was about to be forced to bed by the wicked slave owner, played by Renaldo in padding and false whiskers. In this one, she got to wear a pretty flowered dress. At first, she'd felt uncomfortable that Gregory insisted on pulling the bodice down so low her breasts were clearly visible. But Renaldo winked and teased her and offered such encouragement she swallowed her protests. Gregory professed himself so pleased he doubled her earnings.

Tomorrow they were going to do another of the Darkie sequences. She'd already done Darkie Wedding, which she hated because they were all made to look ridiculous. The only bright spot was that her "husband" was Renaldo, who had his face covered with boot blacking. He smelled so bad, she had to laugh at him. There was another shoot coming up soon, called The Darkie Ball. She'd talked her brother, Fergus, into being in it, but once again the other parts were taken by Renaldo and Clara, who was complaining bitterly about having to dirty her face.

Honoria went into the studio. She had to put out the props and make sure the stage that they used for portraits was well dusted. The long uncurtained mirrors were dark with the night and she could see her own reflection. Briefly, she looked at herself, and wondered not for the first time if there was sufficient attractiveness there to draw her a suitor. And who would that be? There were very few coloured people in Toronto and only Nathan Smith could be halfway considered eligible. Honoria knew he'd got his eye on her but her heart didn't leap when she saw him and to her mind, if you were going to be hitched to a man for the rest of your born days, you had better be more partial to him than that. "You're too particular," said her mother. "You'll be left high and dry, my girl." Honoria dreamed of going to America, to New York or Chicago, to find herself a husband, but she didn't know when she would save enough money for the fare or for living there. They had no relatives in the north and she'd be afraid to go south.

Suddenly, her heart jumped into her mouth. She was standing in front of the set, the one Mr. Gregory called "the Prince's boudoir". She had distinctly seen the cover move on the Turkish couch. For a horrible moment, Honoria thought it was a rat under there. She turned around slowly, picked up her broom, and inched closer to the stage. There was no movement from beneath the cover, but there was something under there, she could see the bulge. Far too big for a rat.

"Whoever you are under there, come out and show your face or I'm going to whack you good."

The scarlet cover shot back and the head of a young girl appeared. Her long hair was loosed and tousled about her thin face and she was wearing an outdoor coat.

"Who in the Lord's name are you?" asked Honoria. "And what are you doing here?"

The girl smiled in a placating way. "Nothing bad, I promise. I didn't have anywhere else to go."

"What's wrong with your own home?"

She averted her eyes. "I had a barney with my pa and I didn't want to stay there."

"Well that ain't none of my business. If you think I'm going to let you doss here, you've got another think coming. Mr. Gregory will have my hide."

"He needn't know. I promise I'll be gone before daybreak. He will never know."

"Well you are surely the most audacious child I've ever seen in a long time." She glared. "How did you get in? Am I going to get the blame for a broken door, now?"

"No, not at all...the front door wasn't locked." Again, the shifting glance. "I was trying to find somewhere to spend the night and I tried this place. I didn't break in or anything. I just walked in. And it looked so comfy in here, I just crawled under the covers and fell asleep."

"I don't believe that. You telling me the most whopping nailer I ever did hear. Mr. Gregory always locks up himself. He would never not do it."

"He must have been in a hurry. You can go and see for yourself. There is nothing damaged."

"I am not going to let you out of my sight, young lady. You'll do a bunk soon as I turn my back. Besides, how can you be so cruel as to worry your parents so? They must be out of their minds wondering where you are."

"They think I'm staying with my sister."

"And where would she be?"

"She lives with her husband over on the other side of Yonge Street."

"What address?"

Honoria was trying to see if she would catch the girl in a lie, but the child answered promptly and easily.

"Number forty-four, Temperance Street. She and her husband rent the upper floor above the grocery store."

"What's her name?"

"Mary. She was Mary Price, but now she's Mary Slade."

"And what name were you christened with?"

"Lydia."

"Lydia what?"

"Lydia Price, of course, same as my sister."

The girl shivered. The stove was allowed to burn down in the night and the studio was cold.

"Please let me stay. I won't be any trouble, I promise. If I go home, my pa will whack me good."

"I don't care 'bout that. You must have done something wicked and you deserve what you get."

She paused, giving so-called Lydia a chance to come up with an explanation, which she expected would be a right old whopper. However, she didn't. Whether she knew she wasn't going to be believed or whether her imagination had dried up, Honoria couldn't tell.

She pushed back the velour cover and stood up.

"Hah, you've still got your boots on," Honoria said angrily. "Don't you go dropping mud on that leopard skin. I'll be blamed."

"They were quite dry. But I'll go now. I don't want to get you into trouble."

Honoria knew she was being played on like a church organ, but the child looked so perishing and woebegone, her indignation began to melt.

"You can't stay here, you just can't. Get off on home and say you're sorry. Or why don't you go to your sister's like they think?"

Lydia gave her a wan smile. "You're right. I was being silly. It's not that late, is it?"

"Yes, it is. It's almost midnight." She picked up her candlestick. "Come on, I'll see you to the door."

The girl didn't argue and Honoria walked her through the outer office. She was telling the truth about the door at least. It was intact. And unlocked, which was very unlike Mr. Gregory.

She ushered the girl into the hall and escorted her down the stairs to the street. Once again, she was jolted. As they paused on the threshold, the light from the street lamp fell across the girl's face. This close, Honoria saw what hadn't been obvious in the low candlelight. What she'd taken as high colour, she saw now wasn't natural. The rosiness of the cheeks was too even, the shadow of the eyelids was too blue. She smelled faintly of scent. Before she could comment, the girl turned and hurried away.

She was a sly one. You don't paint your face like that unless you're up to something wicked. She was nothing better than a doxie. And so young. So very young. She wondered if she should tell Mr. Gregory but almost immediately decided she wouldn't. If you were coloured, you never went to your boss with trouble in your hands. The likelihood was that it would blow right back in your face.

She stared after the girl. Her shoulders were stooped and she thrust her hands into her sleeves for warmth. Honoria shivered in the cold air.

"Wait!" she called.

CHAPTER EIGHTEEN

DAWN WAS ONLY A LIGHTENING OF THE DARKNESS WITH no sun at all showing through the grey clouds. Even the snow on the shore and lake looked dingy. Levi Cross wrapped the strips of linen that he used for boots tighter around his legs and hefted his sack on his back. Although the surface of the snow had softened in the brief thaw and rain had pockmarked it, he could still make out traces of the footprints and the swath of something being dragged out on the lake. He'd been scavenging along the beach when he'd noticed them. He grinned to himself. Along this section of the beach, nobody would tramp out onto a frozen lake, dragging something heavy, unless they were up to no good. People were always disposing of things in the winter. Dogs and cats were the most common, but he'd even found a small donkey once, stiff and mangy. Money saved from the farrier by leaving the beast on the ice until spring. Not that finding a donkey did him much good, but the dogs and cats he carried back to his hut on the beach. When they thawed, he skinned them, cured the hide, and cut it into strips. The cats' fur he sewed into scarves, which he sold to gullible women as mink; the dog skins, if they were short-haired, made good gloves, which he claimed to be kid leather. It was a decent living, all things considered.

The tracks were easy to follow and he could see where two men, for they looked like men's boot prints, had alternately carried and dragged the box. They'd gone to a lot of trouble and he was excited about what he'd find. He could see the tracks returning without the box, so they had left it somewhere. A dog for sure, and a big one at that. Probably the servants being sent to dispose of the dog, a pure breed no doubt, fat and pampered, with good skin.

The soft snow made it difficult to walk and he must have trudged for ten minutes before he spotted the chest. It was shoved under the overhang of a short promontory. Snow had been piled around it to hide it, but some of that had melted in the rain and the lid was visible. Levi hurried over and eagerly brushed away the remaining snow. The trunk was wooden with metal ends, the kind used for travelling. It didn't look particularly expensive, and had obviously been well used. It was tied around with an old leather belt. He tugged at it but it didn't move, held fast in the ice now. That didn't matter, he had his tools. He lowered his sack and took out a saw. The leather belt was stiff but it was easy to cut through. He tried to lift the lid again but it didn't move. There was a brass lock and either it was locked or frozen shut. He picked up his jemmy, inserted it under the lock, and started to pry it open. It was hard going, which told him the trunk was locked, not frozen. He grunted and exerted more pressure with the jemmy. Suddenly, the lock snapped open. He tried the lid again. This time he could lift it and he peered into the chest. There was a piece of velour curtain on top of whatever was in there, and he pulled it away.

At first, unable to take in what he saw, he thought he was looking at a large doll. Then he realized it was the naked body of a young boy, curled up tightly into a fetal position. Levi lost his breath for a moment, every instinct telling him to run. Then sense took over. He'd handled many a dead creature before now. The body was squashed into the trunk, but he was able to feel down the sides. You never knew if you'd find something worthwhile. His fingers touched some silky kind of fabric and he tugged at it until it came free. What the hell? It seemed to be some kind of hat, gold coloured, with a sprig of feathers in the front. There was a metal brooch in the front studded with what were obviously fake rubies. He unfastened it and put it in his pocket. The hat he returned to the chest. Now that he felt calmer he had a closer look at the corpse and he shook his head. Somebody had had a go at the lad good and proper. His hair was caked with blood and his nose was destroyed. He dropped the lid, frightened, and glanced around to see if someone was watching him. Then he picked up his sack and began the trek back to the shore. He supposed he'd better notify the police. They might be glad of the information.

Ruby raked out the ashes from the stove and shovelled them into her cinder pail. She worked quickly, not because she was late, she wasn't, she never was, but because the kitchen was cold. A puff of fine white ash went up her nose and she sneezed. She returned some of the larger pieces of cinder to the bottom of the stove, laid strips of paper on top of them, then added kindling, not a lot, just enough to get the blaze going. She balanced chunks of coal on the wood. She had already blackened and polished the stove and the coal and iron reflected to each other their hard shiny surfaces.

"You're too particular," Mrs. Buchanan had chided her, but Ruby knew she was pleased.

She took a match out of the box, struck it, and lit the paper. The flame jumped up immediately and licked at the dry wood and Ruby sat back on her heels and watched for a moment. Miss Georgina had shown her how to draw flames. *Think of a holly leaf with its sharp points. That's the shape. That and pine tree branches.* She'd got Ruby practising on pieces of scrap paper and she was right. Add some logs, easier to draw than pieces of coal, and you had a believable depiction of fire. *She's a talented girl,* said Mrs. Crofton, and Miss Georgina had ruffled her hair and said, *What would we do without her?* Ruby had flushed with pride. Sometimes in her secret heart, she pretended she was actually Miss Georgina's child who had been snatched away at birth by the gypsies and that someday the truth would be revealed and she would claim her real family and they her.

She waited until she was sure the fire had caught, then closed the door.

Her next task was to drain the large teapot on the draining board by the sink, and she got the strainer and poured the cold tea into a cup. Mrs. Buchanan believed the tea had medicinal qualities and used it to bathe her eyes.

Never squint, child. I used to have the eyesight of a fox but I squinted in poor light and now I'm as good as blind.

Not quite. The housekeeper's keenness of sight was variable, or so it seemed to Ruby. She could detect a hurriedly dusted sideboard from across the room.

A clean house and a clean soul are side by side in God's heart, she'd declare. Mrs. Buchanan was full of sayings and proverbs and offered them daily. Ruby never felt impatient with these repetitions. The words rounded and softened in her mind, pleasant as pebbles worn smooth by the waves rolling in on the lakeshore. She stored them like provisions.

Laying the table in the breakfast room was the next task, but she had plenty of time. Neither of the mistresses rose early in the winter, and Mrs. Buchanan took advantage of this and stayed in her warm bed until eight o'clock.

Old bones feel the cold much more than young ones, she'd declared.

Ruby picked up the heavy housemaid's box. After her other tasks were done, she would come back to light the kitchen lamps and make the room bright and cheerful for the housekeeper. No sense in doing that now.

At the end of the sink, Ruby had tucked a dish of water out of sight under the window ledge. Whenever she was alone either coming into the kitchen or leaving, she dipped the tips of her fingers into the water and touched her forehead and chest. A girl at school had told her that Papists did that when they went to church and they asked for God's blessing. You were supposed to have magic water, but Ruby had collected rainwater from the barrel in the garden, thinking that it would be almost as good. Now she said her own prayer.

"To Lord Jesus and particularly to your mother, Mary. Please keep me safe and in this house forever until I am an old lady. Please keep Mrs. Buchanan in good health and also Mrs. Crofton. Please help her with her bunions."

She dipped her fingers again in the water and wiped her forehead. She needed as much power as she could get.

"Please, Jesus, will you especially take care of Miss Georgina. She is so good and she doesn't mean any harm, she truly doesn't. Please ask your mother to protect her and keep her secret safe."

Even admitting Miss Georgina had a secret was frightening to Ruby, but she thought that in the silence of the sleeping household she could say it to Jesus at least. She needed to unburden herself somewhere.

CHAPTER NINETEEN

THE CHILL WINTER MORNING AIR HAD HIT MURDOCH'S lungs as soon as he stepped outside and he savoured it. He put thoughts of Enid out of his mind. He was struck by what Arthur had said and he felt an awareness of his own health he hadn't had before. He hurried, driven by the cold, aware that he could move fast if he had to, that his legs responded. He was a little breathless by the time he reached the station, but he knew that would soon pass. His body worked.

He entered the warm, snug hall of the station. Sergeant Gardiner was on duty and Constable Callahan was already at the telegraph and telephone desk.

"Early, aren't you?" Murdoch said as he walked by on his

way to his cubicle.

"I'm just trying to keep ahead, sir. Do you want I should bring you a cup of tea? I am not yet officially on duty and you know what it's like trying to get a cuppa when the duty shift changes."

"Indeed I do. They should start coming in any minute now. So yes, in answer to your question. I like it hot, strong, and sweet, if you please."

"Sounds like you're talking about an amour, Murdoch," chipped in Gardiner. "Are you holding back on anything?"

Murdoch liked the sergeant and usually didn't object to getting into randy banter with him. This morning, however, he was in no mood for jokes and innuendos about his love life.

"If I am, I'll tell it to the rushes first, sergeant."

Gardiner looked puzzled, but Murdoch didn't give him an opportunity to say any more. He hung his hat and sealskin coat on the peg by the door and went through to his office. The constables who were on the morning shift would soon be arriving for their inspection. Hales, the patrol sergeant, would make sure they were "all present and correct", then he would march them out to the different beats to replace the bone-chilled, hungry constables on the night shift, who had probably been counting the minutes for the past three-quarters of an hour.

Once in his private space, Murdoch felt a little better. He took some notepaper from his desk drawer, dropping a kiss with his fingertips on the photograph of Liza as he did so. He found writing out his thoughts and impressions helped him when he was on a case. These were for his use, and were not the official notes he handed in to Inspector Brackenreid. Where to start? No avoiding now; no letting softer feelings interfere with rationality –

Amy Slade.

He had been taken aback when the schoolteacher had entered the boarding house, but she had made no secret of her address. Her explanation that her fellow boarder, Seymour, had recommended him was reasonable. But what if there were more to it than that? Murdoch could not imagine Miss Slade being a liar, but he forced himself to examine the possibility. Possessing and taking pornographic photographs certainly constituted an illegal activity. What if Seymour was implicated and she wanted some way to draw attention to this without revealing her identity? If she had a typewriting machine, she could have written the letters, which definitely showed evidence of education. By her own admission, she hadn't told Seymour the precise nature of her visit to Murdoch. Was she somehow in Seymour's thrall or afraid of him and thought the only way out was in this covert manner?

He wrote a large *no* beside that note and underlined it. Nothing he had observed about Miss Slade fitted that notion. She was one of the more independent-minded women he had met in a while. And poor Seymour! Here he was, entertaining the idea that Charlie indulged in a perverted sexual appetite. Murdoch sighed. He wasn't on as sure ground here. Men were capable of splitting off their sexual fantasies and activities and keeping them in some dark secret place while on the surface they lived exemplary lives.

He removed Liza's photograph from the drawer and stared at the blurry face. She'd held strong opinions about the question of sexual activity and the law. *If two grown-up people in their right minds want to do weird and unnatural acts with each other, let them. But if coercion is involved or any misuse of children or animals, I think they should be prosecuted and the punishment should be severe.*

He remembered being shocked when she'd said that, wondering how on earth she even knew of such things as "weird and unnatural acts". He'd finally asked her and she said she'd read about it. He smiled ruefully. If women had been allowed, she would have studied law. What an odd mixture of conventional and radical thinking she'd held. She had insisted they wait until marriage before consummating their love according to their church's dictum. He'd agreed but how he regretted that now.

He returned the photograph to the drawer. Thinking about Liza seemed to affect the way he felt about Enid and he found it hard to shake off vague feelings of discontent. What a shock it had been to see *Enid Murdoch.*

Then there was Miss Amy Slade. He halted. What the hell did he mean, *And then there was Miss Amy Slade?* He hardly knew her. Besides, he wasn't the kind of man who could dally with one woman while promising himself to another. Was he promised to Enid? He didn't feel like answering that question. He glanced up at the portrait of a young and pretty Queen. Even the Queen of India and the Empire was not spared grief. She had been a widow for a long time now and showed no signs of coming out of mourning.

Impatiently, he pulled the notepaper closer. He hadn't got very far with the notes he was supposed to be making.

The talk with Arthur had deeply affected him, as had finding out that the Kitchens were leaving. Nobody had said as much, but it was highly unlikely that Arthur would come back. Murdoch rested his head in his hands. What would it be like if Arthur were to recover? If he and Murdoch did race each other along the edges of the lake? Like all impossible dreams, this one brought a sense of almost unbearable longing.

There was a tap on the wall. Through the reed strips, Murdoch could see Constable Crabtree.

"Come in, George."

Crabtree poked his head in. "The inspector wants to see you right away."

Murdoch didn't move. "Did he say why?"

"No, except to come at once."

Murdoch stood up. "At once, it is."

Crabtree hesitated. "Are you all right, sir? You look a bit peaked."

"I'm well enough, thank you. But I feel as if I have been listening to the hooves of *equis nocti* drawing closer. The sound can make a man grow pale."

"Yes, sir. He does seem in rather a foul mood, I'm afraid."

Murdoch smiled at the constable's misinterpretation.

"Fair or foul, give me Inspector Brackenreid any day. He is mortal after all."

Slightly cheered by his own humour, Murdoch followed Crabtree out into the corridor.

Brackenreid handed him a piece of paper.

"Take a look at this, Murdoch. Different twist." He made no attempt to hide his sneer.

Murdoch unfolded the letter.

Dear Sir. Your acting detective, William Murdoch, is not doing his job. He is not 'acting' at all but sitting on his buttock while Sergeant Seymour continues unpunished. If this matter is not dealt with the entire station will be shamed.

"So what do you say, Murdoch?"

"I wonder if the writer was referring to the left or the right?"

"What?"

"The left or the right buttock, sir. That I am allegedly sitting on."

Brackenreid flapped his hand. "That's got nothing to do with it."

"I presume the letter came with the first post, sir?"

"Yes. The early worm gets the bird."

Murdoch glanced up at him, not sure if he was trying to be

witty. Clearly not.

"Quite so, sir. I'll take this and compare it with the others, make sure they are by the same writer."

The inspector stared at Murdoch. "Of course they are the same. This one is typewritten."

"I just don't want to make any assumptions. I'm wondering how the writer knew that I had been assigned to the case."

Reluctantly, Brackenreid conceded the point. "It doesn't necessarily mean anything. You are the only detective here. It is only logical you'd be given the case."

Murdoch wasn't entirely satisfied with that explanation but he nodded.

"Acorns from mighty oaks do drop, as you might say."

Brackenreid sniffed. His face was normally florid, but this morning it seemed to have taken on a purplish tinge. He had all the signs of a man suffering the aftermath of overindulgence.

He drummed his fingers on his desktop. "I am inclined to agree with the letter writer on one thing, Murdoch. You aren't doing enough."

"May I point out I have only been on the case since Tuesday, sir. Less haste more waste."

That jest sailed right over Brackenreid's head. "Maybe so, but it's not the only place where you're dragging your feet. I haven't seen any progress on the Smithers situation."

"We've questioned everybody, sir. We have no leads."

Brackenreid waved his hand impatiently. "I'm sure the woman lost the damn brooch herself, but she called three times yesterday and insisted on talking to me. The telephone is a menace in the hands of women like that. You'll have to go over or send one of the constables and see if you can appease her. Arrest somebody."

Murdoch couldn't believe he was serious but in this mood he was. Definitely not the time to tell him about the photographs.

"I'll do what I can, sir."

Brackenreid leaned forward on his desk. "Let's put it this way, Murdoch. If you do find out the po-faced sergeant has been up to no good, he will have to pay back every penny he's getting now for sitting on his arse at home."

Murdoch got to his feet. "If that's everything, I'll get going, sir."

The inspector swivelled around in his chair so that he was facing the window, his back to Murdoch.

"I want a full report by Monday. On both cases."

Back in his cubicle, Murdoch took the two other letters out of the file and spread them on the desk, studying each one with the magnifying glass. As far as he could see the latest one had been typewritten on the same machine as the others. The tone was certainly similar. Educated, school-marmish almost. "Buttock," not "arse" or "rear end" or "duff". And his full name. This letter was aimed much more at him than Seymour. He drew in his breath angrily. Who the hell was playing around like this? And where should he start searching? He supposed the only lead he had, if you could call it that, was the faintest suggestion that Seymour was indeed up to something. Whatever it was, the anonymous letter writer knew enough about the sergeant's life to accuse him. It made sense then, that by following in the sergeant's footsteps, or one of his friends at the lodging house, he might find the writer. And what if the sergeant was doing something against the law? What then? Presumably Murdoch would be forced to charge him. He didn't relish that task. What sort of impact would that have on Miss Slade, who considered Seymour one of the most honourable men she had ever met?

There was a tap on the outside wall and he could see Crabtree's shape through the strips.

"Yes, George?"

The constable stepped into the room. "There's a telephone message just come in for you, sir. From Dr. Bryce. He's over at the morgue and he'd like you to come over right away."

Murdoch frowned. "Did he say why, or am I just to admire his finesse?"

Dr. Bryce enjoyed being called as a medical examiner and had no compunction about boasting about his skill.

"Apparently somebody found a body in a trunk on the lake and there's no doubt it's a homicide."

"In that case, I will indeed go right away."

CHAPTER TWENTY

DR. BRYCE WAS A TALL MAN, WITH A BALD HEAD AND a heavy moustache. He had an air of confidence that was perilously close to arrogance, but Murdoch rather liked him. In spite of his brusque manners, he cared about what he was doing and the fact that the bodies he was dissecting had once been living human beings. Not all physicians behaved in that way.

As soon as Murdoch entered the room, the doctor called out to him. "We've got a nasty business on our hands, detective. Come and have a look."

Murdoch walked over to the table where Bryce was standing, a blood-stained apron covering his elegant grey worsted suit. There was a small steamer trunk on the table with the lid open.

"I don't know how much I can do right now," the doctor continued. "The body is still frozen. It's stiff as a board. We can't even get it out."

Murdoch peered into the trunk. Inside was the body of a young man, stark naked, his knees bent up to the chest and his arms folded across each other. His head was pushed sideways. For a brief moment, Murdoch was puzzled why the youth looked familiar, but then with a jolt, he realized it was the same boy who had been in the stereographic photograph. He wasn't wearing the turban, but there was no mistaking him.

"Is he one of yours?" Bryce asked.

Explanations weren't necessary at this point, so Murdoch was evasive. "I haven't met him before. I'll have to take Bertillon measurements to see if he's in our criminal system."

"Well, you'll find him there, I'll wager. The man was a catamite."

"Is that so?"

"Here, touch his chest."

Murdoch lightly touched the icy skin. The chest wasn't as smooth as it appeared.

"He's shaved off the hair," continued Bryce in his lecturing tones, "on the chest and it looks like also at the pubis. Of course, I'll swear to it when I do a rectal probe, but there's not much doubt."

Murdoch wasn't surprised. The painted face and lascivious pose of the photograph had suggested as much.

"How did he die?"

"I can't tell you that, detective! You'll have to wait for my report. I have to do a proper postmortem examination. He could have had a heart attack, he could have consumption, syphilis, who knows?"

Murdoch pointed at the corpse. "He's been badly beaten and I'd say there are marks around his neck."

Bryce nodded approvingly as if he were an observant pupil. "I'd say the poor wretch has been strangled. But there are other traumas. See there. His left shin is quite shattered and there are at least two ribs on the same side that are depressed. You can see the bruises. More than likely he was kicked. He may have a skull fracture, but I won't know that until I remove the scalp."

"Is there any possibility the injuries were caused when he was stuffed into the trunk?"

"No, no. Look at his leg. There has been a flow of blood down to the ankle that could only occur if he was alive when he was hurt. My guess is that he was beaten, then strangled, and then his body bent so it would fit into the trunk, which may have caused further damage. I can verify that later."

"Do you have any idea when he died, doctor?"

"None at all. All deterioration has been halted because of the cold. I see no staining on the body, so that tells me he was put into the trunk almost immediately after death. He could have been killed as long ago as two weeks when we experienced that severe cold weather or as recently as a few days past."

Bryce attempted to move one of the boy's arms but it was still intractable.

"How old do you think he is?"

"His genitalia appears to be fully developed. I'd place him at about twenty years of age." Bryce lifted the corpse's upper lip as far as he could. "His teeth seem decayed. He's thin, probably not well-nourished. I suppose one should feel sorry for him." He looked up at Murdoch, who made no comment. "Well, that's it then." Bryce removed his apron, crumpled it up, and dropped it on the floor. "I can't do anything more for now and I have to attend one of my patients who is at the point of delivering a baby. The bookends of life, eh, Murdoch? Mr. Boys is acting as coroner and he's called an inquest for Monday morning. I should have my report for both of you no later than Saturday."

"Thank you, doctor."

As soon as Bryce had left, Murdoch took his measuring tape from his pocket and did the best he could to at least get the approximate height of the dead man. He was about five feet tall. His hair was dark and cut short, but there were signs around his nails, neck, and the backs of his ears that he hadn't had much opportunity to keep himself clean. Or didn't care to.

The air was stinging with the chloride of lime the doctor used to keep down the smell. The room was bare, lined with shelves that were empty, although some large jars were stacked in one corner. A weigh scale, the kind found in most kitchens, was on a backless chair by the table. This morgue could not be called well-equipped, and Murdoch knew most of the doctors who were called upon to do postmortem examinations preferred to use one of the funeral parlours such as Humphrey's on Yonge Street. He stayed another three-quarters of an hour, taking what measurements he could for the Bertillon files and examining the trunk as closely as he could. It was well used by the look of it, but there were no identifying traces of custom stamps or steamer stickers. No address to help him.

Finally, he straightened up, crossed himself, and muttered a quick prayer for God to have mercy on the boy's soul. Bryce had estimated his age as close to twenty but death had erased care from his face and he looked very young. What the hell was Agnes Fisher doing with his picture and why had she drawn a black border around the card? There was only one answer to that: She knew he was dead.

CHAPTER TWENTY-ONE

THE SACKVILLE STREET SCHOOL WAS CLOSER TO THE morgue than Sydenham Street was so Murdoch decided to go there first just in case Agnes was now in attendance. The weather hovered between snow and sleet with an overcast sky and damp, chill air. Even at this midpoint of the morning, most of the houses showed lit lamps and candles. He couldn't shake off his own inner dreariness either. He'd investigated cases of murder in the past, and one or two of them had brought him to the edge of despair over the darkness human beings were capable of. This case felt equally ugly. He almost doubted that Agnes Fisher was still alive. She could well be implicated in the youth's death, which would have put her in grave danger.

Unconsciously, he braced his shoulders. He'd been accused more than once of being as stubborn as a mule, and he felt mulish now. He intended to find whoever was exploiting Agnes Fisher, but he also knew by removing them he was cutting off only one of the many heads of the Hydra. This was not a happy thought.

There were no children in the playground, and he crossed it quickly and entered the school through the boys' entrance. The corridor was likewise deserted, and this time as he approached Miss Slade's classroom, he heard no animal imitations, just the children chanting their multiplication tables.

"Five times eight is forty; six times eight is forty-eight; seven times…"

He stood outside the door and peered through the window. Miss Slade was at the front of the classroom, waving a stick as if she were conducting an orchestra. Today she had abandoned the pantaloons and was wearing a conventional navy blue skirt and pale mauve waist. Her fair hair was as neatly pinned as usual. The radical New Woman had temporarily disappeared.

"Faster now, eight times eight is sixty-four; nine times eight is…" She caught sight of him but didn't miss a beat. "Girls only."

Shrill voices rang out. "Ten times eight is eighty." "Now the boys." "Eleven times eight is eighty-eight."

These voices were much less confident.

"Twelve times eight is ninety-six."

"Reverse," Miss Slade called out and she pivoted to demonstrate. "Eight times twelve is…? Everybody together."

"Ninety-six."

That was easy but then she took them rapidly down through the numbers until only a few of the children, all of them the girls, could keep up with her. Murdoch thought they were still enjoying themselves and the excitement of competition.

Finally, she lowered her stick. "Excellent, children. That was a great improvement. Well done. I want you to give yourselves a big round of applause."

She clapped her hands and the class joined in with enthusiasm.

"All right, all right. That's sufficient. Save some for the next practice when we will be impeccable. Jane, what does 'impeccable' mean?"

"Clean, Miss Slade."

"Hmm. Yes, you are quite right. The literal meaning of the word is 'without sin', but as with many words in the English language its meaning has adapted to refer to anything perfect, as in with no error, or as Jane rightfully says, 'Clean.'" She clapped her hands again, a habit, he noticed. "Now, take out your slates if you please. I have written some sums on the blackboard. Let's see how quickly you can do them. The first two children who get everything right get a sweetie."

With a flourish worthy of a magician, she pulled back a shawl that she had draped over the blackboard, revealing neat chalk numbers ready to be worked. The class took a few moments to settle down and as soon as they were quiet, Miss Slade came out into the hall.

"Good afternoon, Mr. Murdoch. Sorry to keep you waiting."

She offered her hand and they shook, firmly.

"Has Agnes come to school today?"

"No, she has not." She frowned. "I am worried about her. Do you have any news?"

"Yes, and I'm afraid it is serious. The young man in the photograph has been found dead. There is little doubt he was murdered."

Her hand flew to her mouth. "I see."

"The doctor conducting the postmortem examination places the death between two weeks and two days ago."

She eyed him gravely. "How was he killed?"

"He was strangled. And I'm afraid badly beaten."

Almost on reflex, she glanced through the classroom window to see what her pupils were up to. They were quiet, working for the prize.

"We must find Agnes," she said.

"Is her brother in school?"

"Yes, he is. He has a dreadful bruise over his eye. I believe his father hit him, but he says he banged into the dresser in the dark."

She pulled out a watch from a pocket in the bodice of her silk waist. The watch was unadorned steel and attached to a chain, masculine style. An ebony charm dangled from the fob end of the chain and he wondered what it signified.

"We will be having playtime in only ten minutes. If you will wait until then, I will dismiss the class. I would prefer to keep things as normal as possible for now. I'll ask Ben to stay behind. You can speak to him in the classroom."

"Do you wish to be present?"

She smiled at him ruefully. "Mr. Murdoch, if I am present, there is some chance he will confide in you. If I am not, you might as well put him on the rack, he will not utter a word."

"Very well. Why don't I go back outside so the children don't see me. As soon as I know they are set free, I'll return."

"Thank you, Mr. Murdoch, that is most thoughtful of you."

She went back into the classroom, which was still quiet. Miss Slade might involve her pupils in games but she commanded their respect. He thought they were lucky children. His memories of school were definitely not as agreeable as he supposed those her students would have. The priests and nuns who had taught him firmly believed that the mind was stimulated by corporal punishment. From buttocks to brain. As for learning being fun, that hadn't occurred to them either.

He went outside and walked up and down until the ten minutes was up and both doors burst open and the children surged out. At least, the boys surged, the girls were much more demure. With arms linked, in twos or threes, they proceeded to walk around the perimeter of the schoolyard while the boys immediately began to play tag around the trees. As unobtrusively as he could, Murdoch made his way back to the classroom.

Ben was sitting in one of the desks near the front and Miss Slade was beside him talking. The boy's head was lowered and he was staring at the top of his desk as if there was some excruciating puzzle scratched there. Murdoch gave a tap on the door, then went in. Ben gave one quick, frightened glance at him then resumed his downward, fixed stare. Miss Slade touched the boy lightly on the arm.

"Ben, we are very concerned about Agnes. She has not been in school for the past two days. You say she is with your sister, but we must find her. Will you help Mr. Murdoch?"

There was no response from the child except a slight shrinking down into his seat. He had a nasty bruise and lump above his eye. Miss Slade indicated to Murdoch to take the closest desk and he squeezed himself into the seat.

"Ben, do you know why Aggie isn't in school?"

The boy shook his head, not looking up.

"And she hasn't been at home?"

Another shake.

"She's with your sister, but you still don't know where that is?"

"No, I don't," Ben whispered.

Murdoch hesitated. "You know, son, when I was a lad, my pa used to haul off and give me a stoter when he'd been drinking, just like the one you've got over your eye. When I grew up, I decided to become a police officer because I thought I'd like to do what I could to protect people who couldn't defend themselves against such men, like women and children and the crippled –"

The boy looked at him in alarm. "You're not going to arrest Pa, are you?"

Murdoch couldn't promise that and he glanced over at Amy Slade, not wanting to dump everything into her lap but thinking she might know what to say. She did.

"Ben, do you remember that story we all read about the fox

and the chickens? Well, remember how we all discussed that we can't be angry at the fox because that is his nature to catch and eat chickens?"

The boy looked rather bewildered but he nodded.

Amy searched around for words, for once at a loss. "Do you remember that we said that as human beings we are considered to be superior to the animals. We have brains and souls… Unfortunately, Ben, there are some men who have never risen above their animal nature. They become like the foxes and young girls are like the chickens."

"They eat them, you mean?" Ben asked, his eyes wide with horror.

"Oh my Lord. No, not that but…"

"They do them harm," finished Murdoch. Something flickered across the boy's face and he thought that Ben knew what he was talking about. "The point is we need to find your sister as soon as possible, but we absolutely cannot do it without your help."

"You're like the boy who saves the flock," interjected Miss Slade.

Ben's face lit up. The idea of being a hero obviously appealed to him. He met Murdoch's eyes. "Did you put your pa in jail when you got to be a frog?"

"No…but I sure felt like doing that."

Ben ducked his head again. "You know that picture you showed me? Of the dead baby? Well, I've seen it before. Aggie had it."

"Did she say where she got it from?" Murdoch asked, keeping his voice as neutral as he could.

"No, but she had a bunch of photographs. I think Martha gave them to her."

"Were they all like that one? Were they mourning photographs?"

"Some were. They were scary…She teased me with them, waving them in my face."

"Did she show you any of the others?"

"No. She said they were private and I was too much of a baby to see them."

This had obviously been an ongoing conflict between Aggie and Ben, older sister and young brother.

A bell began to clang from the playground. "The children will be coming back shortly," said Miss Slade.

Murdoch groaned inwardly. "Ben, you said you didn't know where Martha was working, but is there anything at all you can tell us. Did she come home on the streetcar, for instance, or is she close enough to walk?"

"She always walked 'cos she saved money."

"How long has she been in service? When did she find the newspaper?"

Ben thought for a moment. "It was in the summer when it was hot. Just after we got out of school."

Amy interjected. "That would be the end of June."

There was a clatter outside in the hall as the children came down the hall. At the sound, any openness in the boy disappeared and it was as if he had fled to his mental burrow. Murdoch cursed. He looked at the schoolteacher and she gave a little shrug. She knew it was hopeless to continue at this point.

Murdoch stood up. He touched the boy's shorn head. He wanted to say, If your father hits you again, let me know, but he knew the boy wouldn't dare. "Ben, don't forget what I said. Let us know if Aggie comes home."

Ben nodded slightly and Murdoch thought he would at least do that much. Miss Slade told him he could go now and he slunk back to his own desk. She accompanied Murdoch into the hall.

"Please let me know as soon as you have any news, Mr. Murdoch."

"Of course."

She returned to the classroom and Murdoch saw her go to the boy's desk and crouch beside him. He turned to leave.

The children were walking down the hall in an orderly line, all the chatter left outside. Their silence was enforced by the figure of a tall, severe-looking man with a red face and bristling whiskers. Murdoch assumed he was the headmaster, Mr. Kippen. He touched his hat politely as he walked past, knowing that it was on the tip of the man's tongue to ask him what he was doing there. He was only prevented from doing so by the behaviour of one of the boys who seemed to be chewing something. That got him a clout on the side of the head. The lad yelped in protest and the headmaster raised his hand to strike him again. Murdoch stepped forward.

"Mr. Kippen, sir. I am a police officer and I'd say I am a good judge of the criminal character. That boy you have there is as fine looking a boy as I've seen. I doubt you need to worry about him. And I don't hold with beating of boys or horses, myself."

Kippen turned even more red but he released the lad, who scurried away to join his intimidated pals. Murdoch moved even closer to the headmaster and lowered his voice to a conspiratorial whisper.

"In case you're wondering why I'm here, I must tell you, I'm investigating a very serious case of brutality. I suggest you be careful, if you take my meaning. The chief constable is renowned for his soft heart."

That was a complete misrepresentation but Murdoch didn't care. It was either that lie or a punch to the head of the headmaster and he didn't think the latter was wise. With another flick of his hat he walked out. After a couple of blocks, he'd calmed down a little but was still tempted to go back into the school and give Mr. Kippen the thrashing he deserved.

CHAPTER TWENTY-TWO

MURDOCH HURRIED BACK TO THE STATION. IT WAS TIME to inform Brackenreid what was going on and he wasn't looking forward to it. The inspector had the finesse of the old barber surgeons. *Oh, got an ingrown toenail, have you? We'd better amputate that foot then.* Murdoch had a growing and deep conviction that this case required all the delicacy it could get. One slight misstep and Agnes Fisher might be a goner, if she wasn't already. To his great relief, however, Gardiner told him that Inspector Brackenreid was at home with a stomach upset. Murdoch beckoned to Constable Crabtree and headed for his cubicle.

He told him the whole story, beginning with Miss Slade's

discovery of the photographs and the disturbing tie to the body found on the lake. Crabtree's broad face flushed slightly when Murdoch showed him the photographs, but then he looked angry. He had children of his own.

"George, I'd like you to go to visit Agnes's father. Maybe the sight of a uniform will jolt his memory about his older girl's whereabouts. Do whatever you need to do, frighten him to within an inch of his life if you have to."

"Be happy to, sir."

"There's a young woman living downstairs. See if she can give you anything to go on. Ask the neighbours if they have any idea where Martha Fisher is in service. If you get the slightest lead, take it."

"Yes, sir."

"If that's a dead end, I want you to start walking up and down the nobby streets. Start with Jarvis. See if anybody has recently taken on a new servant."

"Can we get some more help, sir?"

Murdoch sighed. "Let's see how this goes first. The girl might have taken a place not too far from home. You might find her quickly."

"And if the younger girl is with her?"

"See if she will come down to the station willingly, but if not, you'll have to make her. She's in danger." Murdoch stood up. "I'm afraid I don't have many leads, just a bad feeling in my stomach that I'm going to acknowledge. I'm going to visit Gregory's Emporium and see if I can shake anything loose there. Let's meet back here in a couple of hours."

"Yes, sir."

At the entrance to the cubicle, Crabtree hesitated, then turned to Murdoch.

"I have a daughter, as you know, sir. I find it incomprehensible what has been done to Agnes Fisher. I don't care if my feet fall off, I'm going to find her."

"Thank you, George."

A slightly tousled Mrs. Gregory opened the door of the studio. She brought a recalcitrant strand of hair under control.

"We're not open for business today."

Murdoch beamed at her. "I do apologize, ma'am, but I'm about to head back home and I'd like to get my photographs. Save you having to post them to me."

She hesitated, then stepped back and let him come in. "I think they're ready. Just a moment."

While she was checking in the desk drawer, Murdoch wandered closer, composing his face into what he hoped was a suitable leer. "Mrs. Gregory, I can tell just by looking at you that you're a liberal-minded woman…I've heard a man can get, you know, er, special cards…Naughty ones, if you know what I mean."

Her expression turned so icy, he quailed. He had no real proof the studio wasn't utterly respectable and now he had possibly insulted a decent woman.

"I have no idea to what you are referring, Mr. Murdoch." She thrust the package into his hand. "Here are your photographs. The balance on account is two dollars and twenty-five cents."

He handed over the money and she snatched it from his hand as if it were contagious.

"We will keep the negative plates for one month and if you want more prints you must let us know at once. Good day, sir." She picked up a pen from the tray and jabbed it into the inkwell so sharply, he almost winced.

There was nothing for it but to leave. When he was in the hall, he heard the door lock behind him.

The light on the stairs was too feeble for him to get a good look at the photographs so he waited until he was outside where the thin winter sun had reappeared and the sky was the pale blue of old, faded eyes.

He studied the photograph, looking for any detail at all that was the same as in the picture of Agnes Fisher. There was nothing. The backdrop was just as Gregory had set it up for him. Perhaps an expert could tell the difference from one camera to another the way Enid could distinguish typewriting machines, but he couldn't.

Then he looked at the whole image, himself in the Prince's study. He grinned wryly. He looked quite distinguished, if he said so himself. Add a desk and bookcase, make your subject stare sombrely into the camera, and you've got a man in the professions with an illustrious career ahead of him. For a moment, Murdoch felt a pang of disappointment. Such a possibility was closed to him. Roman Catholic men with no family connections and no education beyond standard six would never enter any of the professions. Even being accepted into the detective division had been a chance thing. At the last minute one of the applicants had fallen ill and Inspector Stark needed a man to fill his quota. Murdoch was it, although he had been relegated to acting detective for three years now and he didn't know if that status would ever change.

He returned the photographs to the envelope, feeling frustrated again with his lack of progress with the case. Were Mrs. Gregory and the studio what they seemed to be? He couldn't tell, and unless he got a search warrant, he wasn't any closer to finding the telltale props. He thought of going in search of Crabtree but another thought niggled at the back of his mind. The coincidence of the anonymous letters bothered him. Paradoxically, the discovery of the murdered boy had been a relief. Reluctantly, he'd let himself entertain the possibility that his friend, Seymour, might have perverse sexual appetites, but he'd bet his life that the sergeant wouldn't have been party to the vicious beating and strangulation of a young man. He decided this was when discretion could be put aside. Seymour had to come clean.

Murdoch headed along King toward River Street, his thoughts suddenly jumping away to his own situation. The Kitchens and Enid were all on the verge of leaving him. Rationally, he knew that they didn't have much choice. Moving to Muskoka might save Arthur's life and he understood why Enid couldn't ignore the summons to go home. But damn it, all three of them at the same time! He'd even had a fleeting thought after Mrs. K.'s announcement that Enid could move back into the house when they left. He knew she wouldn't, though. Not without a landlady to chaperone them. He'd never quite given up being surprised that she had consented to having connections with him. Not just consented, actually seemed to welcome it. That thought stirred him up, but was followed as quickly by shame.

I saw your face, Will. She saw that he didn't want to marry her. And that was why she was going back to Wales.

By the time he reached Seymour's boarding house, he was thoroughly chilled. The sky might be blue but the price was wind with an Arctic bite to it. He'd walked straight past the planing mill, no dancing on logs today.

Reordan let him in. The livid burn marks on his face seemed even more disfiguring in the winter sunlight. He wasn't very welcoming either.

"Charlie has stepped out. If that's who you're calling on."

"Yes, it is. Do you know when he'll be back?"

"Half an hour at the most."

"Can I wait for him then? I don't want to walk all the way back to the station if he'll be here soon."

Reluctantly, Reordan stepped back so Murdoch could enter.

"I won't disturb you. Shall I wait in the kitchen?"

"That's private quarters."

"Seymour's room, then? I can't just stand here."

"Top of the stairs on the right," Reordan conceded reluctantly.

He shuffled off, leaving a strange, malodorous miasma behind him. Reordan was not a man for washing.

Murdoch went up the stairs. Like the hallway, the walls were bare and painted the same white. The only concession to comfort was a grey sisal runner. Last year, Murdoch had visited his dying sister in the convent where she was a cloistered nun. There had been the same air of austerity and scrupulous cleanliness about the convent halls. He almost expected to see a crucifix here. There wasn't one, but at the end of the landing there was a small table over which hung a large framed photograph.

He went to have a look at it. The table was of polished walnut and on it was a silver candleholder and a little silver dish filled with dried rose petals. He examined the photograph, a formal studio portrait of a balding man, probably in late middle age. He had a strong nose and a white, neatly trimmed beard that couldn't hide the powerful thrust of his chin. The compelling thing about him was his eyes, which were heavy lidded and dark and bespoke both compassion and intelligence. It was an attractive face. There was no name attached to the photograph and Murdoch couldn't identify him. He was about to turn away when he spotted a stamped imprint at the bottom right side of the picture. It was a circle around a triangle with the letters S.O.M.A. written between the circle and the triangle. Murdoch was familiar with most Masonic Order symbols and this wasn't one of them, but he guessed it was some kind of esoteric order. The little dish of flowers, faintly perfumed, and the candle could be some kind of offering or just decoration, he couldn't tell. The unknown man didn't look like the kind who solicited adoration, but who knew for sure. He took out his notebook, copied the symbol, and turned to Seymour's room. The door was slightly open, a low fire in the grate and a lamp lit. Clearly the sergeant hadn't intended to be gone for long. Murdoch went in. He was uncomfortable with anything that might imply spying, but he also knew he wouldn't get another chance like this.

Like the rest of the house, Seymour's room was neat and underfurnished. A narrow bed, covered with a grey blanket, was against one wall. Two cane chairs were arranged in front of the fire, one with a footstool. There was a wardrobe, oaken and plain, a washstand, and a small desk. The only decorations, if you could call them that, were two high bookcases on either side of the hearth. They were loaded with books and binders of newspapers. Murdoch walked over to get a look at the sergeant's taste in reading material but was stopped midway by what he saw on the desk. A stereoscope was lying beside a pile of view cards. For an instant, Murdoch froze, not wanting to go any farther. However, he had no choice. He picked up one of the cards.

CHAPTER TWENTY-THREE

THE CARD READ, *MAKING LADIES WAISTS,* AND SHOWED neatly dressed women sitting across from each other at long tables. Murdoch turned the card over. It was from the T. Eaton Company and explained in glowing terms that the floor engaged more than four hundred and fifty operators and the factory was light, clean, and airy and, even better, the company boasted that they kept a superior class of help. Murdoch put the card into the stereoscope and adjusted the slide until the photograph sprang into relief. The factory certainly looked industrious, with row upon row of women, heads bent over their sewing machines, all definitely looking like a superior kind of woman. He imagined their hands and nails would be inspected by a supervisor every day. Not unlike the constables when they reported for duty, come to think of it. Uniforms checked for spots, shoes for polish, and, of course, breath for any trace of alcohol. He was glad he didn't have to go through that any more.

The next few cards were also from the T. Eaton Company, *The laundry room, The mail room*, the same uninspired photographs of anonymous women and the reverse messages all praising the quality of their work. Murdoch scanned the other cards, about two dozen of them: different employers but all of people working at a trade.

He replaced the stereoscope on the desk. If Seymour was interested in illicit pornographic views he wasn't likely to leave them out for all to see. He hesitated for a moment, then pulled open the drawer. More cards fastened with rubber bands. And an unfinished typewritten letter. He didn't have time to read it, but he noted the same cryptic symbol he'd seen on the portrait in the hall. A triangle inside a circle. There was the sound of the front door opening and almost at once Reordan's voice.

"Your police friend is upstairs, Charlie."

Murdoch went over to the cane chair and sat down. He was highly uncomfortable at what he had just done, even though he believed it was necessary.

He heard Seymour's footsteps on the stairs and in a minute the man came into the room. Murdoch scrutinized his face and was relieved to see no trace of nervousness but rather the opposite. Seymour came over to him, hand outstretched.

"Good day to you, Will. Any news?"

"Not about the letters."

"What then?" The sergeant's expression was enigmatic but Murdoch thought he looked relieved.

Murdoch took the photograph of the turbaned youth from his envelope. "Do you know this fellow?"

Seymour stared at the picture for a moment but after an initial moment of shock, his face was once again inscrutable. "Is he dead?"

"Yes."

Seymour went over to the fire and poked at the coals. "What happened?"

"His body was found on the lake, stuffed into a steamer trunk. Somebody had beaten him then strangled him."

Murdoch saw the tension in Seymour's shoulders. "Poor sod."

"Do you know him?"

There was an indistinguishable mutter.

Suddenly Murdoch felt a surge of anger and he strode over to the fireplace. "Charlie, what the hell is going on here? What are you doing?"

Seymour didn't answer but continued to stab the fire. Murdoch grabbed the handle of the poker, forcing him to stop. "Will you answer me, for God's sake? You've got to stop hiding."

"I don't know what you're talking about."

Seymour let go of the poker and stood up, moving away. Murdoch was after him.

"You bloody *do* know what I'm talking about. You're doing

something that some fart catcher knows about or suspects. Immoral, illegal, at the moment I don't give a frig about fine lines. All those coy little glances and precious allusions. It's obvious you're all involved in some kind of secret society, the special handshakes, the shrine out there in the hall..."

Seymour's lips were tight. "It's not a shrine."

"What the frig is it then? You obviously knew this boy. What was he, your nancy boy? Are you a group of panders who've convinced yourselves it's all right?"

"Will, stop it! You can't talk to me like this!"

Murdoch slapped the photograph. "He's dead, Charlie, and he had a miserable death. I saw the look on your face. You knew him, admit it."

The sergeant flushed. "That has nothing to do with the letters."

"How can you be so sure?"

"Because I haven't seen that lad for several years." Seymour dropped down on the edge of the bed and with a groan put his head in his hands. Murdoch waited impatiently for him to continue. Finally, he looked up. "His name is Leonard Sims and he was one of my nabs when I was on the beat. We raided a brothel where he was working. He was only fourteen or fifteen at the time." He stopped and, for a moment, Murdoch thought he was weeping. "I felt sorry for him and I let him go...Of course he was a guttersnipe to the core. He wasn't grateful. But he saw this as his chance to try a spot of blackmail. He said he'd tell the inspector I'd sodomized him unless I gave him money."

"And did you? Give him money?"

"No. I beat him and dragged him to the magistrate. He was sent to the industrial school for two years. I never heard from him after that."

"Did he make good his threat?"

"Oh yes, but nobody believed him after what I'd done." He shook his head. "I should have admitted at once that I knew who he was but it's an episode I'm not proud of."

"And you're certain that the anonymous letter writer isn't raking up old dirt?"

"I don't think so. The letters refer to my present activities, if you recall."

"Which are?"

"Will, I can't tell you. The story isn't mine alone to tell. I'm sorry."

"Surely, these people wouldn't want you to be dismissed to save their hides?"

"Whether they would or no isn't the point. I told you, I have done nothing that sits on my conscience. You'll have to believe me, Will. And I'm not going to say any more."

"For God's sake, Charlie. What are you, a dried-up old maid of a missionary who wants to kiss martyrdom? I'm not here to burn you at the stake. There are more important things happening than your delicate *conscience*."

Seymour raised his voice in turn. "You know nothing about it. I don't have a delicate conscience, as you call it. I'm not going to reveal secrets that aren't mine alone."

Murdoch reached in his pocket and took out the envelope

with the photographs. He threw it on the desk. "Have a look at these. Miss Slade told you there was a legal matter concerning one of her pupils but she too is of a delicate sensibility and she didn't show you the filth itself. The girl in the picture is the one who drew a mourning band around Leonard Sims's picture so she knows he's dead. As far as I know she could be dead too. Go on, take a look and then tell me if you want to help me find out who did it. That is as long as it doesn't interfere with your conscience too much."

At that moment, there was a tap on the door and Reordan limped in without waiting for an answer.

"What's all the shouting about?"

"Oh nothing much," said Murdoch, who was still steaming. "Charlie and me are having what you might call a philosophical discussion."

For some reason, his words seemed to fling Reordan into a rage and he bellowed, "Are you, indeed? Well that's no call to sneer at him, mister arse crawler of a policeman." He shuffled over to Murdoch with surprising speed and caught hold of the lapels of his coat. "I won't tolerate a copper trying to shout down a pal of mine."

The suddenness of the attack made Murdoch react instinctively and he in turn grabbed the Irishman by the wrists. He was a good foot shorter than Murdoch, which meant he was glaring up into his face like a terrier confronted by a mastiff.

"Don't worry about me being a cripple, Mr. Frog. I'll take you and your kind any day."

In fact, Murdoch could feel the strength in the man's arms. His destroyed face was crimson with rage and there was a speck of saliva at the corner of his mouth. He looked as if he was ready to shift his grip from coat to Murdoch's throat. Either that or throw him to the ground.

"Leave it, John," called out Seymour, and he grabbed Reordan by the shoulder. "Stop this at once. Will's a good friend of mine."

For several more moments, Reordan continued to glare into Murdoch's face, then reluctantly he loosened his hold while Murdoch shifted his weight to the balls of his feet, ready to defend himself again if need be. Finally, the Irishman lowered his gaze and Murdoch released his grip on his wrists. He had no intention of being manhandled again.

"Sir, I don't know what your moan is all about but I won't stand for any man, crippled or not, grabbing me."

Seymour quickly got in between them.

"You've no need to fight my battles for me, John."

Murdoch was about to say, "That's just an excuse for the fellow," but he stopped himself and stepped back a little way. His heart was thudding.

Reordan swayed slightly on his crippled leg and Seymour slipped an arm around his waist to ease him into the chair. "My God, man, we can't be fighting our friends. We've got to save that for the real enemy."

"I didn't like the way he was after talking to you."

"You're not the only hot-head around here. Will can get as

fired up as you but he's a man of honour."

Reordan muttered, "That's hard to believe, he's a frog, isn't he."

"Yes, and I told you he's a friend. Now let's you and him shake hands and, John, you started it, you should apologize."

"That's all right, Charlie," said Murdoch. "Mr. Reordan was correct in saying I was speaking in a certain tone of voice that was uncalled for. I apologize to you for that."

"Well, while we're all apologizing, I'm sorry too, Will. I know you're only trying to help me." Seymour ruffled his own thin hair so it stood up in wisps. "I think we all could do with a nip of brandy. Strictly medicinal, John, don't worry." He walked over to his bookcase, moved aside a couple of fat volumes, reached to the back of the shelf, and took out a bottle. He handed it to Murdoch first. "You'll have to swig, I don't have any glasses up here."

Murdoch took the bottle, unscrewed the top, and swallowed down a gulp, passing the bottle to Seymour, who did likewise, then gave it to Reordan, who indulged in a curiously ladylike sip. He wiped his lips with the back of his hand.

"So why are you riding Charlie?" he said. "Why don't you chase after real criminals? They aren't hard to find. Just look under a rock and you get any number of bosses."

Seymour frowned a warning. "John. We're keeping to my business alone."

"Let him say his piece, Charlie. He might not be aware of the reality of the situation."

"No, Will. It was me you wanted to hear from."

Reordan stabbed his finger in the air. "Say on, Mr. Frog. I'm as aware of reality, as you call it, as the next man. Get it off your chest whatever it is."

Murdoch was thoroughly exasperated by the man and his rudeness and his own voice matched it, in spite of himself and his pity. "You call Charlie a friend and so do I, but he is in danger of losing his job. He's a bloody good sergeant but that's it for his career if it happens. He won't be taken on by any other police force in the country."

"Maybe not such a loss," snapped Reordan.

"To him it would be. If you're such a good friend, you'd know that. It's not just a *job*."

The Irishman glanced over at the sergeant, whose expression said it all.

Murdoch pressed on. "He's been doing something that is against the law, as written on the statutes. Somebody knows about it and has been sending anonymous letters to the inspector in order to get him dismissed. Charlie, however, refuses to clear his name or give me any information so I can help him because he says there are other people involved. I presume you are one of those people, Mr. Reordan. So what is it you're going to do? Let your friend slide down the drain or come clean and let me in on what this is all about?"

Reordan gaped at him, then at Seymour. "Charlie?"

Seymour replaced the cap on the bottle and put it on the lamp table. "I told Will that the secrets weren't mine to reveal."

There was a brief silence, then Reordan grimaced. "Hey, you

can have my secret any time you want. I ain't ashamed of it. If it would help the frog to tell him about the Knights, you have my permission, no question."

Murdoch leaped on his statement. "The Knights? You mean the Knights of Labour? I thought they'd dissolved."

Reordan was indignant. "We ain't going under. We've still got work to do."

"Do you belong to the Knights of Labour, Charlie? Is that it?"

Seymour made fists with his hands and bumped them together. Finally, he answered.

"Yes, I do. And yes, I am quite aware I could get the bird because of it. As our illustrious inspector is forever reminding us." He stuck his thumbs in his waistband and gave a fair imitation of Brackenreid's posture and voice. "'Gentlemen, a police officer must always be without partisanship.'"

"Them's all fancy words for saying that frogs toady to employers and them that already has," scoffed Reordan. "Talk about justice being blind, frogs make up for that by having a great nose for what's going to keep them smelling sweet."

"Give it a bone, Reordan, I'd like to hear what else Charlie has to say."

Seymour got to his feet. His face had brightened and his voice was that of an enthusiast. "This isn't any ordinary labour group, Will. The full name is The Noble and Holy Order of the Knights of Labour and it is an appropriate one."

Murdoch shrugged. "Maybe so but it's still a secret society and a labour group."

"I'm aware of that but hear me out. They – that is, *we* – want to work toward permanent justice for every human soul, not just for one small class of society. I've come to believe deeply in their philosophy."

To Murdoch it was coming to sound more and more like a religion. "The stern-looking cove in the hall with the altar in front of his portrait, I gather he's a Knight too?"

Seymour ignored the jibe. He was too eager to tell Murdoch, for all the world as if he were a young man trying to convince a stern father that his choice of a bride was a good one.

"That's the founder, Uriah Stephens. He began the Order in Philadelphia in 1869. The Canadian chapters have shrunk a bit, more's the pity, but we're still going."

"There was a symbol in the corner, what's that signify?"

"Let me tell him," interrupted Reordan like an eager schoolboy. "The principles of the order are secrecy, obedience, and mutual assistance. The three lines of the triangle indicate the three elements essential to man's existence and happiness: land, labour, and love. The circle is the bond of unity by which the membership is bound together." Like Seymour, Reordan was speaking as fervently as any priest.

"That all sounds very noble – no, hold on, I'm not poking fun at you, it does sound noble. I'm all for it. The problem is that no police officer, including Charlie, can belong to a labour organization." He nodded over at Seymour. "Are you going to resign from the Knights?"

"No."

"And you don't want to resign from the police force?"

"No."

"Christ help us, Charlie, you can't do both."

"Why shouldn't he?" burst out Reordan. "He's been doing both for months now and nobody's come to harm."

"Look, I agree with you, but I'm not the police chief. He'll lose his job."

Seymour did the punching movement again. "God, Will. I don't know what to do. I'm like a man with two wives and I'd swear on the Bible I loved both of them. I don't know how the hell I'm going to choose."

Reordan addressed Seymour. "Perhaps your pal needs to know more about reality as I've seen it, Charlie. Maybe then he'd comprehend better why you ain't going to give up the Knights easily."

Seymour hesitated. "If you want to, John, but I don't think it changes the situation that much. I'll still have to make a decision."

Reordan turned to Murdoch. "Do you want to hear my story?"

Murdoch bit back his reply. "Go ahead."

Reordan touched his scarred face. "You've probably been wondering how I got burned like this. I would never have survived if it weren't for the Knights. They saved me." He stretched out his hand. "But before I go on, you'd better give me a swallow of that brandy." Seymour handed over the bottle and Reordan drank some with the gasp of a man unaccustomed to liquor.

"It weren't no accident. It was done deliberate. I was tarred and feathered, you see."

CHAPTER TWENTY-FOUR

MURDOCH WAITED WHILE REORDAN TOOK ANOTHER drink of the brandy, a much bigger sip this time.

"I got these burns nine months ago. I was working in Ottawa at the Perley and Pettee sawmill. Have you heard of them?"

Murdoch nodded. "There was a big strike there that eventually involved all the mills in the area but it ended badly, I recall."

Reordan scowled at him. "I hope by that remark you mean it ended badly for the workers, not the bosses. They made piss-all concessions."

"I did mean it ended badly for the workers. They couldn't hold out."

His comment agitated the Irishman and he got to his feet and began to hobble up and down the small room. Seymour watched him and Murdoch could see he was ready to jump in at any moment if need be.

"For sure we couldn't hold out because we were almost starving before the strike and even with relief money, men with families couldn't endure. The wives of the bosses sat around in their silk and satin while our wives went in rags and fed their babies cold water to stave off the hunger pangs. All we asked was a ten-hour day and that the wages be restored to what they were, which was pitiful enough. I was bringing in seven dollars a week and I was a single man and could hardly live on it." Reordan's face was contorted with old anger. "All the workers at the Pettee mill and the nearby mills had stopped work. My foreman, a bastard by the name of Napoleon Leblanc, had ordered a shutout. But we had dragged ourselves through a terrible summer of near starvation and we were determined not to give in. We'd have had to, though, if it weren't for the Knights who came in to organize matters." He paused. "The bosses called them 'walking agitators', like their own workers were too stupid or too downtrodden to rise up against them. Well, that weren't the case. When I heard what the Knights had to say, I joined up in a flash…And you despise us, no doubt."

"I rather you didn't put words into my mouth, or thoughts into my head that aren't mine, sir. I have no reason to despise an organization of which I know little but what I do know has been favourable."

Reordan was only slightly mollified. He was hell bent on hating somebody and Murdoch, the policeman, was as good a target as any.

"Like I said, we were determined to hold out. Then on the night of April 13, we heard that the bosses were bringing in scabs from Quebec. A lot of the men were at the boil when they got that news. They wanted to go and burn down the bosses' houses and make a fight of it. But Jamie Paterson, who was one of our leaders, was as smart as a fox. 'That's what the bosses want, lads,' he says to us. 'They want the world to see us as a mob without morals or brains. Well we won't give them that satisfaction.' He says as how he wouldn't put it past the bosses to set the scabs on a rampage and say it was us as did the damage. So he wanted four or five of us to go out on the watch and keep the property safe against anybody who come to pillage, don't matter whether they're calling themselves friend or foe. Well, it took a bit of persuading. There were a lot of hot-heads in our own group at the end of their tether and they were ready to set fire to those big mansions stuffed with the food we had put on their tables. But finally they agreed." He stood still, staring in to space as if he were watching his own story projected on the wall. "So that's how it come that Saturday night, there I was sitting outside the boss's house keeping watch. There was young Sam Gibson and me. We'd been issued with pistols, the both of us, which made us feel we could take on anybody as need be. It had turned cool and we were huddled around a brazier to keep warm, which was why we didn't even see the scabs 'til they was on us. So much for our guns. There were two of them, muffled up with scarves so's they wouldn't be recognized. And they were on us in a flash. Sam was closer to them than me and as he turned to see what was happening, one of them smashed him in the jaw with his billy. They got me pinned to the ground before I could utter a peep and shoved a rag in my mouth. I was trussed and hogtied in seconds."

Reordan wet his lips but didn't face Murdoch. "The one who had hit Sam says to me, 'We heard you fellows was talking of tarring and feathering the scabs. Is that true?' I couldn't answer even if I'd wanted to. There had been loose talk about what we'd do to scabs if they was brought in, but it was just talk as far as I was concerned. 'Is it true?' said the fellow again and he kicked me good in the chest. I tried to shake my head but he weren't looking for an answer. 'We don't like that,' he says with another kick. 'We've as much right to work as you do.' The other fella didn't utter a word, just him. He was the leader. Then he goes, 'So we thought we'd do a bit of tarring up ourselves,' he says. I could smell hot tar and then I saw they'd brought a bucket of pitch with them and a sack. 'It's got to be hotter,' he says to the other cove like he was asking for a cup of tea. 'The feathers won't stick else. And we want them to stick. We want all you lads to see what scabs can do back if they're pressed.' I tried to struggle but they had the better of me. The one talking gave me the boots again and again and I could heard the crack as my thigh bone shattered. He laughed when he heard that, like he was enjoying himself."

He stopped talking and took another swig of the brandy. Seymour stood up and took him by the arm.

"John, you aren't going to find peace in that bottle. Do you want me to tell the rest of it?"

The Irishman was trembling violently and Murdoch's own mouth had gone dry at the horror of the story. Reordan allowed Seymour to lead him to the chair and he collapsed into it, his head in his hands. The older man touched his shoulder gently.

"There wasn't anything you could do to defend yourself."

Reordan looked up and his eyelids were red, the scars on his head livid and raw. "Or Sam, right? I couldn't help Sam either."

Seymour waited for a moment, gripping the man's shoulder until he gained more control. "The leader turned on Sam next –"

"He was just a lad," cried Reordan.

"He was that and he'd been knocked unconscious with the billy so he couldn't resist either. They poured hot tar over him and then rolled him in the heap of feathers they'd dumped on the ground. John was next."

Seymour's voice was matter of fact, not from lack of feeling so much as controlled outrage. "The tar was almost at the boil and immediately burned his skin wherever it touched."

Reordan held up his hand. "I'll tell him the rest," he whispered. "Maybe it'll help him understand." He licked his dry lips. "They rolled me in the feathers the way they had with Sam Gibson. Then the short guy, the talker, looks down at me and says, 'Let's have pity here. Poor cove's burning up. He needs cooling off.' He made a gesture to the other fella. 'Go on,' he says, 'cool his head off.'"

He couldn't continue and Charlie again spoke for him. "The man undid his trousers and made his water – on John."

Reordan held up his hand. "That's enough for now."

Murdoch's neck tightened. "I assume these men were never caught," he said after a moment.

Reordan spoke so quietly he could hardly hear him. "Of course not. They was helped to get away because the bosses were glad about what had happened to us, even though both Sam and me were hurt real bad. They thought it might make us workers buckle under."

"It did just the opposite, I'm happy to say," interjected Seymour. "They held the strike for three more months."

"But there must have been an investigation?"

"I'm ashamed to admit it, Will," said Charlie, "but the local police officers were in sympathy with the bosses. They did almost nothing. The two men have never been found or their identity discovered. Their faces were hidden and all John could offer was a general description of height. The leader was short and he talked with some kind of accent. He had a raspy voice, but the scarf muffled everything and he was most likely trying to disguise his voice. The man who defiled John was about six feet tall and seemed the younger of the two."

Reordan looked over at Murdoch. "I'm going to find them some day, don't you doubt it."

Seeing the look in the man's eyes, Murdoch didn't.

"I didn't get no compensation," Reordan continued. "The

boss said I wasn't injured while doing my work even though it was his frigging property I was trying to protect. I'd have been in a bad way if it weren't for the Knights. They paid for a doctor and gave me a stipend to keep me going. I don't have no family, but Mrs. Pangbourn, who used to live here, is my aunt. She had to go take care of her sister in Vancouver so she asked me to come here and run the house for her. Charlie, here, was already a boarder so he stayed on, then Amy and Wilkinson joined us. I ain't too proud to tell you, Detective Murdoch, that these folks keep me alive. It ain't just the money they gives me, it's that they treat me decent as they would any other human being. And in return I'm what you might call their bulldog. I might be crippled but I'm still capable of a good bite if need be."

Murdoch stood up and walked over to him. "You're as strong a man as I've encountered, John Reordan. Will you shake my hand now? I'm not here as an enemy but as a friend."

At first, he thought the Irishman would spurn him but he stared into Murdoch's eyes for a moment, then smiled slightly. "Like I said, I'm a bulldog sort of fellow. I can smell out friends." He took his hand.

CHAPTER TWENTY-FIVE

REORDAN DECLARED THEY COULD ALL DO WITH A MUG OF tea and he limped off downstairs to make it. At his leaving, Murdoch could feel himself letting out a breath he didn't even realize he'd been holding. Seymour went to the desk.

"Do you fancy a pipe, Will?"

"I do, thank you."

Seymour took out a clay pipe and a packet of tobacco from the drawer. "Badger suit you?"

"It will."

Murdoch had his own utility French briar in his pocket and he stuffed it with the aromatic dark tobacco that Seymour offered. Neither of them spoke until their pipes were lit and drawn.

"That's a terrible story Reordan has to tell," said Murdoch.

"It is indeed and I doubt we'll ever find out who did it, more's the pity."

They smoked in silence for a while, each lost in his own thoughts. Murdoch had no doubt how he would have felt in those circumstances and how corrosive would be the desire for revenge. He sighed and brought himself back to the present.

"So tell me a bit more about this organization you're so enamoured of. I thought they were almost nonexistent in Ontario now. Faded like hothouse flowers in winter." He deliberately made his tone ironic to see Seymour's reaction. He got one. The sergeant's voice was sharp.

"Not exactly. They're smaller in numbers now, unfortunately, but still fighting for justice for every human soul."

"A noble aim indeed but unrealistic, don't you think?"

"I'm surprised to hear you, of all people, say that, Will. You're a man who fights for justice too in your own way."

Murdoch puffed out a cloud of smoke. "I *enforce* the law, Charlie, that's different." This wasn't the time to launch into a philosophical exploration of the problems of enforcing laws that seemed cruel or unfair. It was an issue Murdoch was constantly uneasy about and had not resolved in his own mind, except that on more than one occasion he had chosen to interpret the law morally rather than literally.

Seymour placed his pipe carefully on the lamp table beside him. "Let me read you something, Will." He went to his bookcase and took down a fat binder stuffed with newspapers.

He untied the string, shuffled through the papers, and plucked one out. "Here we are. This was written by Mr. Kilt, editor of the *Ottawa Citizen*, in October of last year. Listen to this. 'What hope is there for a society with such extremes of wealth and poverty as our civilization shows? At the bottom rotting, corroding want and squalor; at the top, enervating luxury, reckless extravagance, useless, purposeless lives.'" Seymour paused and looked at Murdoch to see his reaction.

"I wouldn't mind a taste of 'enervating luxury' before my life is over," said Murdoch with a grin.

Seymour didn't smile back. "It's a taste people get addicted to. Let me continue…'What hope of such a society except that it is susceptible of fundamental reform or radical change? Consider how fruitful it is of meanness, of over-reaching, of envy, jealousy, and all uncharitableness.'" Again he paused but Murdoch didn't risk a comment, just nodded to him to go on. Seymour's normally calm voice was full of passion.

"'How can it be anything else? A society which in its industrial constitution is at war with honour, honesty, and justice, is not likely to beget generosity. It inevitably generates the vices, not the virtues, the baser not the nobler qualities of the soul.'" He put down the paper as reverently as a priest might put down a piece of consecrated parchment. "You asked me if I believe in what The Noble and Holy Order of Knights stands for. That's my answer, Will."

"That's a radical view they hold. The only hope for society is fundamental reform? Smacks of anarchy to me."

"You're wrong about that. They are no destroyers of order, they believe in order, but a fair and just order where workers are accorded respect and treated with dignity. Surely you must agree with that, Will?"

"How can I not? But underneath the dazzling rhetoric that you just read to me, there is a bias. Meanness, envy, and lack of charity are not the exclusive prerogative of the rich."

Seymour frowned. "That is not the point. I am not green, Will. You can't be a police officer as long as I've been and not see depravity and viciousness in all walks of life, but that is no different from saying that a diseased body shows all manner of ugliness on its skin. If society is a balanced and equitable one, it is healthy and manifests such. There is no place for crime where there is no want."

Murdoch thought Seymour was omitting a large proportion of crimes for which the motive was human passion. The envelope of photographs on the desk was a mute testimony to that.

The sergeant went on. "Look at the charges that as police officers we lay. It is the poorer classes who are driven to steal or even murder each other. How many charges are ever laid against the rich culls? One in a hundred?"

Murdoch drew some more on his pipe. "That doesn't mean the rich don't commit crimes, only that they aren't ever charged."

Seymour's normally impassive face was slightly flushed with the ardour of an acolyte. Their eyes met and to Murdoch's relief the sergeant suddenly laughed out loud.

"Will, you're looking at me as if I'm a candidate for the loony bin. I don't have a lance in my wardrobe nor a suit of armour. These are ideals I'm talking about. High ideals I know, but if we don't dare to dream of what might be, what are we?"

Murdoch jabbed at the air with his briar. "That I will concede." The tension between them eased.

"When did you join the order?" Murdoch asked.

"September last year. But I should make it clear, the Knights don't uphold strikes and walkouts. They believe in negotiating with the bosses in a reasonable way."

Again Murdoch was struck by what he thought was sentimental thinking on the part of a man whom up to now he'd considered as down to earth and as clear-eyed as a collector of night soil.

"Do the Knights know you are a police sergeant, by the way?"

"No, but the only occupations officially barred are bankers, lawyers, gamblers, and saloon keepers."

Murdoch laughed. "A motley group who deserve each other."

"Indeed."

"How big are the meetings? Would somebody have recognized you?"

"Oh I can't believe it's one of the members who's doing the dirt. First, we take a solemn oath of loyalty to defend and protect each other and, second, our meetings are quite small. There's been nobody I knew attending. But each assembly has regular meetings. Perhaps by bad chance, the Judas saw me going into the meeting hall. Could have been an old nab of mine wanting to get his own back."

Experienced officer that Seymour was, Murdoch could tell he was falling into the old trap of blame-the-stranger. The truth might be too painful.

"When did you ever know a lag to use such decorous language, not to mention that the letters are typewritten? And what puzzles me is why the man doesn't just come right out and say what you're up to? Why all the circumlocution?"

There was thumping on the stairs and Seymour got up to open the door. Reordan came in carrying a tray with three mugs and a plate of bread and butter. Seymour didn't offer to help him and Murdoch realized it must be a point of pride with the Irishman to manage by himself. He put the tray on the washstand. Unobtrusively, Seymour took over and passed one of the mugs to Murdoch.

Reordan took the other and slurped down some tea. He was noisy about it, not from bad manners but because scar tissue around his mouth made it difficult for him to drink properly.

"I heard the last bit. You two keep saying 'man', but do you know for certain it's a boyo? It could be a missus."

"That's true, but it don't feel like woman's work. Wouldn't you say, Will?"

Murdoch blew on his mug of tea. He'd already discovered it was scalding hot. "We can't totally dismiss that as a possibility." He took a bite of a piece of bread.

"Sorry we don't have no jam," said Reordan. "But the bread's fresh-baked this morning."

"It's delicious," replied Murdoch, and it was. He was

suddenly ravenous and munched through the thick, crusty slice. Reordan watched him, as proud as any cook summoned to the dining room while the mistress sampled the baking.

"What would help is if we had a list of the members of your local assembly," Murdoch said to Seymour.

"I don't have anything like that. We keep all names secret to protect each other. It's not so long ago that men lost their jobs if they were suspected of organizing the workers."

Reordan winked at Murdoch. "I've got one. I earn my stipend from the Knights by keeping track of the dues. I've got a list. Shall I show it to him, Charlie?"

Seymour didn't hesitate. "Thanks, John. A list would be helpful, can you bring it to us?"

Suddenly the Irishman cackled. He fished in his pocket. "I've got it here. Call yourselves police officers. It seems obvious to me that the person doing the letters has to be a member of the Knights or knows somebody that is." So much for Seymour's affirmation of unshakeable loyalty, thought Murdoch. Reordan handed over the paper. "I brought up the membership list of Excelsior. That's the name of his local assembly," he added for Murdoch's benefit.

Seymour stood up and leaned over the chair back so he could read the list with Murdoch. There were twenty-five names, neatly printed.

"Course, the person could be registered under a false name," said Reordan. "It's happened before. The bosses want to keep an eye on their wicked workers, so they send in a spy."

Suddenly, Murdoch stabbed the paper with his forefinger. "No! There it is. Or rather I should say, 'There she is.' Do you know this woman, Charlie?"

"Florence Gripe? Why yes, I've met her. But surely you're not suggesting…?"

"Miss Gripe is presently engaged, and she eventually will become Mrs. Liam Callahan."

"What! The station stenographer?"

"One and the same. I was introduced to her only last night at a typewriting competition. There's your link right there."

"Are you sure, Will?"

"It's a very unusual name. I can't believe there are two of them."

"She seems such a fine young woman, I find it difficult to believe she would betray me." Seymour looked acutely uncomfortable and Murdoch remembered the impression Florence's admiring eyes had made on he himself.

Reordan wagged his finger at them. "There you go again. Overlooking the obvious. Her fiancée might have flushed you out without her intentionally revealing anything. This Callahan, he could have escorted her to a meeting, for instance, and 'Lo, my goodness. Can I believe my eyes. There's our esteemed sergeant filing in with the other plebs.'"

"You said something like that yourself, Charlie," added Murdoch, "and it certainly answers the question of all the beating about the bush. Callahan probably doesn't want his sweetheart to know what he's doing."

"All right. But why has he got it in for me?"

Reordan did the finger-wagging gesture again. "Don't you police officers always ask who stands to gain by this crime? I've heard you talk about that lots of times, Charlie. My guess is that Callahan stands to benefit by you getting the shoot. My guess is that he wants your job."

Murdoch smiled at the Irishman. "You're putting us to shame, John. It makes sense. It's impossible to climb up the ranks of the police force except when a spot opens up ahead of you. We're not expanding at all this year, nor next in all probability. You can stay stuck in the same rank until your hair turns white and your teeth fall out."

"And especially if you're a Papist, which William here is."

Murdoch grimaced. "Especially if you're a Papist."

"I'm one too," Reordan jumped in. "It ain't easy. That's another reason I respect the Knights of Labour, they don't care who you bow to, or bend the knee to, or whatever the Protestants do."

"Hold on, you two. Let's get back on track here. You're saying that Callahan wants my job? But he's only a constable, second class. It wouldn't go to him."

"Not directly," said Murdoch. "The choice would be one of the two first-class constables, Fyfer or Crabtree. Let's say for the sake of argument that you left and George was moved up to sergeant. His position then would need filling. There are several constables, second class, who could take it. In jumps the hard-working Mr. Callahan. Better wages, better conditions."

"Not much better."

"But enough if you want to get married, and he surely does. I thought he was decidedly under Miss Gripe's spell. And my guess is she would be a rather expensive wife. Not to mention that she makes eyes at every man she comes across. Perhaps she trilled on about you to him, and he didn't like it. Come on, Charlie, did you flirt with the girl?"

The sergeant actually blushed. "Not flirt exactly, but she is a very sweet young woman. I didn't know she was engaged to be married. She never spoke of it."

"There you go then. I'd say Callahan got jealous and wanted you out of the way. Or at least disgraced and less eligible."

Seymour was shaking his head. "It's hard to believe, Will. He seems like such a pleasant young fellow."

"Too pleasant for me. He's an arse crawler. No wonder he and our inspector get along so famously. Besides, he's a liar. He told me a lie, a small one to be sure, but it makes me question what else he might be hiding." Briefly he related the story of the type-writing competition and Callahan's unexpected appearance. "He pretended he isn't accomplished when he is, but why not tell the truth? I saw him on that platform and he wanted to win, probably at all costs. Ambition to burn in that young man. One of his jobs at the station is to sort the daily post, so he could easily slip in a letter or two. And he is a stenographer. I haven't had a chance to check his typewriting machine against the letters, but Mrs. Jones, er, a woman I know, says they were typed on a Remington, and that is the machine used in most offices these days. When I asked him about typing, he covered his trouser seat by pretending he didn't know how, not realizing I had a friend who was in the same contest. No wonder he was shocked to see me. It's him all right, Charlie."

"But what do we do now? Even if we unmask him, I'll have to admit my involvement with the Knights and that's it for the police force. He'll probably only get a reprimand."

Murdoch thought Seymour was sitting on the fence. He would have to make a choice sooner or later. But he couldn't abide blackmailers, which was what Callahan was.

"I'll think of something."

The worry left Seymour's face and he laughed. "If I know you at all, William Murdoch, you will most certainly think of something and it will be highly moral but probably quite illegal."

"I'll drink to that," said Reordan and he lifted his mug of tea in a salute.

CHAPTER TWENTY-SIX

SHORTLY AFTERWARDS, REORDAN SAID HE HAD WORK TO do and left them. All this while, the envelope with the other photographs had sat unopened on the desk. Seymour got up and went over and picked it up.

"I'd better have a look at these."

"I warn you, it's ugly," said Murdoch.

The sergeant sat in the cane chair opposite and slid the photographs out. He snorted in derision at the Newly-wed photographs, but when he saw the picture of Agnes, his jaw clenched.

"My God, Will, surely this isn't Amy's pupil? She never told me it was this kind of thing she was concerned about."

"Miss Slade said she discovered them in the girl's desk, but the child would offer no explanation. She wants me to find out who the photographer is and is hoping that I can keep the police out of it officially until we know what's happened. Frankly, I don't know if I can do that and conduct a proper investigation, but I said I'd try."

Seymour, in an unconscious imitation of the schoolteacher's reaction, inverted the photograph.

"You must have thought my little speech about an unhealthy society somewhat naive. I find this kind of thing incomprehensible. Poor Amy to ever have had to see it."

"And poor Agnes."

"Quite. Is she the one who wrote the obscenities on the mourning card?"

"Probably. Miss Slade was fairly certain it was the girl's hand."

Seymour gazed at the photograph of the dead baby. "It's hard to believe that a young girl would deface a picture such as this. Where would she have learned such words?"

"Miss Slade says the girl's father is a complete ne'er-do-well. I met him and I'd concur with that. The mother is dead and there has been no mitigating influence, if there was indeed a maternal one, except for the classroom and Miss Slade."

"And if ever a woman would provide a mitigating influence, as you put it, she would."

Seymour's expression was fond but Murdoch thought it revealed a fraternal fondness and once again he was annoyed with himself for caring about that.

"Do you think Agnes was coerced into posing for the stereoscopic picture? Or was she paid?"

"I don't know. I haven't been able to question her myself. She hasn't returned to school. I spoke to her brother, but other than saying she might be with an older sister who is in service he wasn't helpful. And now that Leonard Sims has been found dead, I'm very worried about the girl's involvement."

Seymour picked up the other photograph. "Have you covered up his parts because he's naked?"

"Yes. I might have to show that picture around."

"The black border and the scratching out of the two faces look as if they have been done with the same pen and ink, so I assume it's Agnes's work too." The sergeant replaced the picture in the envelope. "What have you done so far?"

Quickly Murdoch related his visits to Gregory's Emporium and the other two studios.

"Gregory's is the closest to the Sackville Street School and Agnes's house. I didn't like the fellow who owns the place, but I couldn't find anything to link him to the stereoscopic pictures or the mourning card."

"I can understand your rationale for starting there, but the child could have met them anywhere. We should check every studio in the city."

"I know. Unfortunately, there's nothing to say the photographs have even come from a studio. What do they need? A camera and a set? Not much more."

He took his cabinet pictures from his pocket and handed

them to Seymour. "I had my portrait taken at the Emporium."

Seymour grinned. "You look very prosperous, Will."

"I was imagining I was Inspector Brackenreid. But, as you can see, the backdrops aren't like anything in either of the cards. I managed to have a look inside the cupboard in the studio but there was nothing that corresponded." He knocked out the tobacco from his pipe. "Really, the only two leads I have at the moment are, first, the baby's mourning card and the place where the older sister is working. The baby's picture looks as if it was taken by a different photographer, but it was in Agnes's possession so it might lead us somewhere. Her brother thinks she got them from Martha, the older girl, which is a second reason to find her."

Seymour echoed his gravity. "I agree. What do you want me to do?"

"I'd like you to go to the library and check the death columns in the newspapers for the past six months. Make a list of all the children about three or four months of age who have died. We'll divide up the numbers and go and see if they had mourning cards made and if so what photographer they used. At the same time, I'd like to check the Help Wanted columns and see if anybody was advertising for a servant girl before and including June of last year."

Seymour chuckled. "You'd be surprised at how easy that might be. I don't even have to go outside." He stood up. "Come on."

Murdoch put the envelope in his pocket and followed Seymour downstairs. The sergeant knocked on Reordan's door.

"John, it's me again. Can we have a word?"

The Irishman opened the door promptly and a wave of stale air came out of his room.

"Will here needs to search through some newspapers and we were wondering if you could give us a hand."

Reordan's eyes brightened. "My pleasure. Come in to the library."

The Irishman stepped aside and gestured them into his room. Murdoch had never seen anything quite like it. There were stacks of newspapers on every inch of the floor and little else in the room except a filing cabinet and a narrow bed. Pathways wound in and out of the stacks. The three of them were crowded awkwardly in the tiny space left to let the door open.

"John is the Knights record keeper," said Seymour. "He keeps track of any publicity that the Knights receive in all of the newspapers in the country as well as any news events that might be of concern to us."

Reordan beamed. "I keep a record of everything. This might look like a maze but it ain't. I know where everything is." He was clearly very proud of his accomplishment, but Murdoch was in danger of suffocating from the lack of fresh air in the room and the amount of newspaper there was.

"What are you looking for exactly?"

"We need names and addresses of all families who suffered the bereavement of a male infant over the past six months."

"Right you are."

"I'd also like names and addresses of any people advertising for a servant girl during the month of June last year. And if you can tell me which of those stopped advertising in July, I'll be forever in your debt."

"Done."

"How long do you think it will take?"

"I'll help," interjected Seymour.

"In that case, an hour, an hour and a half at the most." Reordan looked at him. "Am I to know what for?"

Murdoch hesitated. "With regard to the bereaved families we're trying to find out if they have had any dealings with a particular photographer we want to question. The servant girl is somebody we'd like to talk to."

"Good enough."

He shuffled off toward the wooden filing cabinet and Murdoch beckoned Seymour into the hall.

"While you're doing that, I'm going to go see if I can shake some information from Agnes's father."

Seymour grimaced. "Be careful, Will."

"Don't worry. I'm the soul of tact."

"Ha!"

Seymour let him out and, once on the street, Murdoch breathed in deep drafts of the chill air as if he could clean out both Reordan's story and Agnes's plight. He couldn't. He only succeeded in making himself cough.

CHAPTER TWENTY-SEVEN

FISHER WASN'T AT HOME, SO AS MUCH AS HE WANTED TO get his hands on the man, Murdoch couldn't. Once again, young Mrs. Tibbett answered the door and smiled shyly at him. She didn't know where Fisher had gone, she said, but probably to one of the local taverns. Ben wasn't in the house either. Still posing as a truant officer, Murdoch repeated that Agnes's teacher was anxious about her, but, when pressed, Kate could give no further information as to where the girl might be. Murdoch thought she was troubled about something, but one of the twins set up a wail in the background and she hurried away.

He left, briefly contemplated trying to find Fisher's rookery, but decided against it. He wasn't likely to get much information out of him if he was drunk and he was still acting on the premise that the man wasn't aware of what his daughter was up to. Murdoch didn't know how long he could keep the situation quiet, but he could understand why Amy Slade hadn't wanted to report the girl to the police. A couple of years ago, the inspector had received a letter from a woman who claimed that her next-door neighbour was trying to force connections on his own daughter, a girl of ten. She said the girl herself had told her so. Murdoch had been sent to investigate and he found a situation of appalling poverty and misery. The child's mother was a hopeless drunk, as was the father. At that time, the girl, younger even than Agnes Fisher, had, with great fear, whispered it was true what she'd confided to the neighbour. A charge of rape had been brought against her father. However, when the case came to court, the girl, like Aggie, was unable to speak or confirm what she had said. The judge, an arrogant, irascible old man, couldn't or wouldn't understand that she was terrified, and he'd sentenced her to three months for contempt of court. She was sent to the Mimico Girls' Industrial School. And that was the end of her. Murdoch tried to keep track of her after the sentence was served, but the family left the city and she disappeared with them.

He pulled his muffler tighter against the damp, cold air and began to walk in the direction of the Smithers' house on Church Street, near Gerrard. At least he could report back to Brackenreid that he had done something.

The house was large but not in a state of good repair. An elderly butler ushered him into a musty-smelling and cold drawing room festooned everywhere in black crepe. Here, Mrs. Smithers, a woman who must have been well over seventy, was sitting hunched over a meagre fire. She was in mourning dress. Opposite her was another woman in the plain grey gown of a servant. She, too, was elderly and bent with age. She got to her feet when Murdoch was announced and came over to him. Her face was haggard and her eyes were red from weeping. The butler remained in the room.

"Oh, Mr. Murdoch. Thank goodness you're here. Perhaps the mistress will listen to you."

The mistress, in fact, showed no indication that this would be the case. She hadn't even turned around but sat staring into the fire and muttering. Murdoch went closer.

"Mrs. Smithers, I'm Detective Murdoch. Inspector Brackenreid sent me to talk to you. You are missing a brooch, I believe."

The old lady looked up at him. "After all these years, and all I've done for, to turn against me like this."

"Who is that, ma'am?"

Mrs. Smithers jerked her head in the direction of her maidservant. "Her, of course, Carlyle."

Murdoch could see the other woman's body tremble as if she had been struck and he threw a sympathetic glance over at her.

"My mother-in-law gave that brooch to me when I was married," continued Mrs. Smithers. She looked up at a sombre painting that was hung over the fireplace. The frame was also draped in black crepe and the subject, a short, plump woman, bore a strong resemblance to Queen Victoria. A cherub smiled down from the right corner. "It can never be replaced, never," sniffed Mrs. Smithers.

Tears were running down her face and mucus from her nose that she didn't bother to wipe away. Carlyle came over to her and offered her a handkerchief, but Mrs. Smithers slapped her hand away like a petulant child.

"Don't try to make up to me, you thief. I know you've taken it to the Jews."

The maid turned to Murdoch. "Oh, sir. I never touched it, I swear to you. She says she's going to turn me out without a reference. What will I do? How can she believe I would ever rob her? I have been a true servant to this family since I was a girl."

"I can vouch for that, sir," said the butler, casting an anxious glance at Mrs. Smithers.

Murdoch crouched down, closer to the old woman, so he could get her attention. He took out his notebook and pencil. "And when was the last time you saw the brooch, ma'am?"

"It was on my dressing table the night before Mother Smithers passed away. I know that without the shadow of a doubt because I picked it up and showed it to her. She recognized it, I know she did, and she smiled."

Murdoch stood up. "Has the house been searched?" he asked the butler.

"Turned upside down three times, sir. It is nowhere to be found. We only keep three servants. Miss Carlyle and myself and a cook, Mrs. Walden. She too has been with the family for many years and she is above reproach." He lowered his voice. "If I may say, sir, the piece of jewellery in itself is not of particular value. It is what it means to Mrs. Smithers."

She, however, heard that. "It is priceless. A silver circlet with five garnets. I know that Mother Smithers would only have given me a brooch of great value." Her vacuous pale blue eyes stared into Murdoch's. "They are in it together. Both Carlyle and Hunter are in cahoots. They think that I will die soon and they can live off the proceeds. Well, they have another think coming. I have left them provided for in my will but not any more. I'm calling for my solicitor right away to change all that. And I will never give either of them good characters."

Murdoch stood up and beckoned to the butler to move away with him out of earshot. Miss Carlyle was literally wringing her hands and Mrs. Smithers was back to talking into the fire.

"Is there another family member who might help here?"

"Only a nephew who lives in America. I have written to him, to beg him to intervene, but he is not on good terms with his aunt and even if he believed Miss Carlyle and myself, I don't know if he would have any influence with our mistress."

Hunter was a slim, white-haired man of great dignity. Murdoch had the impression that all his working life he had strived to be the perfect butler, loyal, unobtrusive, and efficient, probably a great snob. But now, his world was torn apart and looked bleak indeed.

"Do you have any idea what might have happened to the brooch?"

"I've racked my brains, sir. Mrs. Smithers in the past few years has become increasingly forgetful and we have often found articles that were not in their correct places. But as I say, we have searched the house from top to bottom and not come across anything. We were all quite upset because Mrs. Smithers senior had passed on so I assume in the confusion, madam misplaced the brooch somewhere in the house."

Murdoch gave the butler a warning nod and went back to the old woman. "Mrs. Smithers, Inspector Brackenreid is taking your case very seriously. We have received reports that there are gypsies in the area and we are sure it is there we will find our culprits. I think you can put your mind at rest about your servants, ma'am. I for one believe them to be totally trustworthy and I am a police officer."

She glanced up at the dour portrait and clasped her hands together as if in prayer. She started to rock slightly. "Oh, Mother Smithers would never forgive me."

"I'm sure she will understand it is not your fault, ma'am. She will not hold you accountable."

He'd been shooting in the dark but his words seemed to hit a bullseye. Mrs. Smithers's face flooded with delight.

"Do you not think so, sir? Oh I do hope you are right."

"I'm sure I am. Now can I have your solemn promise that you will not blame Miss Carlyle any more? You need somebody to take care of you after all you've been through. You don't want to drive her away now, do you?"

She shook her head and sniffed. "I promise. How dreadful of

those wretched gypsies to cast suspicions like that. They must be punished."

"Indeed they will be, ma'am."

She caught his hand with her dust-dry fingers. "You will find the brooch though, won't you?"

"We'll do our best, ma'am."

He stepped away and the maid slipped in closer to her mistress, picked up the discarded handkerchief, and handed it to her. This time it was accepted and Mrs. Smithers patted Carlyle's hand.

"May I show you out, sir?" Hunter asked.

"Good afternoon, Mrs. Smithers. I will come back to see you next week."

"Good afternoon. My compliments to Inspector Brackenreid."

Murdoch followed the butler into the hall.

"Should we have concerns about gypsies, sir?"

"I don't think so. Let's say I was stretching the truth a little. Your mistress needs the attention of a physician, Mr. Hunter."

"We are aware of that, sir, but she has been most resistant. And all this dreadful fuss for a trinket. Miss Carlyle has given her lifeblood to the Smithers family, as have I, myself." His polite mask dropped briefly. "My mistress tells anybody who will listen that the brooch was silver with garnets, but in fact it was silver-coated and stones are missing. It is hardly worth two dollars and for this she would cast out her faithful servants."

Murdoch nodded with some sympathy. At the door, the butler paused. "Excuse me, sir. I know this is most unorthodox, but may I shake you by the hand? Both Miss Carlyle and I have been at our wits' end. You seem to have calmed her down."

His voice cracked for a moment. They both knew that the calm was probably temporary and before long the delusions would reassert themselves in a different form. If Mrs. Smithers insisted on dismissing them, there wasn't much they could do to prevent her. Murdoch shook his hand.

Murdoch hadn't walked far when he heard the sound of horse's hooves behind him and, on the spur of the moment, decided he'd take the luxury of a cab ride. It felt as if it had been a long day.

He turned around. The side flag was up, signifying the cabbie was free for hire and Murdoch waved at him. The coachman was heavy with his greatcoat, thick muffler, and fur hat, only his eyes visible. He flicked his whip in acknowledgement of Murdoch's signal and pulled his horse over to the curb.

"Hop in, sir."

"Actually I want to ask you some questions. I'll ride up there with you."

"Suit yourself, sir. Come to the North Pole."

Murdoch climbed up beside him and gave him the address on River Street.

"Walk on," the cabbie called to his horse and off they went. "What you want to know? Don't tell me, you're going to rag on me about Ned, here? He's a miserly looking wretch, but I treat him good. He's always looked that way."

"It's nothing like that. I'm trying to trace the movements of certain men who may have hired a cab to go down to the lake within the past two weeks. They would have been carrying a heavy piece of luggage, possibly at night."

"Wasn't no fare of mine. I'd remember that."

"Did you hear any of the other cabbies talking about it?"

The cabbie's eyebrows were bushy, greying, and eloquent. "Are we referring to smugglers or has somebody absconded with your wife?"

"No, no. Sorry, I forgot to introduce myself. I'm Acting Detective Murdoch from Number Four Station. I'm pursuing an investigation."

"And I'm Mr. Frobisher practising survival in the North Pole."

Murdoch pulled off his glove so he could remove a calling card from his pocket. He handed it to the cabbie, who looked it over carefully, then handed it back.

"All right. I believe you."

He tugged off his glove. "The name's McCrae, Tom McCrae."

Murdoch shook hands, then took out the photograph of Sims.

"Have you ever seen this fellow?"

The cabbie shook his head. "And I'd remember, believe me, if a tarted-up nancy boy in a state of undress got into the cab." He grinned. "Trying to nab him, are you?"

"As a matter of fact, he's dead. He's been murdered. I'm after the killer."

McCrae didn't actually say *serves him right*, but it was obvious from his expression that he felt that way.

"The fellow's name was Leonard Sims and he was involved

in the taking and probable sale of obscene photographs."

McCrae frowned. "There you go then."

"Has anybody ever approached you to buy or sell obscene photographs? Where would they find pictures like that?"

"I've had all sorts of human kind in my cab, Mr. Murdoch, and I've been asked that before and worse, but the answer is no. I make it a point not to know. To tell you the truth, riff raff like that I usually turf out. I stop the cab and open the door."

"Do you think any of the other cabbies would know where to find those kind of photographers?"

"If they did, they ain't likely to tell you. Not all of them are good, hard-working lads like me."

Murdoch thought it was an avenue he'd pursue later if the other search didn't pan out. McCrae seemed to have retreated into his greatcoat and Murdoch was afraid that, in spite of the official calling card, the cabbie thought he was inquiring to satisfy a personal lust. The life of a cabbie!

CHAPTER TWENTY-EIGHT

MURDOCH JUMPED DOWN FROM THE CAB JUST AS AMY Slade was walking up the path to the front door. She turned and Murdoch felt a rush of pleasure at seeing her.

"Mr. Murdoch, how nice. You are coming inside, I presume."

Murdoch paid off the cabbie and followed her indoors. Reordan emerged immediately from the kitchen.

"Hello, Murdoch, come on in, I've got what you wanted. Hello, Amy, you look tired."

"Mr. Kippen insisted on sitting in on my class for the entire afternoon, emanating waves of disapproval, I might add. He intimidated the children, who made all sorts of mistakes they don't usually make. Then I had to remain to correct their papers."

She sounded defeated and both men regarded her sympathetically for a moment. But Reordan was too excited to linger in that mood.

"Mr. Murdoch, we've been waiting. Charlie is in the kitchen. I have your lists for you."

The temperature of his regard for Murdoch seemed to have increased considerably.

Amy and Murdoch divested themselves of their coats and hats and followed him to the kitchen, where they were greeted by a mouth-watering aroma from something cooking on the stove. Murdoch realized it had been hours since he'd eaten the fresh bread that Reordan had provided and he was hungry. Seymour stood up when they entered, greeted Miss Slade warmly, and pulled out two chairs.

"What have you been doing?" Amy asked Murdoch.

"John and Charlie have drawn up a list for me of bereaved families. I'm trying to follow the mourning-card path, see if that will lead anywhere."

Amy cast a warning glance in Reordan's direction, who saw her.

"Look here," he said to Murdoch. "I've been glad to help out, but I'm in the dark as to why. Surely you can tell me something? What do you take me for?"

Murdoch felt like quoting Seymour, "They aren't my secrets to reveal," but Amy took matters into her own hands.

"That seems only fair, John. But why don't we wait until you've finished your business?"

"Right ho," said Reordan. There was a sheet of paper on the table and he pushed it in front of Murdoch. "This is the first list I made. A lot of the announcements were repeated three or four times and several were in all of the papers. But I sifted out as best I could and you've got seventy-seven names there, fifteen of them were children under ten, and twelve of these were infants, stillbirths or babies of three months or less. Eight were males. That's the ones you wanted, right?"

"Correct."

"I marked them out separately. I also arranged them in order, starting with the closest to the house here. I kept them in line, as it were, so you won't have to wander all around the wrekin."

"I had the easier job," said Seymour. "More people were dying than in need of servants." He gave Murdoch another piece of paper. "In June, there were six advertisements. Four were in the *Globe*, two repeated in the *World* and the *News*. Three had box numbers to reply to the newspaper, only three gave an address, but all of those continued to advertise in July and August so I don't think they're the ones we want. Only two didn't repeat their advertisement in July, one was in the Junction and the other, alas, gave only a box number. Both of those were in the *Globe*."

"The Junction is too far, I think. I can't imagine a girl walking from Sydenham Street to there. It would take her all day. But good work, thanks, John. I'll see if I can get the accounts from the newspaper tomorrow. Meanwhile," he stood up, "I'd better get going on this other list before it gets too late to make calls."

"Not until you've had some supper, surely?" Amy said. "I for one am famished and I can smell something delicious that I would suspect is John's famous *ragoût de pattes de cochon*."

"It is. Or, in English, Mr. Murdoch, pig's feet stew. It's a French-Canadian dish."

"We can divide up the list, Will," said Seymour. "It'll go faster that way."

"I stand persuaded. Thank you," Murdoch conceded, as much as to the hunger pangs in his stomach as anything. Reordan beamed and limped over to the stove to serve the meal.

Murdoch turned to Amy. "Miss Slade, I will have to inform Inspector Brackenreid what I am doing. I've already been skating near the thin ice. I don't know if he'd approve of me tromping around the city upsetting people who have recently suffered a great loss." He grimaced. "I'm not implying our good inspector is a man of sensitivity because he's not, but he is jumpy about stirring up complaints."

Amy had laced her fingers in her lap. She didn't look at Murdoch when she said, "Perhaps I could be of help? Three people will make even more headway." She hurried on. "I can be quite truthful about it. I can say one of my pupils is in difficulties and I am trying to trace her nearest relative through the photograph she gave her."

"Why? Why would a teacher go to that trouble?"

"I can only speak for myself. You forget I would be telling the truth."

Seymour interjected. "She's right, Will, and if anybody can

get people to open up, Amy can."

Miss Slade stiffened. "Don't have any fear that I won't appear quite respectable, Mr. Murdoch."

"It's not that," Murdoch said, although the thought had crossed his mind, "Charlie and I are police officers. We have legitimacy."

"I'm not going to make an arrest, surely? We all have the right to ask questions of one another and we have an equal right to refuse to answer."

They were interrupted by Reordan's plunking down three bowls of steaming stew on the table. Thank goodness no little trotters were sticking out of the broth.

"Eat up, argue later."

Murdoch took a taste. The stew was rather on the bland side, the meat cooked to a pulp and mashed into balls. Definitely edible. He couldn't help noticing that Amy made no dainty protestations about how much food was in her dish, but tucked in with as much gusto as the men. The meal was full of odd contrasts. There was no cloth on the scrubbed pine table, but the plates were of fine, patterned china and the knives and forks, silver.

For the next few minutes they spoke little except to make polite comments about the ragout. There was a stiffness between Murdoch and Miss Slade. He decided she was not a woman who liked to be thwarted.

Seymour finally spoke up. "Why not let Amy help? It would be better if you could hold off on letting Brackenreid in on the case until we ourselves know what's going on. Besides, Amy will be a far sight better investigator than some of our constables."

Amy leaned over and gave him a quick peck on the cheek. "Thank you, Charlie. Well, Mr. Murdoch, will you consider it?"

"It's rather unorthodox."

She laughed in delight. "Unorthodoxy and I are close acquaintances, in case you haven't noticed."

Murdoch studied her face for a moment and she returned his regard steadily. There was something about her that reminded him of Liza, although he couldn't quite identify what it was. Physically they were quite different. Liza had been tall and of a dark complexion. Amy Slade had blue-grey eyes and fair hair, and was rather short.

"Well?" she asked.

"All right. I'll agree."

Reordan put a silver tray in the middle of the table and started to load the bowls and cups on to it.

"Isn't it time you told me what is going on?"

Amy looked at Murdoch. "Do you have the photographs with you?"

He nodded and took the envelope from his pocket.

"While you do that, I'll get some writing paper," said Seymour.

He left, and Amy drew Reordan into the chair beside her. "I found these four photographs in the desk of one of my pupils, young Agnes Fisher. They are offensive. Three are obscene, one is both blasphemous and obscene."

Murdoch was about to hand the envelope to Reordan when she stopped him. "I don't want you to show him the picture of the girl." She touched the Irishman's destroyed hand. "This is nothing to do with you, John. Both Mr. Murdoch and Charlie needed to see the picture if they were going to investigate, but I believe strongly that any viewing whatsoever participates in the wickedness." She searched for words. "We become carriers of the evil even if we ourselves are not one of those who would take pleasure from such a sight. This photograph should be destroyed and will be as soon as we find the perpetrator. Do you understand what I mean, John?"

He shrugged. "Not really, but it doesn't matter. If you don't want me to see it, I won't."

She opened the envelope and took out the three cards. Reordan whistled through his teeth when he saw what was written on the back of the mourning card.

"And you believe your pupil wrote those words?"

"It is her hand."

"And who's the dead prince?"

Murdoch answered. "His name is Leonard Sims. He was found murdered this morning."

"You didn't do the in memoriam surely?"

"No. It looks as if the girl was the one who inked in the black borders."

"Which says she knew he was cooked?"

"Yes."

"Bad business."

Reordan picked up the Newly-wed card and seemed to freeze in his chair. To Murdoch's surprise, who thought the Irishman fairly worldly, he appeared shocked by what he saw. He stared at the picture for a moment, then held it up to the light.

"Who scratched out the faces?"

"Probably Agnes, er, my pupil, did," said Amy. "Mr. Murdoch says the ink appears to be the same as that used on the other two cards."

"Is the photograph you don't want me to see an obscene photograph of your pupil?"

"Yes, it is."

Reordan was visibly agitated. He virtually spat at Murdoch. "Do you know who the photographer is?"

"Yes and no. We have no concrete evidence, but I've got my sights on a studio on King Street called Gregory's Emporium. It's close to both the school and Agnes's house. I'm guessing she wouldn't go too far afield. And I didn't like the proprietor at all. Slimy bastard. Oh, sorry, Miss Slade."

"I'm not so delicate, Mr. Murdoch. My ears didn't fall off."

Reordan was studying the Newly-wed card intently and Murdoch could see it was making Amy uncomfortable.

"What did he look like, this Emporium cove?" he asked Murdoch.

"Short and stocky with reddish-brown hair cropped short. He's a cockney and likes to speak in what he called rhyming slang. You don't know him, do you?"

Reordan shoved the card away from him. "Of course not, why should I?" He eased himself to his feet. "Well, I've got washing up to do."

He limped over to the sink and Amy called after him.

"Are you all right, John?"

He didn't turn around but his voice was flat.

"Of course I'm all right. Why wouldn't I be?"

Murdoch found his reaction puzzling. He had been so eager to be involved in the case. What had happened? He was about to press the issue when Amy Slade gave a little warning shake of her head. Just then Seymour returned with paper, pens, and an inkwell.

"Here we go then."

Leaving the Irishman to his task, the three of them huddled around the table with the list in front of them and began to copy out the addresses. Murdoch took three, Seymour three, and Amy was given the two closest to home.

"What do you think, can we reconvene in about two hours, finished or not?" asked Murdoch.

Seymour and Amy agreed and Murdoch managed to hold back on his fussing about what Amy should do or not do. He left, calling out a goodnight to Reordan, who had reverted to his rude self and merely grunted a reply.

When Murdoch got outside, he realized he'd forgotten he'd told Enid he would come to her in the early evening for supper. Damn. He was going to be very late.

CHAPTER TWENTY-NINE

MURDOCH HAD TAKEN THE NAMES THAT WERE ON THE perimeter of the city limits. The first address was on Bloor Street not far from the Church of the Redeemer. However, when he got there, he found the house boarded up. When he inquired at the next-door neighbour's house, he was told that the family had left the city and returned to England.

"Too much sorrow here," said the neighbour, a plump young matron who had a child in her arms and one at her skirt.

The second address was at a large house on Lowther Avenue, and he had to walk there from the end of the Bloor streetcar line. A sweet-faced young maid left him on the doorstep while she went to see if her mistress was "at home". She was, and he was ushered into a drawing room crammed with furniture and, like the Smithers' drawing room, lavishly decorated with black crepe and silk ribbons. The lady of the house was seated at the piano, sorting music, when Murdoch entered. She greeted him politely but her voice was enervated, as if she had no energy left for the world. He explained the reason for his visit and expressed his condolences, which she accepted graciously. She was expensively dressed in a black velvet gown that managed to be a garb of mourning and fashionable as well, with its tight waist, full sleeves, and glitter of jet at the collar and cuffs. He had the sense she hadn't enjoyed the short taste of motherhood she had experienced. There were several framed photographs on the mantelpiece revealing a wife considerably younger than her husband. Yes, they had a photograph taken at her husband's insistence by their friend Mr. Notman. He didn't usually do mourning portraits but had agreed as a favour. At Murdoch's request, and after a search, she unearthed the photograph. It was quite unlike the one Amy had found, the baby was bigger and darker and was photographed lying in a crib sumptuously covered with satin. He thanked her and took his leave.

His last call took him to the north end of Yonge Street, to the home of Mr. and Mrs. James Hickey, who lived above a butcher's shop. There was no maid. Mr. Hickey answered the door and reluctantly allowed him in. His wife was seated on the sofa and he joined her there, sitting close, not altogether to give her comfort, Murdoch thought. He explained his mission again and once more offered condolences. Hickey told Murdoch angrily that no, they would never have a mourning photograph taken because their son was born with a cleft palate, among other deformities. He had died when he was six weeks old. The man seemed to be blaming his wife for delivering a defective product or perhaps his anger was masking dreadful grief and disappointment. The woman hardly spoke, simply sat red-eyed, her hands in her lap. Murdoch left as soon as he could.

He was more than happy to hear the clang of the streetcar coming up behind him as he reached Church Street. He jumped aboard, dropped his money into the conductor's tin box, and sat down, huddling into his coat. The heater at the rear of the streetcar was stoked high, and the mingled smell of coal and damp woollen coats permeated the air. When the conductor called out his stop, Murdoch felt almost reluctant to leave the warmth of the streetcar.

Amy Slade answered his knock. "Oh do come in. You must be perished."

Murdoch tried to wipe the slush from his boots as best he could on the scraper and followed her inside. He suddenly felt shy and awkward, almost missing the hook on the coat stand as he hung up his coat. This time there was no appetizing smell coming from the kitchen and no light showed below Reordan's door.

"Where's the chef?"

"I don't know. He's gone out, which is very unusual for him." She smiled. "I thought we could meet in my room." She hesitated. "Charlie isn't back yet."

"Don't worry, Miss Slade. I won't tell anybody we've met alone in your private chamber."

He was attempting to make a joke, but it fell totally flat. She looked at him in surprise.

"That concern hadn't entered my mind."

They went upstairs, she leading and he studiously focusing on a spot between her shoulder blades. She had changed into her bloomer outfit again, the over tunic was cinched at the waist by a leather belt.

"In here," she said, and ushered him in.

He had expected either the same convent-like furnishings as the rest of the house or, influenced perhaps by the flowing bloomers, a room of drapery and plump cushions. This was neither. Amy had divided off her sleeping area by a tapestry screen and a double set of bookshelves crammed with books. The rest of the room was a sitting area, rather cramped because of the division but pleasant and colourful. Two brocade armchairs were in front of the fire, a dainty mahogany desk was against one wall, and there was a corner shelf unit where he glimpsed a collection of china ornaments. The lamps were turned high and the fire was blazing.

"Here, take this chair. I can offer homemade hot ginger beer, can I pour you some?"

"I'd like that," said Murdoch, not entirely sure if that was true. It was not a drink he'd had before.

She had a small hob on the fire and she removed the steaming kettle, poured the hot water into a jug, added the ginger beer from a bottle, stirred and poured it into a mug.

Murdoch drank some, found it rather stimulating and with a strong aftertaste.

"Very tasty," he said in reply to her inquiring look. He put the mug on a small three-legged table and took out his notebook. "Why don't we start while we're waiting for Charlie. What did you find?"

"Not much, I'm afraid. Neither of the families that I visited could afford photographs. In that respect my help was not fruitful, but I must tell you, Mr. Murdoch, this has been one of the most harrowing experiences I have ever spent. In both cases, the state of the family, especially the mother, was so dire, I, a stranger, could offer them little comfort. The first child succumbed to influenza. They should not even have gone to the expense of publishing a memorial notice but it was a matter of pride. I stayed there for a long time as the mother had a great need to talk about what had happened. When I finally left, I went to the address on Queen Street, which turned out to be the home of a woman I have encountered when I have been shopping. The dead child was her fifth and, like the others, he lived for only two months." She sipped on her own mug of ginger beer. "The poor woman cried out to me for some words of wisdom but I had none, trite or otherwise."

Murdoch remembered how he'd felt when Liza died and how angry he became with the priest who tried to quote church doctrine on the mystery of God's will.

"Sometimes sympathetic silence is the best comfort," he said.

"Perhaps."

They were silent, each in their own thoughts. Finally, Amy said, "Did you do any better with your investigation?"

"Not at all." He relayed to her what had happened. "Let us hope that Seymour did better."

At that moment, they heard the hall door open.

"That must be him," said Amy and she went to the door. "Charlie, we're up here."

Seymour came hurrying up the stairs and into the room.

"Will, good news. I've identified the baby in the picture."

"Well done. Who is it?"

Seymour handed his piece of paper to Murdoch. "They were my last visit, would you believe? They're a young couple and the babe was their first child, a boy. When I went into the parlour, I saw the photograph immediately. They've got it in a fancy silver frame on the mantelpiece. Their name is Dowdell, Geoffrey and Sophie, and the photographer they used was a woman, Miss Georgina Crofton. She lives on Gerrard Street."

"Did you ask the Dowdells if they knew Martha or Agnes Fisher?"

"Of course. They said they didn't. They can't afford to keep a regular servant. I also threw in the name of Leonard Sims, but nothing there either. Here's their address. The other two people on my list had not had pictures taken."

Suddenly, Murdoch couldn't help himself and he had to stifle a yawn. He stood up.

"It's too late to call on Miss Crofton tonight. I'll go first thing in the morning."

"I hope it leads somewhere," said Amy.

"So do I. I'm sorry we're not making faster progress."

She met his eyes. "Do you think Agnes has come to harm?"

"I don't know."

He wished he could say he was certain the girl was safe but he couldn't, and there was something about Amy Slade that precluded platitudes. She looked so pale and tired, his heart went out to her. "If I may say so, Miss Slade, I think you should retire for the night. You have been most helpful."

"What shall I do now?" asked Seymour.

Murdoch fished in his pocket and took out the list he'd made of photographic studios.

"You can start checking on these tomorrow. I'll join up with you as soon as I can."

"John seems to have deserted us," Amy said to Seymour. "I'm worried about him. He was acting so strangely when he saw the photographs."

Seymour shrugged. "He gets that way sometimes. You don't always know what will set him off. And they weren't the easiest pictures to look at. I've known him vanish for one or two days at a time. It's as if his memories press in upon him and all he can do is move like a homeless dog."

Murdoch offered his hand to the schoolteacher. "Thank you again, Miss Slade."

She smiled at him rather mischievously. "You seem in a hurry to leave, Mr. Murdoch. Don't tell me you have another duty to perform."

He could feel himself blush. "Not a duty, ma'am, but a prior engagement. And I'm terribly late as it is."

"I hope your friend will forgive you."

"So do I."

"You will keep us informed of your progress, won't you?" Amy asked.

For a split second, Murdoch wasn't sure what she was referring to.

"Yes, of course. Good night to both of you. No, don't worry, Miss Slade, I can let myself out."

He left them, aware that Amy was gazing after him.

CHAPTER THIRTY

IT WAS PAST TEN O'CLOCK BY THE TIME MURDOCH arrived at Enid's lodgings. He almost expected her to have gone to bed, but there was a light showing at her window. Having no desire to rouse Mrs. Barrett at this hour, he made a snowball and threw it at the window. Immediately, the curtain was pushed aside and Enid waved at him, mimed to him to be quiet, and disappeared to open the front door.

Neither spoke as he entered the house and Enid's welcome was decidedly on the cool side. He went to kiss her, but she avoided him with more warning mimes. Murdoch felt a stab of guilt as it was obvious Enid had been anticipating his arrival for a long time.

She closed the door to her sitting room behind them with a little snap.

"I was worried, Will. I expected you at five o'clock."

He didn't remember specifying a particular time but certainly ten o'clock was well past arrival time.

"I'm sorry, I've been working on a case and I had to trudge all over the city to do my interviews. Is Alwyn asleep?"

"Most certainly, he is. He tried to stay up as late as eight o'clock to see you, but he couldn't."

Another little piece of fiery coal on his head. Murdoch thought Enid had got the matter of reproaches down to a fine art.

"I'm sorry," he repeated.

They were keeping their voices low, which made it difficult to have a flaming row, although Murdoch felt that's what Enid wanted.

"Would you like a cup of tea?" she asked with excessive politeness. "You must be cold and hungry."

Coward that he was, Murdoch didn't feel like explaining he was still full of pig's feet stew so he just shook his head.

"I'm not hungry, but tea would be nice, thank you."

Enid went to the fireplace to fetch the kettle. While she was making the tea, trying to create a distraction to ease the tension and also because he needed her help, Murdoch took his notebook from his inner pocket.

"Enid, I've solved that issue of the anonymous letters. Sergeant Seymour is involved with a labour organization, which he's not allowed to be, and the letter writer knows about it. I don't want Charlie to lose his job, so I've decided to see if I can scare off the fellow. Will you type something for me?"

"Surely you don't mean tonight? I might wake Mrs. Barrett."

"I doubt that. Isn't this the evening she spends with her sister?"

Enid blushed fiercely at being caught in her little lie, and Murdoch thought he'd made matters worse by tripping her up like that. He reached over and pulled her gently into his arms.

"Please don't punish me, Mrs. Jones. I am so happy to see you and if there had been any way of informing you I would be late, I would have done so."

She leaned against him stiffly, not yet ready to yield, but he didn't let go, nuzzling his chin against her hair. Finally she turned her head and looked into his face. He was surprised to see she had tears in her eyes.

"Oh, William, I wish it could have been otherwise."

He knew she didn't mean just the tardiness of his visit but there was nothing he could say. If he made her a proposal of marriage, she would have to return to Wales first and even though with her in his arms he was hot with desire, he knew that he could not pretend a depth of feeling he didn't have. Again he was twisted with guilt, and he kissed her urgently to compensate. She responded slowly at first but more and more passionately. Finally she was the one who broke off the embrace. The brightness in her eyes was unbearable and he reached for her again but she caught his arms.

"Alwyn is fast asleep. If we stay here he is less likely to hear us."

She went to the door, turned the key in the lock, and practically

ran back to him. He drew her to the hearth and they lay down
on the rug. A bed would have been more comfortable but at that
moment Murdoch would have been happy to lie on bricks.

Because of the urgency in both of them, the connection was
over rather more quickly than he wanted but they nevertheless
lay for a while on the rug, until, arm aching, he levered himself
into a sitting position. She stayed there with her head on the
cushion he had pulled down when they started. He'd loosened
her hair and it hung untidily about her face. She was flushed
and he saw that her cheek was reddened from rubbing against
the roughness of his chin. She smiled up at him.

"Did you say you had some work you wanted me to do?"

They both laughed, which led to more kisses.

Finally, he leaned back and grabbed his notebook.

"I wrote it out."

She yawned and, pulling on her robe, got to her feet and
went over to the typewriter. She sat down, inserted a clean
sheet of paper in the machine.

"I'm ready, sir."

He placed the notebook where she could see it. She read
through what he'd written and glanced over her shoulder at
him in surprise.

"Goodness me, is this true?"

He shrugged. "It could be."

"Is it addressed to anybody in particular?"

"Inspector Brackenreid."

She grinned. "I see. What's sauce for the goose is good for the gander."

"Precisely."

CHAPTER THIRTY-ONE

IN SPITE OF THE IMPROVED FEELINGS BETWEEN THEM, Murdoch didn't stay at Enid's much past midnight. A rug on the floor was hardly conducive to a good night's sleep. He slipped away into the quiet streets. The lamps had been extinguished, but the snow reflected light enough to see by. He trudged past the darkened houses, where an occasional lamp revealed a late bedtime.

When he entered his house, he paused as he always did to listen to sounds coming from Mr. and Mrs. Kitchen's quarters. All was quiet, and Murdoch hoped Arthur was having a rare peaceful night. The first shock of their announcement had subsided, and Murdoch wished fervently the move to the fresh country air of Muskoka would bring Arthur health.

Once in his room, he undressed quickly. The fire Mrs. Kitchen always built for him had died to glowing embers and the chill of the winter night had seeped in. Shivering, he jumped into bed, wishing not for the first time there was a warm body waiting for him to lie next to. And again, he cursed himself for not insisting on marrying Liza sooner. He had never experienced her undressed body pressed against his and the regret of that tormented him. He thumped his pillow, rolled on his side, and deliberately tried to wrench his thoughts away from the past and back to Enid and her generous embrace.

He closed his eyes and immediately felt sleep slip away. Damn. He knew what that signified. He tried to lie still but he couldn't, and the tossing and turning began. He sat up to check the alarm clock on his dresser. It was already two o'clock. He thumped the feathers in his pillow and buried his face in it. Arthur Kitchen had once told him that the best cure of insomnia was loving conjugal connections but clearly that wasn't proving true. He'd just had loving connections and he was still wide awake. Arthur may have advised love for insomnia, but Father Fair, the priest at St. Paul's, on the other hand, said the best cause of a good night's sleep was a pure conscience. Murdoch decided that what was keeping him awake was guilt. He sat up again, trying to decide if it was worth it to light a pipe. It was. He reached for his Powhatan, stuffed it with tobacco, lit it, and drew deeply on the stem. What the hell was the matter with him? He'd never describe himself as a randy tomcat, but he did seem to be having divided feelings yet again among three women; one was deceased to be sure, but the other two weren't. And to one of those, he had made promises of the flesh that he didn't think he could keep. The shadow of Liza was present at the best of times when he was with Enid, but now someone else had come into the picture. He couldn't get thoughts of Amy Slade out of his mind.

"And it's not just the pantaloons," he said aloud, punctuating his words with a puff of his pipe. What then? She was pretty enough, but he'd encountered women who were as attractive and he had hardly given them a second thought. Well, to be honest, maybe a second or even a third thought, but nothing like this. He'd just come from intimacy with Enid and like a sly fox his fantasies had slipped away to Miss Slade and the notion of kissing that full mouth. No, that wasn't accurate either. Yes, he would like to hold and kiss her, he wouldn't deny that, but there was something else netting his thoughts. He wanted her good opinion. He wanted her to smile that bright smile at him. He wanted those cool grey eyes to look into his with admiration. Murdoch groaned and puffed away some more. What was he, a green boy mooning over the first girl he'd met? He couldn't remember ever feeling like this about Liza. Their love had been immediate and reciprocal and he'd never doubted that she was his only and complete love. But was he deluding himself? What if she'd lived and they married and then he found himself hankering after somebody else? Was that the kind of man he was? Wanting what he couldn't have, then losing interest when it was his? Why didn't he want to marry Enid Jones, a woman he had been pining after for months?

He realized he was biting so hard on the stem of his pipe he was in danger of snapping it off. His and Enid's difference in religion was a big obstacle but not insurmountable, and he was aware that she had been engaging him less and less in doctrinal discussions lately. If she converted to Catholicism, any priest would agree to the union. Mixed marriages were not unheard of. No, he couldn't make that an excuse. There were other reasons floating at the back of his mind as to why he couldn't marry her. What the hell were they? Was he a man incapable of monogamy? He had become engaged to Liza only a few months after they had met and until she died of the typhoid seven months later, he could honestly say he had not been concerned about any other woman he'd encountered no matter how attractive she had been. But that faithfulness had not been put to the test of time. Would it have lasted? There was no answer to that, of course, except self-knowledge and at this moment he felt a stranger to himself, doubting everything.

Damn, damn. He put his pipe down and swung his legs out of bed. Above the headboard hung a brass crucifix, so familiar he hardly noticed it any more. Now in the dim light, he thought Christ was looking down on him in disappointment. He padded over to his dresser and for the first time in a long while, he took out his rosary. He threaded the beads through his fingers. The wooden beads were smooth and cool to his touch. His mother had given him the rosary when he was six years old on the occasion of his first communion. The crucifix and chain were of silver, the beads olive wood, and he knew she had scrimped for months to save enough money to pay for it. He smiled to himself. He had secretly hoped to receive a bag of marbles even though he knew a rosary was the typical gift. Poor Mamma. He never thought about her without pity and the old stirring of anger that she had died so miserably.

He went to the foot of the bed and dropped to his knees. His inclination was to say the Sorrowful Mysteries, but he thought he'd be better served tonight by acclaiming the Glorious Mysteries. He held the silver crucifix and murmured, "I believe in God the Father Almighty, Creator of Heaven..."

He continued, the rosary a path of prayer that he followed. At the end of the second decade, he stopped. What was the point of repeating prayers that seemed empty to him? He was not connecting with God's presence. Unbidden, memories jumped into his mind: of saying the rosary in the evenings with his mother and Susanna, Bertie joining in with shouts of Happy Christmas, no matter what the season. Harry, his father, was never a part of these sessions, and so the telling of the beads was a moment of happiness, more like a game really, especially when he was younger and he was learning to recite the prayers perfectly. His mother had always been so pleased when he got it right. Susanna soon overtook him though and nothing could match her fervency and accuracy. *Poor Cissie.* All his family had gone now except for Harry, and Murdoch doubted he would ever in his lifetime have fond feelings for his father.

He fingered the small medallion on the rosary, a depiction of Christ holding out his arms to a child. Murdoch thought about Agnes. The priest had told Murdoch at one of his infrequent confessions that he was becoming too worldly and not contemplating the workings of Heaven, but he felt powerless to stop the drift away from his faith. Faced daily with Arthur Kitchen's slow and painful death Murdoch had asked, Where is God's will in this? Priests didn't like questions like that and he'd been sent packing with a heavy penance to perform.

He got to his feet, stiff from the cold hard floor, and returned the rosary to its velvet bag in the drawer. He heard Arthur cough downstairs and the murmur of Mrs. Kitchen's voice as she ministered to him. So much for Arthur's peaceful night.

Murdoch climbed back into bed, rubbing his feet together to warm them. Perhaps it was a blessing that Enid was called back to Wales. He knew he could never be with a woman if he had any doubts at all. It was a dishonourable thing to do. But then what? Would he start to court Miss Slade? He grinned in the darkness. He didn't know what her religious beliefs were, but they weren't likely to be anything conventional. And that thought was quite reassuring.

CHAPTER THIRTY-TWO

SHE WAS IN A HOUSE CROWDED WITH PEOPLE. THEY WERE on shelves along each wall and all of them were dying. They were coughing and crying, calling for water. It was bitterly cold and right through the centre of the room there was a river, filthy and black and moving fast. She was searching for little Patrick, and even above the din she could hear him calling to her from the next room. She walked beside the rushing water, knowing that one false step and she would fall in. She was trying to move as fast as she could, but her limbs were so heavy and cold she could hardly put one foot in front of the other. Then she was at the door. All she had to do was go through and she would be able to get Patrick and they would be safe. But a man was there, sitting on *a high stool. He had a stick that he thrust out in front of her. She tried to tell him that she needed to go through to her child, but no words would come out of her mouth. The man paid no attention but began to push her backwards with the stick. She could see the pleasure this gave him. She couldn't fight him and felt herself falling into the icy river. The foul water flowed up her nostrils and into her mouth and she thought she was going to choke on the stench of it.*

Mrs. Crofton's cries brought Georgina running into the room.

"Hush now, hush. It's all right. I'm here, hush."

Mrs. Crofton was gasping for air, her hands clawing at her throat as if she were drowning.

"Ruby, dearest, fetch a damp cloth." Ruby had been asleep on a cot at the foot of the bed and she got up hurriedly and went to the washstand. Georgina stroked her mother's face, uttering soothing noises as she did so.

"Here, ma'am," said Ruby and she handed her a wet towel, which Georgina placed on the back of her mother's neck. Mrs. Crofton shuddered and tried to shrug it away but her daughter held it on firmly.

"It'll feel better in a moment, Mama. Ruby, light the candle if you please."

Slowly, Mrs. Crofton was becoming calmer but her open eyes were wild, the pupils dilated.

"Lie back for a moment, my dear," said her daughter and she plumped up the cushion for her mother's head. "There, that's better. Good pet. See, we're here. Your own little Ruby and me."

Unasked, Ruby reached for a glass of water that was on the small table beside the bed and offered it to her mistress, who took a small sip.

Georgina tucked a strand of grey hair under her mother's nightcap. Her touch was tender.

"You were having one of your bad dreams, my pet, but it's all right now. See, you're in your own pretty bedroom that you furnished yourself. Look around. There's your bureau and your little stool that Mrs. Buchanan embroidered, just as they are."

Mrs. Crofton caught her hand. "Oh Georgina, I had a terrible vision."

"It was just a dream, Mama…"

"No – not a dream, a vision. I must tell it."

"Of course, my dear. But first why don't I send Ruby to make a hot posset. We can all use one, I'm sure."

"No! It was one of my visions, not like the other dreams. I can tell the difference. I must say it now."

Georgina stared at her. "Tell it to us then."

"There was so much suffering and I could do nothing. I knew I would be able to save little Patrick but a man prevented me. Oh such a wicked man." She sobbed, still in the dreamworld. "I was crying out for help, but no matter how hard I screamed no sound was coming from my throat." Georgina signalled to Ruby to give her the glass of water and she drank greedily.

"Thank you, dearest girl. Did I call out?"

"Yes, ma'am, you did."

"It was a vision. You must write it down, Georgina, you must write it down before it leaves me."

"Very well, Mama. Ruby, will you be so good as to bring me pen and ink and some notepaper from the escritoire."

Ruby hurried to obey and Mrs. Crofton leaned back on her pillow while her daughter took a seat beside the bed, ready to take down what she said. As soon as she began to relate the details of her dream, Mrs. Crofton became distressed again and her Irish lilt was more pronounced.

"The foul water was up my nostrils and in my mouth so I thought I was going to choke on the stench of it."

"Breathe in for a moment, Mama," said Georgina soothingly. "See, there is no stench here. There is only the pleasant lavender cologne that Mrs. Buchanan sprinkles on the sheets and perhaps Ruby has the smell of baking bread in her hair."

Mrs. Crofton was not to be consoled.

"You know whenever little Patrick appears to me in a dream it is a warning that we will hear of a death within the week. Don't you remember, last summer, he came to me and we heard that your Uncle Callum had died? Surely you remember me telling you my dream?"

"Of course I do, my pet, but Uncle Callum was very ill. His death was not unexpected."

Mrs. Crofton ignored her. "This dream is a warning to us, Georgina."

"If this is a warning, my pet, what should we take from it?"

"Somebody is in grave danger. Death is approaching. Kiss me, my dear one. And you too, Ruby. Oh kiss me so I know that you are quick and not dead."

Dutifully, her daughter did so and Ruby managed a timid peck on her mistress's cold hand.

"Oh it was dreadful. Such fear and sorrow coming from your poor dead brother and I could not help him and I knew that stinking river would take me."

"The people on shelves sound like the passengers in their bunks," said Georgina. "And the stinking river running through the room is the bilge of the ship. You are dreaming of the crossing again."

"Oh Gina, don't make fun of me."

"I'm not at all, Mama, but we know how terrible the voyage here was. How many times have you dreamed of it? More than we can count."

Mrs. Crofton was almost weeping. "No matter that it has the look of my memory, this was a premonition. It must be respected. That man in my dream was as wicked as the devil himself. He was evil, I tell you. I could see his delight as he forced me into the river. He was enjoying my suffering and that he had the power to keep me from my poor little boy. He was happy others were in such need and he was not."

"That sounds very like any one of the English peers who let our people starve," said Georgina.

Her mother shuddered. "It is true. There was the same cold indifference and I, alas, I was as helpless as I was then."

Ruby moved closer to Georgina and they were quiet for a moment, watching Mrs. Crofton as she looked into the horror that never left her. She said with great weariness, "This is no mere dream. I have not lost the true gift, the sight. We are being sent a warning of tragedy. There is danger all around us and wickedness. We must beware."

"And we will be, Mama."

Georgina looked over at Ruby, who was pale and wide-eyed. "Remember how Mama was telling you last month about the Great Hunger when the potato blight destroyed the harvest?"

Ruby managed to nod.

"Her nightmares still visit her, alas."

Mrs. Crofton had closed her eyes and already seemed to be drifting off to sleep. Georgina put the ink pot, pen, and paper on the side table. She said softly to Ruby, "The entire village where Mama lived was starving to death. Her own family was decimated. The landlord finally paid their passage to Canada. No, child, this was not an act of kindness. He wanted to get rid of them so he could claim their paltry sliver of land. There were others in the same plight, of course, and the boats were so overcrowded it is a wonder they could sail at all."

Mrs. Crofton moved her head restlessly and Georgina waited until she settled down. Ruby was hardly breathing and even though her bare feet were icy cold by now, she dared not move. She wanted Miss Georgina to continue with her tale because she loved to be spoken to in that special way, but she could hardly believe that her mistress had suffered from the same poverty that she herself understood all too well.

Georgina sat back in the chair. "Mama was the only

remaining child, and her father, my dear grandfather, died before they even got to the port. Her mother had no choice but to continue. The conditions on board the ship were almost too terrible for us to contemplate. The ship owners took on as many passengers as they could for the money…"

Ruby couldn't bear it and she burst out. "But the captains, ma'am. Didn't they refuse? Captains are the kings of their ships, you told me so yourself."

Georgina sighed. "Perhaps one did, perhaps even two, but we have no record of them. All we know is that many, many people died on the journey over. Typhoid fever swept through the hold where the poorest people had been crammed and stuffed like so much baggage. There was no one to take care of the sick and the dying and Mama's mother, my dear grandmother, died. For two days, Ruby, for two long days, nobody came down to tend to those who were ill. Mama, who was a mere child, much younger than you are now, was forced to lie beside the corpse of her own mother."

Ruby was trembling, as much with fear and cold as with sorrow, but she whispered, "Oh Miss Georgina, I am dreadful sorry to hear it."

"Fortunately for her, another family, who had lost their only child, took her in. They prospered when they came to Toronto, which was why Mama was able to make such a good match when she grew up." She smiled at the girl. "But I am giving you such a long face. That part of the story is a happy one and I shall tell it to you another day. You looked perished, you poor little mite." She lifted the quilt. "Why don't you get into Mama's bed. It will keep you both warm. I'm going to stir up the fire and sit in the armchair for a while. She'll be right as rain in the morning, you'll see."

Ruby did as she was told. Mrs. Crofton's body was warm under the covers and soft. The older woman stirred for a moment and pulled her close, whispering drowsily, "What would we do without our precious jewel, Georgina? What a comfort she is."

Georgina blew out the candle and went to the big armchair by the fire. It wasn't long before Ruby heard her light snore. Mrs. Crofton's breathing deepened and she knew that they were both sound asleep.

She lay watching the shadows of the flames flicker on the wall until the fire died down. The feather pillow smelled faintly of the lavender water that Mrs. Buchanan sprinkled on the pillowcase when she was doing the ironing. Mrs. Crofton was lying against her and her breath was on her neck. Ruby cautiously touched the silk of her mistress's nightgown.

She had a good idea why Mrs. Crofton had dreamed what she had. She had met that evil man who took pleasure in others' suffering. Ruby covered her ears with her hands as if she were blocking out cries. No matter what happened, she would never give up this sanctuary she had found. There was nothing she could do.

CHAPTER THIRTY-THREE

RALPH TIBBETT STROKED HIS WIFE'S BREAST, SWOLLEN with milk, the nipple dark. Kate was half asleep but instinctively shifted to make herself more available. As if sensing the movement, the smaller twin woke up, snuffled, then started to wail.

"Leave him," whispered Ralph into Kate's neck. But the brother was disturbed and he woke too.

"I've got to see to them," said Kate and she rolled away.

Ralph caught her arm. "Let them cry. They'll fall asleep in a minute."

Kate hesitated, reaching down to rock the cradle beside the bed. Her nipples were already oozing milk in response to the infants and both babies smelled it, making jerking movements with their arms as if they would get right out of the cradle and grab hold of her.

"I'll feed them first."

She sat up in the bed, pulled the pillow onto her lap, and picked up Jacob, who immediately stopped crying. She laid him on the pillow so he could latch on to her right breast and took the other infant, James, out of the cradle and placed him at the left breast.

Ralph was propped on his elbow, watching. "You spoil them," he said.

Kate tried to smile at him, although she quailed at the disapproval in his voice. "Ma always said there's no use in letting a babe cry itself into a fit. They're much happier if they know I'm here."

"And your husband would be much happier if he had a wife he could count on."

"I'm sorry, Ralph. I can't help it."

"Can't you? I don't know about that."

"It's true. I was so sore at first and then...I don't get much sleep." She glanced over at him with a sudden uncharacteristic resentment. "You aren't here when it's the worst."

"Thank goodness for that."

He swung his legs over the side of the bed. "I said I'd be in to work early anyway. Did you wash my shirt?"

"Yes, it's in the wardrobe."

He got up and padded across the floor. "It's bloody cold

in here."

"We're almost out of coal. You said you'd bring a bucketful in last night."

The twins were slowing down on the suckling, their cheeks flushed with pleasure and exertion. Kate watched her husband as he dressed. He'd got fatter since they'd married. The handsome young lad she had fallen so wildly in love with seemed to be vanishing daily. But she was filled with yearning.

"Ralph, can you stay a bit longer? I get so lonesome when you're not here."

"Do you? You have the babies, how can you be lonesome?" His tone was mocking. "Don't tell me you don't love those little ones. I thought they were your heart's delight."

"They are, of course they are, but sometimes I am so tired and I have just fallen asleep when one or the other wakes up. And then I could scream, Ralph. I feel so bad about that but I can't help myself. I do love them so much but I think if I could just have a rest, I'd feel better. That's not wicked, is it? If you could only mind them for me for just a few hours, sometimes. Please, Ralph. They're your children too."

"Are they? I hope so."

He was standing in front of the washstand fastening his silk cravat. He watched her in the mirror. "Oh don't fret so, Kate. You know I'm just trying to get some extra money for us. That's why I work so much."

"That's a new tie, isn't it? We could buy two buckets of coal for what you spent on that."

She'd never challenged him before, and they were both momentarily surprised at her outburst. Ralph picked up a jar of pomade and applied a good helping to his hair. "It is new to me but not new bought. You know how important it is that I look up to scratch. He gave it to me."

He had no need to say who "he" referred to. His employer was a real go-getter, as Ralph described him. Kate was growing to hate this man she'd never met because of the unpredictable and, to her mind, often unjustified demands he put on Ralph's time. Ralph was vague about his duties, which he said varied but were generally in the realm of helping customers. He was just as vague about his weekly wage. Unfortunately, his job as night watchman at the brewery was also unpredictable, sometimes he was called in and sometimes he wasn't. And he'd made her swear not to reveal to anybody that he was employed there. He was embarrassed at having to do such a menial job, a far cry from the glamour of the office and the swell clients. He only did it so he could provide for his family, he said, but Kate, in her rare honest moments, had to admit she seldom saw the extra money.

Kate placed Jacob back in his cradle. James snuffled but then relapsed into sleep as well and she put him in the other end.

"Can you come back to bed now, Ralph?"

"Don't be silly, Kate. I'm dressed. It's too late." He came over to the bed and gave her a kiss on the cheek. "Look, I promise I'll bring home some coal or at least the money to buy some."

"When will you be home?"

"Late, I'm afraid. We have an important client coming in from Hamilton and I have to be on my toes. I'll be needed." He took a dollar out of his pocket and put it on the dresser. "Here. Get Ben to fetch more coal for you."

Kate got out of bed. "He'll be going to school in a minute. You'd better ask him now."

"All right, I will. Bye, Kate, no need to fret. Things are looking up for us."

She didn't trust herself to answer.

Ralph went into the hall just as Ben was coming down the stairs.

"Morning to you, lad. Off to school, are you?"

The boy nodded. He was muffled in a long ratty-looking scarf but he had no gloves or hat and bare leg was visible between the top of his boots and his too-short trousers.

"Tell you what. I'm going in that direction. I'll walk a ways with you."

Ralph led the way outside, pulling his soft lamb's wool muffler around his chin. His gloves were fur-lined pig skin. They walked on for a bit, then Ralph said, "Where's your sister? I haven't seen her recently. Not ill, is she?"

"She's staying with Martha."

"And where would that be?"

"I don't know, sir. She's never told us."

A gust of cold wind made Ralph jam his astrakhan hat more tightly on his head. Ben tried to wrap the thin muffler around his face. Ralph tapped him on the shoulder.

"If you don't mind me saying, young fellow, you could do with some warm clothes."

Ben didn't answer.

"Tell you what," continued Ralph. "How would you like a job? No, I'm speaking God's truth. Why don't you come along with me? It don't matter if you're a bit late for school. We'll think up a good excuse."

The boy looked at him doubtfully.

"What sort of job?"

Ralph beamed down at him. "Well, I work for this real toff, you see. It's very well-paid work."

"What do you do?"

"I'm a sort of jack of all trades. Somebody needs meeting at the train station, I'm there. Need a good-looking sort of fellow, I'm your man. Very varied kind of job. But you know he's so busy these days that he said to me the other day, he said, 'Ralph, I could do with a bit of extra help. Do you know of any lad might be willing to run errands a few times a week?' So I thought to myself, 'By Jove, I do know a lad who might be willing to make himself a bit of dash.' And you're the lad I have in mind, Ben."

Another pause. They were almost at the corner of Sydenham and Sackville, where the boy had to turn for school.

"Is it against the law what he wants me to do?"

Ralph clapped him on the shoulder and burst out laughing. "What a bright lad you are, Ben, I knew it. No flies on you. But no, of course, it ain't against the law. I wouldn't ask you to do anything that'd get you into trouble. But I wager this job would bring you enough for a hat and some gloves. And if you do it properly and prove you are a reliable lad, there might be more work and you can get some socks and new boots. Those you've got on wouldn't look good on a stiff."

At the corner where he would normally turn to go to school, Ben halted.

"All right," he said.

"That's my lad," said Ralph and he rubbed the boy's shorn head. "It's a bit of a walk but it'll do us good. Get some colour into those pale cheeks of yours." He took Ben's arm. "Heigh ho, now let's think of what we will tell your teacher."

CHAPTER THIRTY-FOUR

NIGHT AND MORNING HADN'T QUITE CHANGED PLACES, the station lamps were fully lit, and Murdoch experienced his usual tug of pleasure at the sight. From the beginning, when he was merely a constable, he had loved the job despite the dull hours of walking the beat. He liked being in a world that was both outside of society and paradoxically at its very heart. He couldn't imagine doing anything else. This was why he could understand Seymour's being so disturbed by the malicious anonymous letters. He and the sergeant shared the same loyalty to their work and colleagues. And he was about to put that loyalty into operation.

This early in the day, the main hall of the station was empty of any miscreants shifting their rear ends on the polished bench. The stove was hot, and the smell of burning coal mingled with the lingering sour odours of fear and poverty. Fresh sawdust on the floor was needed by the look of it. The duty sergeant, Gardiner, was sitting behind the high charge desk, writing in the day book.

"Hello, Will. Don't tell me you've been ill too. We didn't see you yesterday."

"I've been working, sergeant, don't worry."

"I'm not worried. It's just that we're short-handed with Seymour off sick. I wondered if it was something catching that was going around."

"Could be. You'd better wear your flannels."

Murdoch hung up his hat and coat and strolled over to the desk where Callahan was pecking at the typewriter. He slapped him on the back.

"Come on, Liam. You can't have lost your skill overnight. Or did you get a mote in your eye?"

Callahan's fair skin flushed making his freckles vanish. "No, I was just being careful."

"Good idea. But probably unnecessary considering how well you performed in the competition."

Gardiner, who loved a good gossip, overheard as he was meant to.

"What competition you talking about? Shiniest boots?"

"Our young constable here is an expert typewriter. You got a fourth place, didn't you, Liam?"

Callahan nodded. Gardiner laughed. "I can see why he's keeping his light under a bushel. You know how things are in here. He'd never get out from that desk if the inspector thinks he's a prize."

"That is for certain. He likes his trophies," said Murdoch. "But I didn't know you were hungering to be out on the beat, Liam."

Callahan flashed his boyish smile. "It's more interesting than sitting here all day."

"Tell him the truth, Will. In winter, you get frostbite and in summer you bake like bread in an oven but you don't smell as good. Why he'd want to leave this cushy job, I can't fathom."

Murdoch spoke to the sergeant. "Too bad there's no position open. Especially now that the city council has turned down the chief's request for more money." He grinned down at Callahan. "Sorry, lad. Typewriting it is. No advancement for you. Maybe you could train as a Bertillon clerk."

"No, thank you, sir. I'm quite happy doing what I'm doing."

"Are you then? I'm glad to hear it." Murdoch reached in his pocket for his notebook. "Speaking of Bertillon, I'd like you to telephone headquarters for me. I've got some measurements on somebody I'd like them to check. We've even got a name, so that should make their job easier."

The Bertillon system the police force used was notoriously difficult to learn and required a skilful and trained clerk.

At that moment, an elderly woman came into the hall. She was neatly dressed in a black bonnet, a brown fur caperine, and black serge skirt. A widow for some years by the look of her.

She sent directly to the sergeant.

"I have lost my purse, it may have been stolen from my pocket."

Gardiner tut-tutted sympathetically. "Let me get the details down, ma'am. We'll get it back for you."

Murdoch tore the page of notes from his notebook and gave it to Callahan. "Tell them it's urgent, will you." He glanced over his shoulder at Gardiner, who was studiously writing down what the woman was telling him.

"By the way, Liam, this letter was inside the door. I picked it up." He took another envelope from his pocket. "You deal with the post so I thought you'd better have it."

Callahan took the envelope curiously.

"I noticed it was addressed to the inspector," continued Murdoch, "but it's odd that somebody just dropped it off like that, don't you think? He told me he'd been receiving some complaining letters lately. Maybe it's one of them."

"Right." Callahan put the envelope in a tray on his desk. "I'll take it up later."

The sergeant was still busy with the widow who was deaf and both their voices were raised as she described at length where she was when she missed her purse. Murdoch bent close to Callahan's ear.

"You know what, young Liam, I saw that the envelope wasn't sealed. It might be better for our inspector's frame of mind if he wasn't troubled by silly nuisance notes at this time. Why don't we have a look at what that letter is all about? I take responsibility. If we think it's worthwhile, we'll pass it on to him; if it's a load of horse plop, we won't bother him with it. He's already had three letters that really bothered him, I know that for a fact."

Callahan began to look afraid. He knew what Murdoch was getting at but wasn't ready to crumble just yet. He didn't move and Murdoch picked up the envelope.

"Why don't I open it and you can be completely innocent of all wrongdoing, if it is wrongdoing, which I doubt."

He removed the letter from the envelope, turned so that his body shielded them from Gardiner. Fortunately, the widow was garrulous.

Murdoch held the paper in front of Callahan. "My, my, it's a good thing Brackenreid hasn't seen this."

To Inspector Brackenreid.

What is this station coming to? You harbour a viper in your bosom in the presence of constable, second class, Liam Callahan. This is what he does in his spare time. He is planning to send it to the newspapers. You will be a laughing stock, sir.

                                                    A well wisher.

On a separate sheet of paper Murdoch had drawn a picture of the inspector, with his bald head and bushy sideburns, slumped at his desk, clutching a bottle of whisky. A caption came from his mouth: "Don't bother me, I'm working." If he said so himself, Murdoch thought it was a good likeness and he'd inked the nose with the red of a serious toper. He almost felt sorry for Callahan, who gasped in horror. "I never did that."

Murdoch grimaced. "That's the problem with letters like this. There's no way to prove they're not true. You say you're innocent, but who'll believe you? When the dirt flies, somebody's going to smell."

"But why would I do anything like that? I have no reason."

"Liam, I believe you but I don't know if anybody else will. Miss Gripe is loyal though, isn't she? She won't mind if you lose your position. She'll stick by you."

Callahan looked at him directly. The pretence dropped. He knew what Murdoch was doing. He almost snarled, the fresh-faced youth vanished.

"What shall I do?"

Murdoch folded the letter and drawing and replaced them in the envelope he put in his pocket.

"I'll help you even if thousands wouldn't. Type the following letter. Quick, before Gardiner hears us...Dear Inspector Brackenreid. Regarding the matter of Sergeant Seymour. I am happy to inform you that I completely retract my former accusations which were based on error and mistaken identity. He is a fine officer and you need have no concern for his conduct at any time. You have my guarantee I will let the matter drop completely."

Callahan was in his best form and typed as quickly as Murdoch was speaking. Silently he rolled the paper from his typewriter and handed it to Murdoch, who put it in an envelope he had brought with him.

"I'll deliver it to his office right away."

The constable was staring straight ahead but Murdoch could feel his hatred. He squeezed his shoulder hard.

"It's reassuring to know that the matter is settled and there will be no more anonymous letters to distress the inspector." He tapped his pocket. "We don't want him to see this, do we? Ever."

Gardiner was escorting the old lady to the door.

"What have you two been doing? Didn't I hear you clacking away like a train, Liam? That was very good."

"Constable Callahan was obliging me in a personal matter," said Murdoch.

"You shouldn't be doing that on police time."

"Don't worry, it won't happen again." He took his hat from the peg and held out the new envelope. "Gardiner, this letter is for Inspector Brackenreid. Will you see that he gets it? Don't worry, I think he'll be very happy to receive it."

CHAPTER THIRTY-FIVE

GEORGINA CROFTON'S HOUSE WAS ON GERRARD STREET, facing onto the Horticultural Gardens. In good weather, the Gardens were a popular gathering place, dapper mashers in their straw hats strolled the paths covertly eyeing the nursemaids wheeling perambulators or the servant girls and seamstresses on their days off chattering together on the benches, also covertly eyeing the dandies. But on this bleak January morning the park was deserted.

The house was large and elegant, built of pale buff-coloured brick with a green door and window trim. The front steps curved to the door and the path was paved with slate. It was possible Miss Crofton made a good living from her work, but

Murdoch thought the look of the house more suggested long entrenched wealth. He tugged on the bell and while he was waiting for the door to open, he banged the muddy snow off his boots. He was just about to pull more heartily on the bell when the door was opened by an elderly woman in the plain navy dress of a housekeeper.

"Yes?"

The woman's tone was supercilious, her expression disdainful. Murdoch had encountered the snobbishness of servants many times before but it still irritated him. He handed her his card.

"Good morning, ma'am. I'm Acting Detective Murdoch and I would like to speak to Miss Georgina Crofton."

He expected more disdain but her reaction was the opposite. She looked alarmed.

"Oh dear, so there are thieves in the neighbourhood. We feared as much. Come in, please. Miss Georgina is in her studio. I'll get her at once." She started off down the hall, then turned back to him.

"Shall I fetch Mrs. Crofton as well? She is in her chambers."

That sounded rather legal but Murdoch knew it was just a pretentious way of saying Mrs. Crofton was not dressed yet.

"No, don't bother her. Miss Georgina will be sufficient."

The housekeeper pulled back the brocade portieres from the drawing-room door.

"You can wait in here, sir. It's a bit chilly, I haven't got the fire going yet."

Murdoch gave a little deprecating shrug. "It's what I deserve for calling at such an early hour, ma'am."

She looked flustered and, pushing aside another set of curtains, she ushered him into the room and hurried away down the hall.

The air of the drawing room was cool but the decorations were not. Murdoch had never seen anything quite like them. His first impression was that the room was spacious and full of sunlight, but he realized that this was an illusion created by a screen of mirrored panels at a right angle to the wall. The room was actually fairly small and much of the space was taken up by three Turkish couches covered by woven blankets of deep blue with a sun yellow and fire-red zigzag design. The woollen curtains looped across the threshold were of the same pattern. The most unusual features, however, were the window frames, which had a facade of slender white columns supporting arched lintels with scalloped edges, decorated in gold filigree. In the window bays were two earthenware pots, each filled with man-high pale green plants with flat, oblong spiny leaves. The marble fireplace was reflected several times over in the mirrors as was a brass birdcage where a pale yellow bird cocked its head at him curiously. Murdoch felt as if he had entered a foreign country.

He was about to test the tip of one of the spiny plants to see if it was as sharp as it appeared to be when the portieres were pushed aside and a woman made her entrance, heading straight for him, her hand outstretched. The housekeeper was behind her.

"Detective Murdoch, I'm Georgina Crofton. Mrs. Buchanan tells me you are in pursuit of thieves."

He shook hands although initially she had crooked her hand as to almost invite a kiss. She wasn't in the least imperious, however, and he put the gesture down to finishing-school training. Like her drawing room, Miss Crofton was exotic. She was tall, past middle age, with a face that seemed all nose and chin. Her hair was braided on top of her head and wrapped with a flowered scarf. She was wearing a long holland smock so bedaubed with paint it might have been used for her palette and she smelled faintly of turpentine.

"As a matter of fact, ma'am, that is not why I am here. I have no knowledge of thieves in the area."

She turned to the housekeeper. "But I thought you said…"

"That's what he told me, ma'am."

Murdoch had done no such thing but he didn't want to wrangle with the woman.

"Not thieves, ma'am, but a very serious matter I wish to discuss with you."

He thought an expression of wariness flashed across Georgina's face, but she said affably, "Of course, perhaps, Mrs. Buchanan, you would be so good as to bring us some chocolate. I haven't had my morning chocolate, Mr. Murdoch, so I do hope you will join me."

"No, thank you, ma'am."

"Dear me. I'd better wait then. Hannah would you mind… perhaps Mrs. Crofton needs your assistance?"

The housekeeper didn't look happy about having to leave but she did so, pushing through the curtains like an actress making her exit.

"Please sit down, Mr. Murdoch." Georgina waved at one of the couches and took the one opposite. Murdoch moved aside a red tasselled bolster so he had room to sit while Miss Crofton reached over to one of the lacquered tables beside her, snapped open an ornate silver box, and took out a thin brown cigarillo.

"Would you like one, Mr. Murdoch?"

Briefly, he was tempted, they didn't come his way that often, but he shook his head.

"I hope you don't mind if I do. I'm quite an addict to the demon tobacco." She put her cigarette in a little clip on a stick, lit it, and drew in a deep grateful breath. The tobacco smell was slightly perfumed.

"So what is the nature of your business, sir?"

Murdoch took the envelope from his pocket, removed the mourning card, and held it in front of her.

"Did you take this photograph, ma'am?"

She held out her hand. "Let me see."

"I'll just hold it for you, if you don't mind, ma'am."

He leaned closer and she peered at it with myopic eyes. "Why yes, that's the Dowdell infant, isn't it? Poor lamb, he was with us such a short time and his parents were devastated at his loss." She blinked at Murdoch. "I don't understand why you, a police officer, are asking me about this photograph. How did it come into your possession?"

He didn't have a chance to answer before the door opened and Mrs. Buchanan returned, wheeling a tea trolley.

"You know what you're like if you don't have your chocolate," she said to Georgina, ignoring Murdoch.

Georgina smiled. "Hannah has been here since I was born. She feels she has the right to supersede my decisions."

The housekeeper lit a spirit lamp on the trolley and set an exquisite china pot on top of the ring.

"Please continue, sir," said Miss Crofton.

"I prefer to wait, ma'am."

"My goodness, you can say absolutely anything in front of Mrs. Buchanan. We have no secrets from her."

Maybe you do and maybe you don't, thought Murdoch, *but I'm not about to flash photographs like these in front of an elderly servant.*

"I'll wait," he repeated and saw the tightening of the housekeeper's lips. She desperately wanted to put him in his place and establish hers but didn't quite dare. She picked up a grater and a block of chocolate and shaved slivers into the pot. She gave it a thorough stirring, then poured some of the hot liquid into a china mug.

Behind Miss Crofton, Murdoch caught a glimpse of his own reflection. In his grey sealskin coat, he looked as out of place as a sparrow among parrots.

Mrs. Buchanan handed the mug to her mistress but made no attempt to leave.

"Mr. Murdoch is inquiring about one of my photographs,

Hannah, but so far he hasn't said why. Surely you are not come to offer me a commission for the police are you, Mr. Murdoch?"

"No, ma'am."

Miss Crofton extinguished her cigarette on a silver dish. "Hannah, would you be so kind as to bring me a slice or two of that delicious seed cake you baked yesterday. I find I'm quite peckish."

Mrs. Buchanan shot a poisonous look at Murdoch and she flounced away, as much as a woman who is stiff with rheumatism can flounce.

As soon as the door closed, Georgina frowned at Murdoch.

"I have hurt her feelings, sir, and I never wish to do that to somebody as valuable as my good nanny. What can possibly be so serious that it necessitates this secrecy?"

He handed her the card. "Look on the reverse if you will, ma'am."

She turned the photograph over, then held it closer to her face so she could read the words.

"Good gracious me. How disgusting. Who wrote such things?"

"I don't know for certain. That is what I am trying to find out. The photograph was discovered by a teacher in the desk of a young pupil at one of our schools."

"Has the boy been charged?"

"It was actually a girl, ma'am. And no, she has not been charged as yet. She denied all knowledge of the photograph and how it came to be in her desk."

"Somebody is trying to cause trouble for her then?"

Murdoch shrugged. "Perhaps. When was the photograph taken?"

"Three months ago."

"Who else would have a copy of this photograph, ma'am? Other than Mr. and Mrs. Dowdell?"

"I can't really say. They ordered ten cards, which I made and delivered to them, but they no doubt gave them out to various people."

"Do you have a copy yourself?"

"Yes. I have the original plates and I usually retain a print in my files."

"Who else has access to your files, Miss Crofton?"

"They are not under lock and key if that's what you mean. Anybody in my household can open them if they wish."

Murdoch had taken out his notebook. "Who is in the household, Miss Crofton?"

"My mother, Mrs. Buchanan, our housekeeper, and our maid, Ruby."

"Her last name?"

"Adams."

"How long has she been in your employ?"

"About six months I suppose, surely that is irrelevant."

"Would you mind checking your files to see if the card is still there?"

"Of course it's there. Why on earth would it not be?"

"The brother of the girl in question says she had several photographs in her possession and some of them were mourning cards. Unfortunately, he didn't know where she obtained them. There is an older sister who is in service, we don't know exactly where. The girl has disappeared and is supposedly staying with her." Murdoch closed the notebook. "I would like to speak to your maid, if I may."

Georgina lit another cigarette. "I can assure you, Mr. Murdoch, we are not harbouring any lost child. We have a small household, and unless she is stowed in the water closet, I have not seen her." She puffed again and stared at him. "I do hope you believe me?"

Murdoch thought her distress seemed genuine, but he wasn't about to assume it was all righteous indignation. Not yet, not by a long shot.

"It isn't a matter of whether or not I believe you, ma'am. I would like to talk to Ruby Adams."

"In other words, you don't take my word."

"I'm a police officer, Miss Crofton. It's my job to be thorough."

She flushed at his response. "Very well, but I cannot permit you to speak to Ruby. She is timid enough as it is and speaking to a policeman would frighten her out of a week's growth. We have worked hard to bring her to the point she is now. Besides, she is not the girl you are looking for. Ruby is an orphan. She had no family connections whatsoever. She came with excellent references and has never given a moment of trouble."

"I must insist, ma'am."

"Very well, if you must." She got up and tugged on the embroidered bellpull beside the fireplace. Mrs. Buchanan came in through the curtains so quickly, Murdoch wondered if she'd been eavesdropping in the hall.

"Ah, Hannah. Is Ruby in the house?"

"No ma'am. She is out on an errand."

"Ah, there you are, Mr. Murdoch. She isn't here. She is probably gone for the morning."

He turned to the housekeeper. "When do you expect Ruby to return?"

"Like Miss Georgina said, she has gone for the entire morning."

"A long errand."

"Yes, it is."

Miss Crofton extinguished her cigarette. "Hannah, will you go to the studio and look in my filing cupboard. I need to know if the Dowdell photograph is still there. That's Dow-dell. You can bring it here."

The housekeeper left with the air of one who has won a victory. The bird gave a soft peep, and Georgina took yet another cigarette from the box and lit it. Murdoch thought that the action covered up the woman's uneasiness. She had dropped all pretence of polite manners and they sat in silence until the housekeeper returned.

CHAPTER THIRTY-SIX

THE CURTAINS WERE SHOVED ASIDE AND HANNAH returned. "Is this what you wanted, Miss Georgina?"

She handed her mistress a folder.

"Yes, that's the one and, see, Mr. Murdoch, the card is safely within." She reversed it. "And not defaced, needless to say."

She gave him the photograph and, aware of the intensity of the housekeeper's curiosity, he compared it to the one he had.

"The image in this card seems somewhat lighter than yours, Miss Crofton."

"Really?" She held the two cards side by side. "Yes, you're quite right. You've got good eyes. The process of development is a delicate one and sometimes I will lighten or darken a photograph by exposing it for various periods of time. That card is more exposed than mine."

"Is that significant?"

"It is possible that the copies I sold to the Dowdell couple were exposed to that degree, I don't really remember."

"But you did develop them all at the same time?"

"Yes. I always do, unless my client wants to order more."

Murdoch handed back the card. "I'd like to see your studio, if you please, ma'am."

"See my studio? What on earth for?"

"He wants his photograph taken," muttered Mrs. Buchanan.

"I feel that the girl is in grave danger, morally and perhaps even physically. It is most important that I track her down."

"What's he talking about?"

"Never mind, Hannah, I'll explain later." Georgina looked at Murdoch. "I quite understand your concern, detective, but I fail to see how visiting my studio will in any way further your investigation."

Murdoch stood up. "Allow me to best determine that, Miss Crofton."

"Very well." She stubbed out her cigarette in the silver dish and took a gulp of her chocolate. "Hannah, we'll be all right, thank you. Mama will be needing her breakfast soon, I'm sure." She swirled her way out of the room, leaving Murdoch to follow like a lackey. Mrs. Buchanan brought up the rear, then reluctantly left them to go back to the kitchen.

The studio was on the second floor of the house, facing

onto the park. This time mirrors weren't necessary to give the illusion of spaciousness; the room was genuinely large. Two deep windows gave plenty of light, but Murdoch saw that the room was also equipped with electric lights.

"Here we are, Mr. Murdoch. My den of iniquity."

He didn't particularly like Miss Crofton's flippant tone. "I don't know how it can be that, ma'am, considering how many angels are watching over you."

In the corner of the room were at least a half a dozen plaster sculptures of angels occupied in such angelic tasks as playing the harp or praying. There were even a couple of fat cherubs suspended by wires from the ceiling. Georgina looked discomfited and waved her hand in the direction of the large easel that was in the centre of the room. "My speciality is painting people who have passed on. The families often like me to include depictions of heavenly beings."

Murdoch indicated a raised dais near to the window. There was a plain upholstered chair in the centre, behind it a frame with a neck brace for holding the subject immobile. The rather ghastly image of a corpse being so propped up flashed through his mind but he thought it was more likely Georgina used it for restless children. There was a camera on a tripod in front of the dais.

"Do you take stereoscopic pictures, ma'am?"

"Not any more. They don't really suit my clients."

"Where do you keep your props? I assume you stock the usual plants, birdcages, leopard-skin rugs, and so forth."

"I use very little. My subjects rarely desire any elaborate photograph. A simple back cloth and the chair is all I need. I transpose the photograph to my canvas and I can add whatever I wish. And as I said, most of my work is done outside of the studio."

At the far end of the room were two doors. "Where do those doors lead, ma'am?"

"One leads to the servant stairs, the left one is the dark room. And don't ask if you can look in there because you can't. I am developing some prints."

"I beg your pardon, Miss Crofton, I must check."

He strode over to the doors, ignoring her protests. The left door did open onto a small room that was completely dark. It smelled strongly of what he presumed must be developing fluid. The door let in sufficient light that he could see a clothesline with several pieces of paper pegged on to it. He snatched one off the line. It was a photograph of a woman lying in a bed. The peacefulness of the position made it obvious he was looking at a corpse. He replaced the print and closed the door.

Miss Crofton glared at him. "You have probably ruined my photographs, sir, and they are irreplaceable."

"I apologize, ma'am," he said and opened the second door. It led to a narrow uncarpeted flight of stairs. If Miss Crofton was guilty of creating pornographic images, she had to be doing it somewhere else because in this room there was nowhere to store all the elaborate sets he had seen in the stereoscopic pictures.

"Are you satisfied, Mr. Murdoch? I can understand your

concern about a young child who is presumed to have defaced one of my photographs but I am completely at a loss to know why you seem so determined to implicate me in the sordid situation. I am not responsible for what people do to my pictures."

Murdoch took out the photograph of Leonard Sims. "Would you take a look at this photograph, ma'am?"

She had to hold the card close to her face and he saw her look of shock and the quick recovery.

"Do you recognize the young man?"

"As a matter of fact, I do. He did some work for us recently. I'm afraid I don't remember his name, Simpson or something like that."

"Leonard Sims."

She pursed her lips. "That is possible. I see that somebody has drawn a black border around the card. Is that wishful thinking?"

"What do you mean, ma'am?"

"He was a thoroughly unpleasant young man. Quite untrustworthy. I gave him the sack. I suspected he was a deviant and I assume from his pose I was right."

"He is, in fact, dead. He was murdered."

Her hand flew to her mouth. "God forbid. I truly did not mean to be flippant, Mr. Murdoch. Even Mr. Sims cannot deserve such an end."

"Indeed."

"Why are you asking about him, Mr. Murdoch?"

"At the moment, I know almost nothing about the young man and I need to find out whatever I can. This card was also in the desk of the girl I mentioned. She likely inked in the black borders. I fear she may know what happened to him. And if that is the case, she is in grave danger."

"Poor child."

Georgina's response seemed genuine, but Murdoch was puzzled about her reaction to the Sims card. It wasn't only the response of somebody being shown a photograph of someone she had known. That would elicit more curiosity than the flash of fear he'd seen in her eyes. She was hiding something, but for the life of him he didn't know what it was.

"Do you know where Sims lived?"

"No. I don't. He was here only for one day."

"He didn't mention any friends to you, or family?"

"Mr. Murdoch, you will probably see me as a callous and indifferent employer, but I had virtually no conversation with the young man. I told him what we needed and what his wages would be and that was that."

"Did he do the job?"

"Not well but yes, he did do most of it. Mrs. Buchanan paid him, and off he went."

Murdoch wasn't sure quite how to proceed and he might have taken Miss Crofton at her word if at that moment, a sudden flash of sunlight hadn't gleamed on something on the far side of the room. Tucked into one corner was a brass birdcage. He'd totally missed it when he first looked around. He got to his feet and walked over to it.

"Do you use this as a prop, ma'am?"

"Yes, I do. My little bird won't sing. I thought a larger cage would help but it hasn't. I use that empty one now as symbolic of the soul's flight from its earthly imprisonment. It is very popular."

Murdoch took Agnes's photograph from the envelope and compared the two cages. He thought the Crofton one was richer but it was hard to tell. They could be the same. He came back to Georgina.

"Miss Crofton, I'd like you to sit down if you please. There is something more I must show you."

If she was as innocent as she appeared to be, he didn't want her to faint, or pretend to faint for that matter. Reluctantly, she did as he asked and perched on a paint-splattered stool near the easel. He stood beside her and handed her the envelope.

"These other two photographs were also in the girl's desk. Please take a look at them, but I warn you they are most graphic."

Her reaction to the Newly-wed photograph was a quick blink, but when she peered at the picture of Agnes, she recoiled and put the card down.

"If a grown man wants to make a complete exhibition of himself by not wearing his trolleywags, that is his business, but the child...who would do such a thing, Mr. Murdoch?"

"Who indeed? Do you recognize the girl, Miss Crofton?"

"Of course I do not. How could I?"

"Her name is Agnes Fisher."

"That means nothing to me."

She quickly returned the stereoscopic cards to the envelope and handed it to Murdoch, not meeting his eyes. "I can hardly comprehend that you have made a point of searching my studio, Mr. Murdoch. Surely you cannot for a moment believe I am in any way involved in the taking of these disgusting photographs?"

Her face was quite pink, but he couldn't tell if it was from indignation or embarrassment. She might dress like a Bohemian and smoke like a man but underneath it all she was no doubt a well-brought-up woman who had never before in her life looked at such explicit scenes.

"As I said, Miss Crofton, I am afraid for the safety of this girl. I have to find the photographer and that means I cannot afford to stand on ceremony. If I have offended you unjustifiably, I apologize."

She turned away from him and he could see she was trembling. "Please leave me, sir. I presume you have seen all you need to see. You can let yourself out."

Short of getting a warrant to search her entire house, there was nothing much more he could do. He walked over to the door.

"I am at Number Four Station on Parliament Street. If there is anything else that comes to you that you might think is helpful, please send for me."

He'd half expected Mrs. Buchanan to be in the hall ready to leap on him, but there was no one.

CHAPTER THIRTY-SEVEN

BEN FISHER WAS SEATED ACROSS THE TABLE FROM RALPH Tibbett and he'd just finished mopping up the gravy on his plate with a crust of bread.

"You liked that, eh?" Ralph beamed at him.

"It was good. That's the second beef pie I've had this week," added Ben, who thought that might impress Ralph.

"That so?" Ralph took a silver case from his pocket and removed a slender cigar.

"The truant officer bought me one," said Ben.

"Really?" He had Ralph's interest now. "I've never heard of a truant officer standing a boy to a beef pie. When did that happen?"

Ben picked up something in Ralph's tone and he began to

feel uneasy. He'd been presenting his story to make himself look clever, but he thought it unwise to let drop that Murdoch was a police officer.

"He came to the house looking for Aggie."

"What exactly did he say?" Ralph clipped his cigar and lit it with a match.

"Aggie fainted in class and Miss Slade our teacher was worried about her so she sent this man. But Aggie weren't home so he couldn't talk to her."

"Talk to her about what?"

Ralph held the cigar between his teeth, which made him look as if he was grinning, which he wasn't. The boy shrank down in the seat.

"I don't know. Just why she'd fainted, I suppose."

"Does Aggie ever have good old chins with you, Ben? You know, sister to brother heart to hearts?"

"Not our Aggie. Pa says she don't have two words at a stretch in her head. She's a quiet one."

Ralph was studying him and Ben began to find it hard to breathe. "Didn't she ever mention that she helps us out as well?"

"No, sir, never."

"Well she does and does very good too. She models for my employer. She's a pretty girl, your sister, and he uses her in certain photographs. You know, dressed like a shepherdess or an angel looking down on a baby. Did she never show you the pictures?"

"No, sir. I ain't seen anything."

"You wouldn't fib to me, would you, Ben? These pictures are

what's considered private property. Some people want them all to themselves. They don't want anybody gawking at their own private pictures. You can understand that, can't you, Ben?"

The boy had no idea what he was talking about but he nodded vigorously.

"Did this man from the school mention pictures?"

"No, sir. He just said that Aggie was in trouble and he wanted to help her."

Ralph knocked off some ash on the edge of the table and Ben saw it land on the bare plank floor. There was no carpet, no cloth on the table either. Ralph had said that his employer was a wealthy man but nothing about his apartment revealed that. In fact, Ben would have thought he wasn't much better off than they were by the look of things. He wished he hadn't agreed to come, that he was safely in his desk at school, making foghorn noises. He'd been practising and he thought Miss Slade would be pleased by his rendition. But he had been here with Ralph since this morning and, except for the beef pie, it had been a boring time. He'd been left to wander around the studio. He could stand boredom, however; he was used to it, but since Ralph had returned, the atmosphere had changed. He hadn't raised his voice or looked angry, but Ben's heart was pounding. He scurried around in his mind trying to find the words to appease him. What did he want to hear? Everything he said seemed to make matters worse.

"What kind of trouble is Aggie in, Ben?"

"I don't know, sir. Maybe she has a bun in the oven."

"What makes you think that?"

"Momma used to faint when she had a bun in the oven."

Ralph grimaced. "And how many buns did your mother bake before she passed away?"

Ben wasn't sure what he meant. Ralph scowled, his voice impatient. "Babies. How many babies did your mother have?"

"At least three that I remember. The last one got stuck in her belly, which was why she died."

"Indeed. How tragic. But Aggie isn't married. How could she have a baby inside her? You know you have to be married in a church before that happens, don't you, Ben?"

In fact, Ben knew that babies were made in a hot bed where they incubated like eggs and that if a girl grew fat and had a baby without having a husband, she was a wicked girl and would go to hell. Martha had explained it all to him one day. She had been instructing him on the necessity of not touching a girl until they were married in the eyes of God because if he did he would go to hell and have his member chopped off by the Devil.

At that moment the door behind Ralph opened and a chubby man with a red face came in. Close behind him was a young woman whose fair hair was hanging loose and unbrushed about her shoulders. To Ben's intense discomfort she was not wearing proper clothes, only a red silk gown that gaped open at the neck and looked as if it might come undone at any minute. Ben had never seen such a garment before but he guessed this was what well-to-do ladies wore in their bedrooms. Martha had told him as much on one of her infrequent visits after she had gone into service. She said her mistresses both wore silk gowns in their bedrooms and no stockings or shoes. They had thick carpets to walk on so they didn't get cold.

"What's this about being married? He's a bit young to have a trouble and strife, isn't he?" The man's voice was loud and should have sounded friendly but didn't. He had a funny way of pronouncing his words that Ben had heard occasionally at the market. He was from over the pond, he knew that. Ralph almost stood up.

"Afternoon, sir."

"Who's this woeful scrap of badness?"

"This is young Ben Fisher that I told you about. He's just had some good grub and we was having a chin about this and that."

Ben knew at once that Ralph was afraid of this new man and that he had to be even more careful what he said. Then to his dismay, the young woman walked over to Ralph and, plopping herself into his lap, kissed him hard on the lips.

"Hello, Renaldo, my pet. I missed you."

Ralph gave a warning glance in Ben's direction and the girl giggled. "Oops, sorry. I forgot…Mr. Tibbett and I are long-lost cousins," she said to Ben. "What you might call kissing cousins."

Her words were slurry, and except that she was so young and clean and in a red silk gown, Ben would have thought for certain she was hickey.

The man leaned and caught the girl by the wrist. Ben saw her wince but she didn't protest.

"Clara, my dear. Go and make us all a nice pot of char. Be quick. A very important customer is due in an hour."

She got up promptly and walked to the door, staggering and almost colliding with a brass birdcage that was standing in the corner. There was no sign of a bird, Ben had made sure when he came into the room.

Not even waiting until the door had closed behind her, the man spoke to Ralph.

"Miss Clara is trying my patience."

Ralph nodded. "She's certainly becoming a handful."

The other man put his forefinger against his temple. "A note to self. Do not allow Clara to have any of her, er, her cough syrup until the evening." He smiled at Ben. "In case you're wondering, little titch, I find it helps to say, 'Make a note to self.' Keeps everything tidy in my idea pot." He tapped himself again a couple of times. "I've got a lot of business matters to keep straight. Now what were we saying? Oh yes, the boy getting married."

Ralph smiled a false smile. "What we were talking about was actually Ben's sister, Agnes. Seems like a truant officer was visiting the house because Aggie was taken ill at school. According to our laddie here, this man says Aggie's in some kind of trouble and he wants to find her so he can help."

"That so?" Uninvited, he picked up Ralph's cigarette case and helped himself to a cigarillo. Ralph lit a match for him. "Did he say what kind of trouble, young Ben?"

"No, he didn't, sir."

"Aggie fainted in class and Ben was worried that she might

be having a baby, which was why I was explaining to him that that weren't possible. Aggie ain't got a husband."

The man drew on his cigarillo and watched the red-hot ash eat into the paper. "That's right, never mind her being so young, she's what the reverend would describe as 'pure.'" He chuckled. "At least I hope she is. I can't go around photographing girls to be angels if they aren't pure. That right, Mr. Tibbett?"

Ralph was lighting up another cigar and Ben could have sworn his hand shook. Without even being conscious of it, the boy eased himself away from the table so he would be free to run if a fight broke out.

"Tell me, young fellow, did this helpful officer have a name?"

Ben felt a shiver of fear run up his back. "I don't remember, sir."

"What did he look like then? Was he an old dodgy codger dressed in a black suit?"

"Oh no, sir. He wasn't old."

"But he had a beard for sure and a bald head?"

"No, sir. No beard, but he did have a moustache and he wasn't bald at all. He had wavy hair."

"A carrot top, I'll wager?"

Ben laughed. He seemed to be pleasing the man now. "Not at all. His hair was dark brown, sort of like mine."

"Ah. Was he as tall as me?"

"Not much taller, sir. About as big as Mr. Tibbett."

The man nodded at Renaldo. "Anybody you recognize?"

"No. Do you?"

"Maybe. Then again there are a lot of coves look like that.

The point is if they're sending truant officers to the house, it's time we found Aggie ourselves. Poor girl might need our help and I've come to look on her as a daughter." He felt in his inside pocket and took out a paper bag. "Ben, I'm partial to sweeties and this bag is full of them. Here." He shoved one across the table to the boy. "Where might we find your sister, Ben?"

"I don't know, sir. She hasn't been home for the last two nights. Nor at school neither."

If telling this got Aggie into trouble but meant Ben had less of it, he didn't mind.

"Sometimes we have to work late into the night," the man continued. "In which case your sister has been known to stay here with my good wife in charge. But she wasn't working yesterday." He tapped his finger. "Think, Ben. Where might she be staying?"

"They have a sister who's in service," interjected Tibbett. "Didn't you say she was with her, Ben?"

"Yes, sir. That's where she is most likely."

"That so? Where's your sister work, Ben?"

Ben hardly paused. It was one thing to risk Aggie's ire, another entirely to aggravate Martha. He had sworn with a blood oath, painfully inflicted, that he would never tell anybody where she was.

"I don't know. sir. She didn't want Pa dunning her for her wages. She told Aggie but not me."

"Any guesses then?"

"I think the house is one of the grand ones up in the end of the city. Where the bridge is."

"Bloor Street, you mean?"

"Yes, sir."

Bloor Street wasn't far, not far enough at all, but it was the first place he thought of.

"You're not fibbing me, are you, Ben?"

Ben looked him in the eyes in the way he had perfected over the years. "No, sir. Never. I'd tell you if I knew."

The man grunted. "All right then." He leaned forward and wiped off a speck of pie crust from the side of Ben's mouth. "I can't abide fibbers, little titch. I'd never hire anybody to work for me if I didn't think I could trust them. Honest and close-mouthed, that's the kind of boy I like. Are you that kind of boy, young Ben?"

He hadn't moved his finger and he was pressing it hard into Ben's cheek. His eyes were the colour of the lake in winter.

"Yes, sir."

He let him go and held out the bag of candies. "Have a sweetie."

"What are we going to do about the girl?" Ralph asked, and again Ben trembled at his tone of voice.

"Do? We'll do nothing. She's probably tucked away nice and safe with her loving skin and blister. I don't think we need worry. She's a quiet girl. Isn't that right, little Ben?"

"Yes, sir."

The man shook the bag of sweets. "If Aggie shows up at your house and you come and tell me, or better still bring her with you, you can have the whole bag."

Ben made himself look happy about that.

The man scrutinized him for a moment, then he said, "Now, my lad, did Renaldo, that's what we call him here, did he tell you about our little business proposition?"

Tibbett answered, "No, I haven't said anything yet."

"Well then, here's the story, young Ben. A gentleman we know likes to see photographs of boys who are all dressed up like princes. He's an odd cove, I'll give you that, but who am I to judge? He'll only look at boys that are small like you and refined, just like you. Is there any boy at school that you could bring over for a test? I warn you, the gentleman nor me will not tolerate any rowdy rough boys who'll boast to everybody what they've been up to. The fellow must be a quiet sort, bit on the shy side if you like. Like princes are. And he must be able to keep a close mouth, just like you. This gentleman is very particular about his affairs being private. Now if you can bring us such a lad, young titch, you will get a whole bag of sweeties between you and a dollar for you alone. How's that suit you then, good deal, wouldn't you say, Renaldo?"

"The best. I wish I got as much when I was a calf."

"So, Ben, old son, is there any lad you know of who might suit us?"

Ben thought. He didn't have any friends to speak of and the only one he ever really got along with was Emmanuel Hart and he wasn't at all small and refined. But there was a boy. He was younger, small and dark-haired, and he hung on the fringes of the playgroup and the groups of rowdy boys just the way Ben did.

"There's a boy I could bring. I take him home from school sometimes. His ma works because he doesn't have a pa."

"Poor laddie. That might make him all the more willing to earn a bit of dash to help his ma. What's his name, this cove?"

"He's from Wales. He's got a funny name. It's Alwyn Jones."

CHAPTER THIRTY-EIGHT

BY THE END OF THE DAY, MURDOCH WAS TIRED AND discouraged. He felt like a dog in a revolving cage, plodding on but going nowhere. He'd had the satisfaction of hauling Fisher out of bed but the man was so full of liquor, he was incoherent. Murdoch had only managed to shake out of him that he didn't know where Martha or Aggie were, and he had to accept that.

A prim clerk at the *Globe* newspaper office told him that they had no records of past transactions. If the account was paid that was an end to it. Why should they clutter the office with unnecessary pieces of paper? Murdoch had considered giving her an answer, but the question was rhetorical and the woman of middle age, so he swallowed his irritation and left.

Seymour had agreed to interview the people to whom the Dowdells had sent mourning cards and Murdoch went to check on the remaining photographic studios on his list. He offended several of them by asking about "naughty" pictures, but nobody admitted to having photographed such a thing, and they all seemed to be sincere. He made a brief stop at the Sackville Street School just as Miss Slade was entertaining the class by whistling a lively waltz that made him want to practise a few reverse turns in the hall. She came out to him right away. Neither Agnes nor Ben Fisher had been in school. Promising he would come to the boarding house that night, he left to seek out the final three studios on his list. By dusk and the lighting of the street lamps, he had checked off the last studio.

Briefly, he was undecided as to whether to go directly to the lodging house to see if Seymour had any luck, or to go after he had visited Enid. He'd promised her he would redeem himself and come for the supper he'd missed the day before. That promise won out and he trudged off to Mrs. Barrett's house.

Enid opened the door and he knew without asking that this was another evening when the landlady was not at home. Enid was wearing her best blue silk taffeta dress and her hair was freshly and elaborately pinned. If he didn't know better he'd think she had applied a touch of rouge.

"My you look lovely, Enid," he exclaimed.

"This is in the way of a celebration. I received a banker's draft in the amount of ten dollars today from the competition."

She lowered her voice. "And Mrs. Barrett is away to her sister's for two days."

Murdoch stepped into the hall, caught her in his arms, and gave her a hearty kiss.

"More cause for celebration."

"She was in an uncommonly good humour and she has given me permission to use the dining room." Enid smiled at him. "She got a notion in her head, how I don't know, that I would be entertaining some of my fellow competitors and I did not disabuse her."

He kissed her again. "Clever wench."

She took his hand and began to lead him down the hall. "Alwyn is in bed. I'm afraid he might be sickening for something, he has been so low and quiet. Perhaps after we've had our meal you could go up and say goodnight to him. That might cheer him up."

Murdoch thought that the only thing that would cheer up Enid's son was if he gave up all claim to her affections. He flinched. That was coming soon.

Enid ushered him into a dining room crammed with heavy dark furniture. She had lit a good fire and all the lamps in an attempt to make the room bright and welcoming but nothing could overcome its ugliness. The tablecloth at least was a white damask and Enid had laid it with her own china.

"Sit down and I'll bring in the dishes."

He took his place at the table and she left with a slight swish of taffeta and a waft of essence of roses. Murdoch leaned his head in his hands. Enid was making it clear that she welcomed his love but she was leaving the country and he couldn't see any future for them. And that was separate from the confusion of feelings he was having for her and Amy Slade. He grinned to himself. Maybe he was being entranced by the charms of the whistling waltzes, the way he'd heard Indian fakirs entranced snakes.

Enid opened the door carrying a tray loaded with covered dishes. "You're looking quite peaked, Will. You're not ill as well, I hope."

"No, not at all. I'm just tired and cold and foot sore and I seem to have spent a wasted day. I've made no progress in the case I'm working on. Although I did deliver the letter to Mr. Callahan, and it did the trick. Thank you very much for your help."

She smiled with pleasure. "I'm happy for that. Now, look you, I've made a roast of pork with boiled potatoes and cabbage, so I hope you have a hearty appetite."

He clutched the knife and fork in his fists, held them upright, banged them on the table, and proclaimed, "I have the stomach of a lion."

He tucked in to the meal and had eaten about two mouthfuls when Enid said, "I've never seen Alwyn so dispirited. I'm worried that something happened this afternoon."

"Hmm?" said Murdoch, his mouth full of potato.

"One of the boys at school sometimes accompanies him home for me when I have to be out. I know you think I mollycoddle him, Will, but I feel more easy in myself if I know he is with somebody."

Murdoch nodded. He did think that, but he wasn't going to bring it up now.

"The other boy isn't much older than he is really so they can play together. I give him five cents and something to eat and the poor chappie is always after asking me if I'll be out." She poked at a piece of cabbage on her plate. "According to Alwyn, instead of coming here as they usually do, Ben took him to a photography studio." She stopped, seeing his expression. "Will, what's the matter?"

"Did you say Ben?"

"Yes, Ben Fisher. He goes to the same school."

"My God." Murdoch pushed back his chair. "I have to talk to Alwyn."

"He's probably asleep by now. Please tell me what's the matter, you're frightening me."

He stared at her. "Enid, did Alwyn mention the name of the studio?"

"No, he didn't."

"Where was it?"

"I, er, I don't know. I wasn't paying a lot of attention."

She was preparing the meal in anticipation of his coming, Murdoch realized.

"What has happened? Did you receive a complaint? Did the boys break something?"

"No, nothing like that." Murdoch leaned forward and touched her hand. "What did Alwyn tell you?"

"Nothing at all. I think he regretted even saying where he'd been. But when I pressed him, he said he'd promised not to talk about it. Heaven knows why. All he would say was that he was supposed to be a prince and he was to wear some nice clothes."

She shook her hand free from Murdoch's. "Will, you have a face like thunder. What is wrong?"

"Enid, a few days ago, a schoolteacher came to me because she found a photograph of one of her pupils hidden in a desk. It was vile. The girl is Agnes Fisher, Ben's sister. She wouldn't say a word to Miss Slade and now she has vanished. She could be in grave danger and I've been trying to track down the photographer."

Enid's hand was at her throat. "Are you trying to tell me that my son has been used in the same way?"

"Let's talk to him."

They hurried up the stairs to the little box room. There was a lamp turned low on the dresser.

"I'll wake him," said Enid. Gently, she called to her son and he stirred. She sat on the bed and said something to him in Welsh. He shifted to a sitting position, but seeing Murdoch, he shrank back into his pillow and spoke to his mother anxiously. She answered in English.

"Mr. Murdoch isn't angry at you, Alwyn. He is troubled about a case he's working on and he wants to ask you some questions."

"What sort of questions?" The boy's eyes were large and dark in the shadowy light.

Murdoch perched on the end of the bed and tried to make his face less frightening.

"Your mamma was telling me about you and Ben Fisher going

to a photography studio this afternoon. Where was it, Alwyn?"

"I don't know, Ben took me."

"But you must know where you went. Was it north up to Gerrard Street? South to King Street? Where?"

Alwyn whimpered. "I don't know. We were playing with the snow in the gutters and I was just following Ben."

Murdoch stood up. "What is wrong with you? Surely you must know if you were going in a northerly direction or not…"

Alwyn yelped as if he had hit him and shrank into his mother's arms.

"Will, please! He's a child. He doesn't have a good sense of direction."

"Enid, there are very serious matters at stake here. I have not asked him a difficult question. He must answer it."

Suddenly, Murdoch had an image of himself at Alwyn's age cowering in his bed as his father shouted at him about some misdemeanour far more trivial than his fury warranted. Damn it anyway. He forced himself to calm down and he walked around to the other side of the bed.

Alwyn was sniffling against his mother's chest and Murdoch bent over and stroked his hair. "I'm sorry, lad, the reason I am so upset is because there are other children involved whose safety I am concerned about. One of them is Ben's sister, Agnes."

Alwyn's tear-stained face peeked out at him.

"Do you think you can talk to me now?"

A hardly perceptible nod.

"I'm not angry at Ben or Agnes. I want to help them. And

I'm not angry with you either…but it would be a big help if you'd answer my questions."

Enid spoke to her son and reluctantly he straightened up.

"That's my brave lad," said Murdoch. "Now, first question. Was Aggie at the studio as well?"

"No," in a whisper.

"Was the person at the studio a man or a woman?"

"A lady."

Damn, thought Murdoch. "What did she look like?"

"She was like Mamma."

"In what way?"

"She was pretty and she had on a silk frock."

Enid gave her son a quick kiss on his forehead.

Murdoch frowned. He couldn't imagine even a small boy describing Georgina Crofton as pretty.

"Was there anybody else there?"

"Ben's friend…"

"A grown-up or another boy?"

"A grown-up. He's an actor."

"Did he tell you his name?"

"They call him Renaldo for the stage. He was getting me some work so I could help Mamma."

"What sort of work, son?"

"Being a prince in a photograph. I was going to get some sweeties and half a dollar. He was nice, but I didn't like the other man."

Murdoch couldn't help himself. He snapped his fingers.

"Name? They must have used names when they spoke to each other, what were they?"

Alwyn whimpered again. "I didn't notice, but Ben told me the name of his friend but I forget what it was. He lives downstairs."

"What! Downstairs from Ben?"

"Yes. They have twins and Ben said he hears them crying a lot."

"Was his name Tibbett?"

"It could have been."

Murdoch had an image of a young mother kindly offering him a candle. Surely she was what she appeared to be.

"Did Mr. Tibbett take the photograph or the lady?"

A shake of the head from Alwyn. "No. There was another man there. The lady took us to get the nice clothes. We were going to be young gentlemen."

"Did you hear the name of this other man, Alwyn?"

Alwyn was still eyeing him nervously and he didn't want him scurrying back to his burrow like a timid rabbit. Murdoch softened his voice again. "Well, did you?"

Another shrinking back and a quick warning glance from Enid.

"I didn't hear it but I saw the sign on the door when we were leaving. His second name is Emperor. I could read it."

Murdoch let out a rush of breath. So he had been right. It was hard to hold back his impulse to run out of the room down to the Emporium.

"Did this man take a photograph of you in the nice clothes?"

Alwyn shook his head. "We didn't even have a chance to put them on. He said there was a gentleman coming who wanted to see what we looked like, to see if we'd do but he came before we were ready." He gazed up at his mother. "He was so rude, Mamma, he didn't knock or anything, he just walked in. Mr. Emperor was angry with him."

"What happened then, Alwyn?" asked Enid.

"Mr. Emperor took him into the front room, but we could hear them shouting. Then he came back and was in a bad skin." Tears started to roll from Alwyn's eyes. "I was afraid, Mamma. He grabbed me so hard, it hurt." He held up his arm and Murdoch could see the bruise near his wrist. Enid pulled her son close to her so she was speaking over his head.

"What does this mean, Will?"

Before he could answer, Alwyn burst out. "He said we wouldn't do any pictures today and Ben had to take me home but I mustn't say a word or I couldn't come back and get my wages." He was crying in earnest now. "I wanted to help with our passage to Wales, Mamma."

"Hush, darling, hush."

But nothing could stop the rush of words as the boy finally let go of his terror. Murdoch could only just make out what he was saying.

"The man that came was so ugly, Mamma. I tried to be a good boy but he frightened me so. And Ben too. I could tell. He was a monster, Mamma. Something had happened to him like the king in the fairy story. The one who'd been turned into a beast until the princess loved him."

Murdoch stiffened. "What do you mean something had happened to him?" He had to wait until the racking sobs subsided sufficiently for him to be heard.

"Alwyn, describe this man to me."

"Enough, Will. He's had enough. Don't be so cruel."

"He must answer, Enid."

"He didn't have any hair…and his face was all white and wrinkled." The boy held up his hand, squeezing the fingers together. "His hand had got melted so it was like a bird's claw. And he couldn't walk properly."

Enid looked at Murdoch who had jerked back. "Do you know the man?"

All Murdoch could say was, "I bloody well do."

CHAPTER THIRTY-NINE

LEAVING ENID TO MINISTER TO THE BOY, MURDOCH hurried down the stairs and began to trot as fast as he could along River Street. Alwyn's voice ran over and over in his head: *We were waiting for a gentleman who had to see if we would do*, and in had come Reordan. The boy said he had argued with Gregory. Had Reordan told him Murdoch was on his tail?

When he got to the lodging house he didn't wait politely on the doorstep but went straight into the hall. He was heading for the Irishman's room when Seymour came out of the kitchen, Amy Slade at his heels.

"Will, what's happened?"

"Is Reordan here?"

"He went out almost an hour ago."

"Did he say where he was going?"

"We didn't see him, we just heard him come in and go out again immediately after. I called to him to join us but he didn't even answer."

"What's the matter?" Amy asked.

As succinctly as he could, Murdoch told them Alwyn's story.

Amy sat down suddenly on the coat-tree seat. "And you think the man they were waiting for was Reordan?"

"No, I'm not certain of that. But he was undoubtedly the one who showed up at Gregory's studio at that moment."

"And Gregory is the photographer we've been looking for?" Seymour asked.

"He's the one, all right. There was another man present who they said was an actor who might be in the scene with them. He's called Renaldo, but Ben told Alwyn his real name was Tibbett. He lives in the rooms below the Fishers."

"So he would know both Agnes and Ben," said Amy.

"Yes."

"Just a minute," said Seymour. "I've got to check something." He went down the hall and tried Reordan's door. It was unlocked and Seymour entered the room. Murdoch waited with Amy in the hall. She had replaced her severe navy jacket and white waist with a short-sleeved, green silk loose top. Her hair was down and tied back in a ribbon. She looked much younger and more vulnerable than he'd yet seen her.

"I cannot comprehend Ben taking the Welsh boy to that studio. How could he do such a thing?"

"We don't know anything yet. Ben might be an innocent himself. He told Alwyn that Gregory promised him a dollar and some sweets if he could find a suitable boy."

Seymour emerged from Reordan's room. "John had a pistol in his drawer. It's gone."

"What the devil...now what?"

Amy looked up at Murdoch. "You don't know Reordan as we do. He couldn't be involved in abusing children."

Murdoch shrugged. "We'll find out, won't we."

She frowned at him. "I am not speaking only about his character. He never leaves the house except for dire necessity. He is so ashamed about the way he looks. We would know if he was going out a lot."

Murdoch was skeptical. "Neither of you are at home during the day."

She shook her head. "I cannot believe it."

"I must admit, Will, I find it incredulous as well."

"It always is," said Murdoch. "But let's think logically, can we? Where might he go and why has he taken his revolver?"

"I think he's been in a very strange mood since we showed him that photograph," said Amy. "I thought he was dreadfully shocked."

"Could it be he has taken the law into this own hands?" asked Seymour. "Remember, he asked you if you had any suspicions as to who was the photographer."

"It's more likely he's done something like that. I refuse to believe he'd be a purchaser," said Amy.

"He could also be trying to destroy any evidence."

"No! I don't believe it."

"Regardless, we'd better get over to the bloody Emporium quick."

Amy reached for the cloak that was on the peg behind her. "I'll come with you."

"Don't be ridiculous," said Seymour. "This has all the indications of a dangerous situation."

"The only person John will listen to at all is me. If he's planning something harmful, I can talk him out of it...Please don't waste time trying to dissuade me, Mr. Murdoch. There is no time to argue. I am quite capable of taking responsibility for my own actions. I will not be a liability."

She was right, there was no time to argue, and he could tell arguing wouldn't work anyway. Short of tying her up, he had no way to stop her. Besides, what she said made sense and he already knew that Miss Amy Slade was a woman of her word. She would not be a liability.

Seymour hurried off to get his coat and hat. He came back downstairs carrying a policeman's short stick with a leather looped strap at the end.

"I kept this from my days on the beat. It may come in handy."

The three of them set off, Amy in the middle of the two men. Murdoch was prepared to hire any cab that came by but the street was deserted. Amy kept up with them even though they were jog-trotting. At the corner of King and River, they paused to get breath, just as a streetcar came rumbling by.

"Come on," shouted Murdoch and he set off at the run. The ticket collector saw him and signalled to the driver to stop. Seymour and Amy were right at his heels as Murdoch climbed aboard the streetcar. There were only a handful of passengers on board. He pulled out his official card and showed it to the driver.

"I'm commandeering this car on police business. No stops, as fast as you can to Church Street."

"What about my passengers?"

"They'll have to get out and catch the next car."

"There isn't one for half an hour."

"They'll survive."

Seymour was already moving down the aisle of the streetcar, telling the passengers they had to disembark at once. Fortunately they all looked like able-bodied men who wouldn't freeze to death waiting for another streetcar. They were curious but compliant, there were only a few grumbles. As soon as they were out, the driver started off, getting up the car to top speed. Amy sat on the bench.

The ticket collector came up to them. "Who's she? A police officer too?"

Murdoch didn't answer but something must have showed on his face because the man averted his glance. Seymour clung to one of the leather straps hanging from the ceiling of the car.

At top speed and with no need to stop for passengers, the streetcar was at the corner of King and Church in a matter of minutes.

"Stop here," said Murdoch. "Thanks, and keep my card so you can report what happened."

"I will," said the driver. "I hope it was worth it. If I get the can, I'll come after you."

The three of them jumped down.

"Will, look!" Seymour grabbed his arm and pointed at the roof of the Emporium building. A drift of black smoke was coming from around the frame of the top window. In the seconds they watched it, a tongue of flame appeared.

"My God, the place is on fire." Murdoch swirled toward Amy Slade. "There is an alarm box at the corner of Jarvis Street. Here's my key. There's a hook inside the box that you have to pull down. Let it slide back and the alarm will ring. You will have to stay there until the firemen arrive so you can direct them."

She took the key and set off on the run, her pantaloons making the going much easier than the encumbrance of a heavy skirt would have done.

Murdoch and Seymour raced across the road to the Emporium. A quick glance in the front window showed them the fire had not started in the empty downstairs store. The house was quiet, no shouting of occupants, no roaring of flames as yet. Murdoch tried the door leading to the upper floor and they went into the hallway. Seymour shone his lantern on the stairs, and they headed to the studio. There was an acrid smell of gathering smoke in the air.

The upstairs door was slightly ajar. Murdoch pushed it open and they stepped inside. A woman, bound and gagged, was in a chair in the middle of the room. It was Mrs. Gregory.

Her head was drooping on her chest and for a moment he thought she might be dead. However, as he crossed the floor toward her, she jerked into consciousness, her eyes widened in terror.

"Mrs. Gregory, we are police officers."

The gag was a woollen scarf that had been tightened cruelly around her mouth. Murdoch tugged it free and the woman began to scream.

"It's all right, ma'am. You are safe," he said, even though she probably couldn't hear him above her own screams.

"Charlie, take her outside. I'll check the studio."

Thick smoke was rolling underneath the door to the adjoining room. Murdoch thought he could hear the crackling of flames.

Seymour began to untie the woman's arms, and all the while she never stopped screaming. Murdoch left him to deal with her. He ran over to the other door and threw it open.

"Reordan? Are you in here?"

The smoke was so dense, he started to cough violently. Holding up his arm to shield his eyes he managed to get to the window. He'd snatched up Seymour's night stick, and he used it to smash the glass. The fresh air came in with a rush and the smoke billowed and rolled but began to pour out of the window. Murdoch turned around, able to see more clearly.

On the dais in the very chair he himself had sat was a man, also tightly bound. He was not tied or gagged because there was no danger that he would run or call out. The entire side of his head was destroyed from the blast of a revolver, by the looks of it. There was enough of his face left for Murdoch to recognize the young man he had encountered when he first went to the Emporium. Ralph Tibbett. His upper torso was drenched in blood from the head wound but what was worse was that his trouser buttons had been opened and blood still seeped from the injury that had been inflicted on him. He had been castrated.

CHAPTER FORTY

THERE WAS A LOUD CRACK FROM THE OTHER SIDE OF the room and more smoke gusted underneath the door and through the frame. Murdoch knew he couldn't wait for the fire truck to arrive. He didn't know if anybody was alive or where Reordan was. He wrapped his muffler around his nose and mouth and shoved open the door that led to Gregory's apartment.

The entire opposite wall seemed to be on fire, flames licking at the window frames and mantelpiece. However, opening the door had allowed some of the smoke to escape and he could see well enough.

In the centre of the room, as yet untouched by fire, was one of the most macabre scenes he had ever witnessed and it was to haunt him ever after.

Gregory was bound hand and foot to one of the central pillars. He was gagged but his eyes were open and he was alive. Stacked all around him in a pyre were dozens of photographic cards and loose papers. John Reordan was in the process of emptying a drawer of folders on to the heap. Hearing Murdoch, he spun around. He had a revolver in his hand and he immediately pointed it.

"Don't come any closer, Will. You don't deserve to die, but I'll kill you if you try to stop me." His voice was hoarse.

"What the hell are you doing?"

Reordan continued to shove papers toward the pyre with his foot but without taking his eyes off Murdoch for a moment. "That's it exactly. I'm sending him to hell." He uttered a cry that was half sob. "I have very good reasons, Will."

"John, he'll be tried and sent down for a long time, I promise you."

"That's not enough."

Murdoch went to say something, but Reordan yelled at him. "There's more to it than you know. It's personal."

He was coughing from the smoke and very agitated but the gun was steady. Out of the corner of his eye, Murdoch saw Gregory heave against his bonds. Reordan saw him too and responded by throwing another folder on the pyre. He jerked his head in Gregory's direction.

"He's the one who tarred and feathered me...When you

showed me that photograph of a man with his cock exposed, I recognized that man too, or should I say *it*. He has scars from the clap on his shaft. I dealt with him next door, and now I'm dealing with this one."

Murdoch risked a glance at Gregory, whose frightened eyes fastened on his in desperation.

Reordan barked out at him. "Charlie told you he pissed on me, but he didn't know the worst. Both of them raped me afterward." Murdoch tried a small step forward but Reordan kept the revolver steadily aimed at his head. "When you said you suspected Gregory of doing those photographs and that he was an Englishman, I knew it was him. And I was right, of course. I'd know his voice if I was dying. If I'd gone blind, I'd know that voice." He kicked some more cards to the heap, which Murdoch could see had been splattered with fluid. A smashed lamp on the floor indicated what that splatter was. Reordan was seized with a spasm of coughing but didn't break his focus on Murdoch.

"I'm not the first person he's raped. You should see these cards and photographs. He was going to set something up with two young boys. I saw them when I came here."

Murdoch eased forward again. The smoke was worse and his eyes were stinging and watering so badly he could hardly see. He raised his voice over the noise of the flames.

"John, don't do this, I swear I'll bring him to justice."

Reordan gave a sort of laugh. "Come on, Murdoch. You must have seen Tibbett out there. There's no going back for me.

Can you blame me? They're getting what they deserve."

Murdoch didn't know how much of this Gregory could hear but he was still struggling futilely with the bonds. He obviously knew what Reordan intended.

With his gun still aimed at Murdoch, Reordan reached to a table behind him where there was a lit candle in a holder.

Murdoch yelled at him. "John, stop. I'm not going to stand by and watch you burn a man alive."

He tried another step. Reordan cocked the hammer of the gun. "Don't be a fool, Will. This toe-ragger isn't worth it." Quickly, he stooped down and applied the candle flame to the paper. With a whoosh, the paper, soaked with lamp oil, burst into flames.

Then they both heard the bell of the fire truck as it raced toward the building. For one crucial second, Reordan was distracted and glanced over his shoulder. Murdoch leapt forward and grabbed his wrist, and they locked in a bizarre dance, pivoting and twisting. But his assailant had a demented strength and he flung Murdoch to the ground. He rolled to one side, expecting to be shot, keeping his eye on Reordan. The Irishman lowered the gun, then suddenly thrust it underneath his own chin and pulled the trigger. The impact threw him backward into the heart of the fire. Murdoch scrambled to his feet and waded into the burning pile, kicking away the cards and paper. The flames had raced greedily toward Gregory and his clothing and hair were on fire. The rope cords that were binding him were also burning. At the edge of his consciousness, Murdoch could feel pain in his own legs, but he tugged Gregory free, and dragged him away from the flames.

Suddenly he was aware of Seymour beside him. He had a blanket, which he threw over Gregory to smother the flames. By now the gag had burned off and the man was screaming, not the full-bodied cry of his wife but a thin, shrill wail, just as persistent.

Behind them, where the windows had been, there was a sudden, explosive hiss of water as the hoses were directed at the wall from the fire truck below. Dense, choking smoke billowed toward them.

"Get his legs," said Murdoch and he lifted Gregory underneath his arms. Gasping, almost blind, they managed to carry him into the studio, where there was less smoke, and lie him on the floor. His exposed skin had turned black and blistered, and in places the burns were more severe and oozed blood. Coughing and spluttering, both Seymour and Murdoch fell on their knees, struggling for air. Then the door was shattered and what seemed like an army of firemen burst in.

"Get out of here," one of them yelled, and Seymour and Murdoch scooped up the injured man again and staggered to the stairs. Halfway down they met with more firemen and one of them unceremoniously took Gregory from them, tossed him over his shoulders, and ran down the stairs. His lungs burning, Murdoch followed, Seymour behind him.

Outside, a crowd of people were being held back by two constables who had answered the alarm. Amy Slade was among them and she ducked under the restraining arm of the officer and ran toward them.

"Where's John?"

Murdoch found himself suddenly sitting on the curb. His hand, legs, and feet were excruciatingly painful and he saw in surprise that the bottom of his trousers were in blackened shreds and that his boots were smoking.

"He shot himself."

Seymour was in better condition than Murdoch. "We've got to get Will to hospital."

Amy turned and called to a man who had pulled up in his carriage and in spite of the nervousness of his horse was leaning out of the carriage window, intent on watching the proceedings.

"You, sir. These men are police officers. They must be taken to hospital immediately."

The man obeyed without the slightest hesitation. He recognized an Amazon when he met one. He jumped out and opened his carriage door.

Amy and Seymour helped Murdoch to stand and all three climbed into the plush interior of the carriage. The last thing Murdoch saw as they drove away were the billowing clouds of smoke and fire as the Emporium was consumed by flames.

EPILOGUE

MURDOCH WANTED TO TAKE ONE LAST LOOK AROUND the house to make sure it was sparklingly clean for the new arrivals. Not that he needed to. Mrs. Kitchen had spent two entire days before she and Arthur left for Muskoka, polishing and washing everything, floor to ceiling. Murdoch limped into the parlour. His right foot had blistered badly, and he still found it painful to draw in a deep breath, but he was on the mend. He'd been given two paid weeks leave of absence, which was astonishingly generous coming from Brackenreid. However, he was in the inspector's good books. The case had received a lot of attention in the newspapers and Brackenreid felt his police officers had come off in a favourable light. He had even intimated that Murdoch would be promoted to full detective as soon as the opportunity arose.

Bartholomew Gregory had not survived his injuries, and his widow told the police everything they needed to know about her husband's sideline. Clara Hill had been at her boarding house when the fire happened, but she too testified to her role in the taking of pornographic photographs. As far as Murdoch could tell, she was unrepentant. It was a job like any other. Both she and Mrs. Gregory swore they knew nothing about the misuse of children, but Murdoch didn't believe either of them. He was sorry when Clara got a reduced sentence by providing a list of Gregory's customers. As far as Murdoch was concerned it was a depressingly long list.

It turned out that Agnes Fisher was safely hidden away at the home of a coloured woman, Honoria Davis, who cleaned the studios and sometimes modelled for the more benign photographs. The day after the fire, when Honoria discovered what had happened, she had brought Agnes to the police station where she told Brackenreid what she knew, including details concerning the murder of Leonard Sims. Later, Murdoch discovered that the inspector had been openly skeptical of Agnes's story and profession of innocence but Honoria supported what she had said. Honoria wasn't charged but Agnes was placed at once in the Girls Home on Gerrard Street.

Murdoch brought Brackenreid the photographs that Amy Slade had found because they would be needed in the inevitable investigation. In the meantime, however, he slipped the Dowdell photograph into a folder. When Agnes went before the police magistrate, she could plead coercion with regard to the obscene picture but she would be in serious trouble if the magistrate saw what she had written on the back of the mourning card. Murdoch didn't think it necessary for anybody else to know about it. Amy Slade had engaged the services of the hirsute Mr. Wilkinson, and Murdoch felt confident that Agnes wouldn't be sent to the Mercer Reformatory.

Aggie had revealed the address of her older sister and Murdoch wasn't surprised to hear it was the Crofton residence, Martha Fisher metamorphosed into Ruby Adams. When he limped over with Seymour to inform them of the situation, Georgina and her mother had declared unswerving loyalty to their maid and had promised they would act charitably toward the younger sister and brother. Murdoch had noticed the ambivalence on Ruby's face, and he felt sorry for her. She had obviously hoped to make a clean break from the squalor of her family life. He thought there was still something covert about Miss Crofton, but he didn't know what it was and frankly didn't care. She seemed to him to be a generous-hearted woman, eccentric yes, but basically decent. Ruby's adoration of her counted for a lot as far as he was concerned.

Ben was left with his father, but Seymour and Murdoch had paid a visit to Mr. Fisher and scared the life out of him. They made it clear they would not tolerate any misuse of the boy and if Ben so much as had a scratch when he showed up at school, Fisher would be held accountable.

Murdoch glanced at the clock on the mantelpiece. It was a handsome piece of ormolu and brass, a parting gift from Enid. She'd managed a smile when she gave it to him. "Perhaps when you check the time, you will think of me." He'd taken her in his arms at that, but she had not returned his embrace. She had already left him. For a week, Murdoch had moped around the empty house, relieved only by daily visits from Charlie Seymour. It was he who had come up with the request. With Reordan dead, his aunt who owned the River Street house had decided she would sell at once. Seymour, Wilkinson, and Amy would soon be homeless. Wilkinson moved back into his parents' home, and Seymour asked Murdoch if he could rent a room in the Kitchens' house. Murdoch was more than happy to do so.

"What about Amy?" he asked.

"Well, I was wondering if she could move in as well. She's reluctant to approach you herself, she doesn't want to impose, so I'm asking for her."

Murdoch was flustered. His previous experience of attractive boarders had been with Enid, who had lived here for a while. She had moved out, claiming that proximity should not be mistaken for love. In that case she was probably right, and Murdoch didn't want to repeat the mistake with Miss Slade, around whom his feelings swirled and surged like an adolescent boy's.

However, it seemed churlish and embarrassing to refuse her lodgings and he'd agreed. Yesterday, both she and Seymour had brought over their belongings. Charlie was taking Enid's old room and Amy was in the front parlour.

Over the evening meal, which Murdoch had cooked to perfection, if he said so himself, Amy had made her own request. "My situation is shaky enough," she said. "I don't want my school board to know I'm living with two bachelors." She had a proposal and this Murdoch had accepted willingly. This afternoon, he was getting his third lodger.

There was knocking at the door and he limped off to answer it. Amy Slade was standing outside. She had an infant in her arms, bundled up against the cold. The baby's mother was holding the twin.

"Will you hold Jacob for a minute?" Amy asked. "I have to pay the cabbie."

She thrust the baby into his arms. Alarmed by the sudden transition, Jacob let out a wail of distress. His brother immediately answered in kind.

"Mrs. Tibbett, do come in, and welcome," said Murdoch. He had to raise his voice above the din. Shyly, Kate came into the house. She looked pale and ill-nourished, although the babies seemed bonny.

"Your room is down here. I hope it will be suitable for you," said Murdoch. Kate looked as if she was about to burst into tears but she followed him down the hall to the room that the Kitchens had occupied. Little Jacob's cries were unabated and Murdoch held him close against his chest, jiggling him slightly. Abruptly the baby stopped crying, reduced to some snuffles.

His tear-filled eyes looked up at Murdoch, who smiled down at him.

"There you are. I'm not so bad, am I?"

Jacob reached up with his plump hand and grabbed Murdoch's moustache, causing him to yelp in pain.

"What have I got myself into," he wondered.

AUTHOR'S NOTE

ONE OF THE UNFAILING PLEASURES OF RESEARCH FOR ME is discovering pieces of history I didn't know about before. The Noble and Holy Order of Knights is one such example. A North American labour organization that numbered almost a million members at its peak, it had started to fade by the turn of the century but was still a force to be reckoned with. The aims and principles I have related in the book are those of the Knights. The workers strike in Ottawa did happen but not the injury that I have ascribed to one of my characters.

In 1895, the magnificent typewriting machine was becoming common, and a popular form of entertainment was the typewriting competitions. Miss Orr was indeed the champion of typewriters.

Unfortunately, what exists now existed then in terms of pornographic photographs and the misuse of children.

ACKNOWLEDGEMENTS

I NEVER CEASE TO BE AMAZED AND GRATEFUL THAT SO many people are willing to share their time and expertise with me. Thank you especially to Gregory S. Kealey, who, together with Bryan D. Palmer, is the author of *Dreaming of What Might Be*, the story of the Knights of Labour in Ontario, and who took time to answer my questions. Maurice Farge was once again available for the finer points of Catholicism, and our wonderful neighbour, Tim O'Dacre, a firefighter, gave generously of his time to explain to me how fires behave. Jean Rajotte made a delicious pig's feet stew for me, and Gail Hammer tested some of my ideas about photography.

Thank you to my editor, Dinah Forbes, for her perceptive

comments and to my agent, Jane Chelius, for her unfailingly cheerful support.

Poor Tom Is Cold

In the third Murdoch mystery, the detective is not convinced that Constable Oliver Wicken's death was suicide. When he begins to suspect the involvement of Wicken's neighbours, the Eakin family, Mrs. Eakin is committed to a lunatic asylum. Is she really insane, he wonders, or has she been deliberately driven over the edge?

AVAILABLE APRIL 2012

Let Loose the Dogs

Detective Murdoch's life and work become tragically entwined when his sister, who long ago fled to a convent to escape their abusive father, is on her deathbed. Meanwhile, the same father has been charged with murder and calls on his estranged son to prove his innocence. But, knowing his father as he does, what is Murdoch to believe?

AVAILABLE APRIL 2012

TITANBOOKS.COM

Vices of My Blood

The Reverend Charles Howard sat in judgment on the poor, assessing their applications for the workhouse. But now he is dead, stabbed and brutally beaten in his office. Has some poor beggar he turned down taken his vengeance? Murdoch's investigation takes him into the world of the destitute who had nowhere to turn when they knocked on the Reverend Howard's door.

AVAILABLE JUNE 2012

A Journeyman to Grief

In 1858, a young woman on her honeymoon is abducted, taken across the border to the US and sold into slavery. Thirty-eight years later, the owner of one of Toronto's livery stables has been found dead, horsewhipped and hung from his wrists in his tack room. The investigation endangers Murdoch's own life – and reveals how harms committed in the past can erupt fatally in the present.

AVAILABLE JULY 2012

TITANBOOKS.COM